Math Review

Computation · Algebra · Geometry

Copyright © 2014 by Houghton Mifflin Harcourt Publishing Company

Printed in the U.S.A.

ISBN   978-0-544-26184-6

1 2 3 4 5 6 7 8 9 10   0982   22 21 20 19 18 17 16 15 14

4500460777   A B C D E F G

Core Skills Math Review

Table of Contents

Table of Contents
Core Skills Math Review

Common Core State Standards for Mathematics Correlation Chart

Grade 6	
Ratios and Proportional Relationships	
Understand ratio concepts and use ratio reasoning to solve problems.	
6.RP.1	76, 77
6.RP.2	78
6.RP.3	
6.RP.3.a	77, 84, 129
6.RP.3.b	78
6.RP.3.c	55, 56, 57
6.RP.3.d	215

The Number System	
Apply and extend previous understandings of multiplication and division to divide fractions by fractions.	
6.NS.1	42, 43, 44, 45
Compute fluently with multi-digit numbers and find common factors and multiples.	
6.NS.2	6, 7, 8
6.NS.3	25, 26, 27, 28, 29, 30, 31, 32, 33, 34, 35, 36, 37, 38, 39, 40
6.NS.4	9, 10, 11, 12, 13
Apply and extend previous understandings of numbers to the system of rational numbers.	
6.NS.5	16, 17
6.NS.6	
6.NS.6.a	16, 17
6.NS.6.b	122, 134
6.NS.6.c	16, 122
6.NS.7	
6.NS.7.a	18, 51
6.NS.7.b	51
6.NS.7.c	14, 15
6.NS.7.d	15
6.NS.8	122, 123

Expressions and Equations	
Apply and extend previous understandings of arithmetic to algebraic expressions.	
6.EE.1	21, 65, 93
6.EE.2	
6.EE.2.a	94, 95
6.EE.2.b	96, 97
6.EE.2.c	83, 97, 98
6.EE.3	92, 99
6.EE.4	99

Reason about and solve one-variable equations and inequalities.

6.EE.5	103, 117, 130, 153
6.EE.6	95, 103, 153
6.EE.7	104, 105, 106, 107
6.EE.8	153

Represent and analyze quantitative relationships between dependent and independent variables.

6.EE.9	125

Geometry

Solve real-world and mathematical problems involving area, surface area, and volume.

6.G.1	165, 166, 168, 169, 170, 172
6.G.2	179
6.G.3	173
6.G.4	183, 184, 186

Statistics and Probability

Develop understanding of statistical variability.

6.SP.1	201
6.SP.2	201, 207, 208
6.SP.3	207, 208

Summarize and describe distributions.

6.SP.4	201, 208
6.SP.5	31, 32, 33, 38, 39, 40
6.SP.5.a	201
6.SP.5.b	201
6.SP.5.c	205, 206, 207, 208
6.SP.5.d	207, 208

Grade 7

Ratios and Proportional Relationships

Analyze proportional relationships and use them to solve real-world and mathematical problems.

7.RP.1	79, 80
7.RP.2	103
7.RP.2.a	81, 85, 86
7.RP.2.b	85, 86
7.RP.2.c	85
7.RP.2.d	86
7.RP.3	58, 59, 60, 61, 62, 63, 82, 85, 86

The Number System

Apply and extend previous understandings of operations with fractions to add, subtract, multiply, and divide rational numbers.

7.NS.1	
7.NS.1.a	46
7.NS.1.b	46
7.NS.1.c	47
7.NS.1.d	19

7.NS.2	
7.NS.2.a	48
7.NS.2.b	49
7.NS.2.c	20, 48, 49
7.NS.2.d	23, 24
7.NS.3	79, 216, 217

Expressions and Equations

Use properties of operations to generate equivalent expressions.	
7.EE.1	100
7.EE.2	101
Solve real-life and mathematical problems using numerical and algebraic expressions and equations.	
7.EE.3	222, 223
7.EE.4	
7.EE.4.a	108, 109, 115, 116
7.EE.4.b	150, 151, 152

Geometry

Draw, construct, and describe geometrical figures and describe the relationships between them.	
7.G.1	87, 88, 89, 90
7.G.2	163
7.G.3	187
Solve real-life and mathematical problems involving angle measure, area, surface area, and volume.	
7.G.4	174, 175, 176
7.G.5	155
7.G.6	167, 171, 178, 180, 185

Statistics and Probability

Use random sampling to draw inferences about a population.	
7.SP.1	202, 203
7.SP.2	203, 204
Draw informal comparative inferences about two populations.	
7.SP.3	209
7.SP.4	209
Investigate chance processes and develop, use, and evaluate probability models.	
7.SP.5	189, 190
7.SP.6	193, 194, 195, 196
7.SP.7	
7.SP.7.a	191, 192, 194, 195
7.SP.7.b	193, 195, 196
7.SP.8	
7.SP.8.a	197, 198
7.SP.8.b	197, 198
7.SP.8.c	199

The Number System

Know that there are numbers that are not rational, and approximate them by rational numbers.

8.NS.1	50, 52
8.NS.2	53

Expressions and Equations

Work with radicals and integer exponents.

8.EE.1	66, 67, 68
8.EE.2	73, 74
8.EE.3	69, 70
8.EE.4	71, 72

Understand the connections between proportional relationships, lines, and linear equations.

8.EE.5	131, 132
8.EE.6	135, 159

Analyze and solve linear equations and pairs of simultaneous linear equations.

8.EE.7	
8.EE.7.a	118
8.EE.7.b	110, 111, 112, 113, 114
8.EE.8	
8.EE.8.a	139
8.EE.8.b	119
8.EE.8.c	119, 139

Functions

Define, evaluate, and compare functions.

8.F.1	124, 128
8.F.2	137
8.F.3	126, 127, 131, 135, 136

Use functions to model relationships between quantities.

8.F.4	133, 134, 136, 137
8.F.5	138

Geometry

Understand congruence and similarity using physical models, transparencies, or geometry software.

8.G.1	124, 128
8.G.1.a	145
8.G.1.b	145
8.G.1.c	145
8.G.2	142, 143, 146
8.G.3	141, 144, 147
8.G.4	148
8.G.5	156, 157

Correlation Chart
Core Skills Math Review

Understand and apply the Pythagorean Theorem.	
8.G.6	158, 160
8.G.7	161, 162
8.G.8	162
Solve real-world and mathematical problems involving volume of cylinders, cones, and spheres.	
8.G.9	181, 182

Statistics and Probability

Investigate patterns of association in bivariate data.	
8.SP.1	210
8.SP.2	211, 212
8.SP.3	211, 212
8.SP.4	213

Preview

Divide.

1. $54\overline{)4{,}271}$

2. $24\overline{)1{,}488}$

3. $39\overline{)5{,}350}$

4. $57\overline{)2{,}579}$

_____ _____ _____ _____

Find the GCF of each pair of numbers.

5. 15, 30

6. 24, 36

7. 14, 38

8. 32, 64

_____ _____ _____ _____

Simplify.

9. -8 + 6 =

10. -20 − (-9) =

11. -76 ÷ -4 =

12. 13(-6) =

_____ _____ _____ _____

Evaluate each expression.

13. $14 \times 2 \div 7 =$

14. $3(10 - 4) =$

15. $(8 + 12) \times 5 =$

16. $21 - 6 \div 3 =$

_____ _____ _____ _____

Write each decimal as a fraction or mixed number.

17. 0.3 =

18. 4.65 =

19. 3.06 =

20. 0.125 =

_____ _____ _____ _____

Write each fraction as a decimal.

21. $6\frac{7}{10} =$

22. $\frac{51}{20} =$

23. $\frac{4}{25} =$

24. $\frac{5}{1{,}000} =$

_____ _____ _____ _____

Find each answer. Write zeros as needed.

25. $\begin{array}{r} 4.28 \\ + 0.26 \\ \hline \end{array}$

26. $\begin{array}{r} 82.6 \\ - 5.93 \\ \hline \end{array}$

27. $\begin{array}{r} 0.00132 \\ \times \quad 45.5 \\ \hline \end{array}$

28. $0.3\overline{)12.03}$

Divide. Simplify if needed.

29. $4 \div \frac{7}{8} =$

30. $\frac{5}{8} \div \frac{3}{8} =$

31. $1\frac{3}{4} \div 2\frac{1}{2} =$

32. $24 \div \frac{5}{6} =$

_____ _____ _____ _____

Find each answer.

33. What is 80% of 50? _____

34. 40% of what number is 34? _____

1

Name _____ Date _____

Find the simple interest using Interest = principal × rate × time.

35. \$175 at $3\frac{3}{4}$% for 2 years _____

36. \$400 at 9.2% for 1 year _____

Find the absolute value of each number.

37. $|-3|$

38. $|2|$

39. $|-4|$

40. $|-601|$

_____ _____ _____ _____

Write an algebraic expression for each verbal expression.

41. a number times 50 _____

42. 17 less than z _____

Evaluate each expression if $m = 5$, $n = -2$, and $p = 3$.

43. $n - 3p =$

44. $17 + mp =$

45. $n(2 + 2m) =$

46. $\frac{2mp + 5}{m} =$

_____ _____ _____ _____

Solve for x.

47. $x + 11 = 40$

48. $x - 7 = 17$

49. $9x = 45$

50. $3x + 5 = 32$

_____ _____ _____ _____

51. $3x + 4x = 84$

52. $15x - 3x = 72$

53. $42 + x = 81 - 2x$

54. $8x + 6 = 9x + 1$

_____ _____ _____ _____

Simplify.

55. $(6^2) =$

56. $(-2)^3 =$

57. $\sqrt{49} =$

58. $(9^7) \div (9^5) =$

_____ _____ _____ _____

Change each number from scientific notation to standard form.

59. 3×10^3

60. 1.2×10^4

61. 6.07×10^5

62. 8.9×10^2

_____ _____ _____ _____

Circle all points that lie on the graph of the given function.

63. $3x - 3y = -3$ $(2, 3)$ $(0, -1)$ $(-4, -3)$

Solve.

64. Carpet sells for \$36 per square yard. How much will $8\frac{3}{8}$ square yards cost?

65. A book that cost \$25.00 was on sale for 35% off. How much would you save on the book?

_____ _____

2

Name _____ Date _____

Solve each equation using the given value of *x*. Write the ordered pair that makes the equation true.

66. $2x + 2y = -4$ when $x = 2$ **67.** $x - 3y = 9$ when $x = -1$ **68.** $2x + y = 10$ when $x = 3$

_____   _____   _____

For each equation, find and graph three solutions. Draw a straight line through those points.

69. $2x + y = 1$ **70.** $x - 2y = -2$

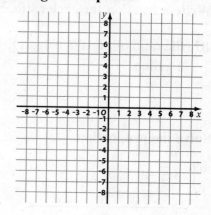

Find the slope of each line that passes through the given points.

71. $(1, 4), (2, 3)$ **72.** $(1, 0), (3, 7)$ **73.** $(-2, 1), (5, 10)$

_____   _____   _____

Solve.

74. $2x - 10 > -44$ **75.** $49 \geq x + 17$ **76.** $-4x \leq 60$ **77.** $3x - 13 > 19 + 7x$

_____   _____   _____   _____

Solve.

78. Shane hiked 15 miles in 5 hours. What was Shane's unit rate?

_____ miles per hour

79. Kimbra ran 4 miles in 44 minutes. What was Kimbra's unit rate?

_____ minutes per mile

80. What is the constant of proportionality for the relationship shown in the table?

_____

Gallons of Gasoline	4	5	6	7
Total Cost ($)	13.80	17.25	20.70	24.15

Preview
Core Skills Math Review

Name _____ Date _____

Change each measurement to the unit given.

81. 15 qt = _____ gal _____ qt

82. 40 m = _____ km

83. 32 oz = _____ lb

84. 40 in. = _____ ft _____ in.

85. 56 kg = _____ g

86. 334 mL = _____ L

Write a fraction for each ratio. Simplify.

87. the ratio of pints in a quart to pints in
a gallon

_____

88. the ratio of days in a week to months in
a year

_____

Solve the proportion.

89. $\frac{7}{8} = \frac{x}{40}$

90. $\frac{x}{9} = \frac{10}{3}$

91. $\frac{x}{3} = \frac{12}{18}$

_____   _____   _____

Solve.

92. Triangle *ABC* is similar to triangle *XYZ*.
What is the length of side *XY*?

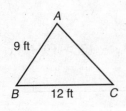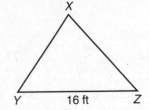

93. Triangle *MNO* is similar to triangle *TUV*.
What is the length of side *MO*?

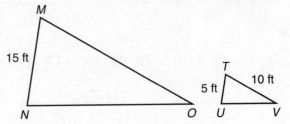

_____   _____

Find the length of the missing side in each right triangle.

94. $a = 3$, $b = ?$, $c = 5$

95. $a = 8$, $b = 6$, $c = ?$

96. $a = ?$, $b = 12$, $c = 13$

_____   _____   _____

Solve.

97. What is the area of a triangle that has height
14 inches and base 24 inches?

_____

98. What is the area of a picture that measures
9 inches by 12 inches?

_____

Name _____ Date _____

Add or subtract each expression.

99. $(2x + 5) + (8x - 3)$ 100. $(7x + 10) - (3x + 1)$ 101. $(9x - 6) - (4x - 3)$

_____   _____   _____

Solve each system algebraically.

102. $-5x + 4y = 16$
       $x + 4y = -2$

103. $x - 3y = 7$
       $-2x + 2y = 6$

104. $4x + y = 32$
       $2x - 3y = 2$

_____   _____   _____

Graph each inequality.

105. $g > -6$ 106. $h \leq 8$

Solve.

107. What is the circumference of a circle that has a diameter of 14 cm? Use 3.14 for pi.

_____

108. What is the area of a circle that has a radius of 9 ft? Use 3.14 for pi.

_____

109. Find the volume of a rectangular prism that has height $2\frac{1}{2}$ inches, length 3 inches, and width 7 inches.

_____

110. The radius of a cylinder is 1.3 cm, and the height is 15 cm. What is the volume of the cylinder? Use 3.14 for pi. Round to the nearest tenth.

_____

111. A box contains 4 green marbles, 16 yellow marbles, 2 red marbles, and 6 gray marbles. What is the theoretical probability of randomly choosing a gray marble?

_____

112. Kirk tosses a coin. It lands on tails 33 out of 60 times. What is the experimental probability that the coin will land on tails on the next toss?

_____

Dividing Large Numbers

To divide large numbers by a 2-digit divisor, decide on a trial quotient. Multiply and subtract. Check to make sure the quotient is great enough, but not too great. Write the remainder after the quotient.

Find: 96,446 ÷ 26

Divide.
Multiply. Subtract.

```
        3,
26)9 6, 4 4 6
  −7 8 ↓
    1 8 4
```

Divide.
Multiply. Subtract.

```
        3, 7
26)9 6, 4 4 6
  −7 8
    1 8 4
  −1 8 2 ↓
        2 4
```

Divide.
Multiply. Subtract.

```
        3, 7 0
26)9 6, 4 4 6
  −7 8
    1 8 4
  −1 8 2
        2 4
      − 0 ↓
        2 4 6
```

Divide.
Multiply. Subtract.

```
        3, 7 0 9 R 12
26)9 6, 4 4 6
  −7 8
    1 8 4
  −1 8 2
        2 4
      − 0
        2 4 6
      −2 3 4
            1 2
```

Divide.

1.
```
          3
75)2 3, 5 5 0
  −2 2 5 ↓
    1 0 5
```

2. 42)54,364

3. 62)60,202

4. 89)95,720

5. 92)77,777

6. 28)14,118

7. 39)67,612

8. 59)10,830

Dividing by Hundreds

When you divide by hundreds, look at the first 3 or 4 digits of the **dividend** to determine your first trial quotient. From that point on, use the same steps: divide, multiply, and subtract.

Find: 52,386 ÷ 388

Divide.
Multiply. Subtract.

```
              1
    388)5 2, 3 8 6
      - 3 8 8  ↓
        1, 3 5 8
```

Divide.
Multiply. Subtract.

```
             1 3
    388)5 2, 3 8 6
      - 3 8 8   |
        1, 3 5 8
      - 1, 1 6 4  ↓
          1, 9 4 6
```

Divide.
Multiply. Subtract.

```
             1 3 5 R6
    388)5 2, 3 8 6
      - 3 8 8
        1, 3 5 8
      - 1, 1 6 4
          1, 9 4 6
        - 1, 9 4 0
              6
```

Divide.

1.
```
            2 3
   341)7 9, 5 6 0
     - 6 8 2  ↓
       1, 1 3 6
     - 1, 0 2 3  ↓
         1, 1 3 0
```

2. 453)18,327

3. 236)3,317

4. 426)3,966

5. 863)63,043

6. 904)75,000

7. 506)435,160

8. 246)123,456

9. 716)69,464

7

Multiplication and Division Practice

Multiply.

1.   72
    × 4

2.   319
    × 3

3.   1,728
    ×   9

4.   50,800
    ×   4

5.   37
    × 24

6.   78
    × 56

7.   485
    × 92

8.   6,948
    ×   89

9.   9,967
    ×   36

10.   45,847
     ×   65

11.   592
     × 231

12.   6,342
     × 358

Divide.

13. $63\overline{)834}$

14. $9\overline{)8,452}$

15. $4\overline{)2,563}$

16. $7\overline{)36,533}$

17. $24\overline{)96}$

18. $27\overline{)5,776}$

19. $14\overline{)1,032}$

20. $268\overline{)8,174}$

21. $85\overline{)71,995}$

22. $60\overline{)28,988}$

23. $57\overline{)34,676}$

24. $357\overline{)44,982}$

Name _____ Date _____

Factors and Greatest Common Factor

List the factors of each number.

1. 16 _____   2. 39 _____   3. 50 _____

Find the GCF of each pair of numbers.

4. 40 and 48 _____   5. 10 and 45 _____

6. 6 and 21 _____   7. 60 and 72 _____

8. 21 and 40 _____   9. 28 and 32 _____

10. 28 and 70 _____   11. 45 and 81 _____

12. 30 and 45 _____   13. 55 and 77 _____

14. Mrs. Davis is sewing vests. She has 16 green buttons and 24 yellow buttons. Each vest will have the same number of yellow buttons and the same number of green buttons. What is the greatest number of vests Mrs. Davis can make using all of the buttons?

_____ vests

15. A baker has 27 raisin bagels and 36 plain bagels that will be divided into boxes. Each box must have the same number of raisin bagels and the same number of plain bagels. What is the greatest number of boxes the baker can make using all of the bagels?

_____ boxes

16. Lola is putting appetizers on plates. She has 63 meatballs and 84 cheese cubes. She wants both kinds of food on each plate, and each plate must have the same number of meatballs and the same number of cheese cubes. What is the greatest number of plates she can make using all of the appetizers?

_____ plates

17. The Delta High School marching band has 54 members. The Swanton High School marching band has 90 members. The bands are going to march in a parade together. The director wants to arrange the bands into the same number of rows. What is the greatest number of rows in which the two bands can be arranged?

_____ rows

Write each sum as a product of the GCF and the sum of two numbers.

18. 75 + 90   19. 36 and 45

_____   _____

20. 56 + 64   21. 48 + 14

_____   _____

9

Greatest Common Factor

List the factors of each number. Then find the GCF.

1. 18, 27

    18: _____

    27: _____

    GCF: _____

2. 28, 35

    28: _____

    35: _____

    GCF: _____

3. 12, 15

    12: _____

    15: _____

    GCF: _____

Use prime factorization to find the GCF.

4. 15, 35

    15: _____

    35: _____

    GCF: _____

5. 24, 36

    24: _____

    36: _____

    GCF: _____

6. 21, 45

    21: _____

    45: _____

    GCF: _____

Forest City has ordered 36 maple trees and 54 dogwood trees to be planted in groups in a city park. Each group will have the same number of maple trees and dogwood trees.

7. Can the trees be planted in

    6 groups? _____

    8 groups? _____

    9 groups? _____

8. What is the greatest number of groups of trees that can be planted? How many trees of each kind would be in one group?

    _____

    _____

Find the missing numbers. Explain the pattern.

9. 1, 3, _____, 15, 25, 75

10. 1, 2, 7, _____, 49, 98

11. 1, 2, 4, 5, 10, 20, 25, _____, 100

12. 1, 2, 3, 4, 6, 8, 12, _____, 24, 48

_____

_____

Exploring Least Common Multiples

Draw a number line or list multiples to solve.

1. Name three multiples of 4 greater than 0. _____

2. Name three multiples of 5 greater than 0. _____

3. Name two multiples of 3 that are also multiples of 4. _____

4. Name two common multiples of 9 and 2. _____

5. What is the least common multiple of 6 and 12? _____

6. What is the least common multiple of 5 and 8? _____

Use the table for Exercises 7–9.

7. Hester is making necklaces using three kinds of beads. She buys the beads in boxes, and she wants to use all the beads she buys. If she wants to use the same number of beads of each kind, what is the least number of beads she can put in one necklace?

_____

Number in a Box	Kind of Bead
9	
12	
4	

8. Hester wants to make a bead bracelet. She plans to use only the small and the large round beads. If she uses the same number of each size of bead, what is the least number of beads she will need?

_____

9. Hester makes another bracelet using only the small round beads and the beads with flat surfaces. If she uses the same number of each size of bead, what is the least number of beads she will put in the bracelet?

_____

10. Use the diagram to find the least common multiple of 3 and 4.

_____

multiples of 3   multiples of 4

multiples of 3		multiples of 4
3, 6, 9, 15, 18, 21	12, 24	4, 8, 16, 20

Name _____ Date _____

Least Common Multiple

List multiples to find the LCM of each pair of numbers.

1. 4 and 9 _____

2. 18 and 24 _____

3. What is the LCM of two numbers when one number is a multiple of the other? Give an example.

_____

_____

4. What is the LCM of two numbers that have no common factors greater than 1? Give an example.

_____

_____

Find the LCM of each pair of numbers.

5. 6 and 9 _____

6. 9 and 21 _____

7. 8 and 56 _____

8. 16 and 24 _____

9. 12 and 30 _____

10. 6 and 10 _____

11. At a restaurant, on every 12th visit, you receive a free beverage. On every 15th visit, you receive a free dessert. On which visit will you first receive a free beverage and a free dessert?

Visit _____

12. Starting today (day 1) Lee will swim every 3rd day and jog every 5th day. On which day will Lee first swim and jog?

Day _____

Use the train schedule for Exercises 13 and 14.

13. The red line and the blue line trains just arrived at the station. When will they next arrive at the station at the same time?

In _____ minutes

Train Schedule	
Train	**Arrives Every...**
Red line	8 minutes
Blue line	10 minutes
Yellow line	12 minutes

14. All three trains just arrived at the station. When will they next all arrive at the station at the same time?

In _____ minutes

Using the GCF and the LCM

Solve.

1. Toby fertilizes the plants in a nursery every sixth day, and May prunes the plants every fourteenth day. They are both fertilizing and pruning plants today. How many days will pass before both will again fertilize and prune on the same day?

_____

2. Ramona is cutting tags for trees from a 27-inch strip of paper and from a 30-inch strip of paper. Each tag will be the same length. Each strip of paper will be cut into equal lengths. What is the longest length she can cut for each tag?

_____

3. Viola is arranging mixed bouquets of carnations and roses in vases. Into each vase she places an equal number of each type of flower. If there are 48 carnations and 60 roses, what is the largest number of vases Viola could use and still have the same combination of flowers in each vase?

_____

4. Pam can wash a car in 8 minutes. It takes Rob 10 minutes to wash a car. They begin at the same time. How long will it be before they have both washed a whole number of cars?

_____

5. Mort has a certain number of Venus' flytraps to sell at his booth at a school science fair. It is possible to arrange the total number of plants into groups of 9 or 12. What is the smallest number of Venus' flytraps he can have in his booth?

_____

6. A 126-inch board and a 168-inch board are being cut for steps at a nursery. All steps are to be the same length. Each board is to be cut into equal lengths. What is the longest length that can be cut for each step?

_____

Write the prime factorization, using exponents when possible.

7. 24

8. 32

9. 58

_____   _____   _____

Understanding Numbers and Absolute Value

The **absolute value** of a number is its distance from 0 on a number line. Look at 2 and -2. They are both 2 units away from 0.

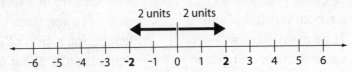

2 is 2 units from 0. The absolute value of 2 is 2.

-2 is 2 units from 0. The absolute value of -2 is 2.

$|2| = 2$ is read as *the absolute value of 2 equals 2.*

$|-2| = 2$ is read as *the absolute value of -2 equals 2.*

$|3| = 3$ $|-4| = 4$ $|1| = 1$ $|-5| = 5$

Find the absolute value of each number.

1. $|6| =$ **2.** $|-9| =$ **3.** $|-8| =$ **4.** $|-13| =$

_____   _____   _____   _____

5. $|18| =$ **6.** $|-3| =$ **7.** $|10| =$ **8.** $|-15| =$

_____   _____   _____   _____

9. $|-7| =$ **10.** $|0| =$ **11.** $|-17| =$ **12.** $|22| =$

_____   _____   _____   _____

13. $|-12| =$ **14.** $|-19| =$ **15.** $|-11| =$ **16.** $|26| =$

_____   _____   _____   _____

Name the two numbers that have the given absolute value.

17. 30   **18.** 14   **19.** 32   **20.** 29

    30, -30

_____   _____   _____   _____

21. 21   **22.** 23   **23.** 42   **24.** 99

_____   _____   _____   _____

14

Absolute Value

Graph the following numbers on the number line.

1. -7   5   7   -2   4   -4

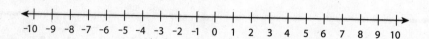

Use the number line to find each absolute value.

2. $|-7|$ =

3. $|5|$ =

4. $|7|$ =

_____

_____

_____

5. $|-2|$ =

6. $|4|$ =

7. $|-4|$ =

_____

_____

_____

8. Which pairs of numbers have the same absolute value? How are these numbers related?

_____

_____

9. Do you think a number's absolute value can be 0? If so, which number(s) have an absolute value of 0? Explain.

_____

_____

10. If a number is _____, then the number is equal to its absolute value. If a number

is _____, then the number is less than its absolute value.

11. Negative numbers are less than positive numbers. Does this mean that the absolute value of a negative number must be less than the absolute value of a positive number? Explain.

_____

_____

The Number Line

> **Positive numbers** are numbers greater than 0. They are located to the right of 0 on a number line. **Negative numbers** are numbers less than 0. They are located to the left of 0 on a number line. The number 0 is neither positive nor negative.

The elevation of a location describes its height above or below sea level, which has elevation 0. Elevations below sea level are represented by negative numbers, and elevations above sea level are represented by positive numbers.

1. The table shows the elevations of several locations in a state park. Graph the locations on the number line according to their elevations.

Location	Little Butte A	Cradle Creek B	Dinosaur Valley C	Mesa Ridge D	Juniper Trail E
Elevation (ft)	5	-5	-8.5	8	-3

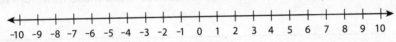

2. What point on the number line represents sea level? _____

3. Which location is closest to sea level? How do you know?

   _____

4. Is the location in Exercise 3 above or below sea level? _____

5. Which two locations are the same distance from sea level? Are these locations above or below sea level?

   _____

6. The table below shows winter temperatures of several world cities. Graph the cities on the number line according to their temperatures.

City	Anchorage, AK, USA F	Fargo, ND, USA G	Oslo, Norway H	St. Petersburg, Russia I	Helsinki, Finland J	Budapest, Hungary K
Temperature (°F)	-4	9	-6	-10	7	6

Core Skills Math Review

Name _____   Date _____

Integers and Opposites

Integers are the set of whole numbers and their **opposites**. Integers can be shown on a number line.
Positive integers are greater than 0. **Negative** integers are less than 0.

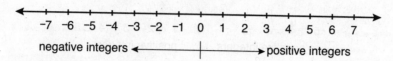

The integer –5 is read *negative five*. The integer 5 can also be written as +5, or *positive five*. These two integers, 5 and –5, are opposites.

Positive and negative numbers are used in many everyday situations.

10° below zero	–10
loss of $7	–7
gain of 12 yards	+12 or 12
profit of $100	+100 or 100

Write the opposite of each integer.

1. 4

_____–4_____

2. –7

_____

3. –21

_____

4. 45

_____

5. –19

_____

6. 33

_____

7. –66

_____

8. 0

_____

Write an integer to describe each situation.

9. 33° above zero

_____+33_____

10. 8° below zero

_____

11. deposit of $150

_____

12. loss of 10 yards

_____

13. gain of 6 yards

_____

14. profit of $88

_____

15. 3,500 ft above sea level

_____

16. 50 ft below sea level

_____

17. up 7 floors

_____

18. down 4 floors

_____

19. debt of $30

_____

20. 9 units to the left of 0

_____

17

Unit 1
Core Skills Math Review

Comparing and Ordering Integers

To compare integers, think about their positions on a number line. An integer is less than any integer to its right. An integer is greater than any integer to its left.

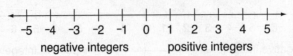

negative integers   positive integers

4 is to the right of 2.   3 is to the left of 5.

2 < 4 and 4 > 2   5 > 3 and 3 < 5

-1 is to the right of -2.   -4 is to the left of -3.

-2 < -1 and -1 > -2   -3 > -4 and -4 < -3

Compare. Write <, >, or =.

1. 4 ___<___ 5   2. -2 _____ 9   3. 4 _____ -4

4. 6 _____ -3   5. 0 _____ 0   6. -8 _____ -1

7. -2 _____ -6   8. -7 _____ 3   9. 10 _____ -15

10. -10 _____ 1   11. -14 _____ -12   12. -4 _____ -9

13. 14 _____ 14   14. 7 _____ -5   15. -6 _____ -6

16. 1 _____ -2   17. 0 _____ -3   18. -9 _____ 5

19. -7 _____ -9   20. 16 _____ 16   21. -5 _____ -8

22. -15 _____ -11   23. -8 _____ 5   24. -4 _____ -5

Write in order from least to greatest.

25. 0, 7, -6 _____-6, 0, 7_____   26. -5, -9, 7 _____

27. 1, -1, 11 _____   28. 27, 12, -21 _____

29. 8, 3, -2 _____   30. -3, -13, 0 _____

31. 5, 4, -11 _____   32. -20, -16, 19 _____

Adding and Subtracting Integers

To add integers, use the absolute value of the numbers.

Adding Integers with the Same Sign	**Adding Integers with Different Signs**
$(-3) + (-4)$	$-6 + 2$
Find the absolute value of each integer.	Find the absolute value of each integer.
$\lvert -3 \rvert = 3 \quad \lvert -4 \rvert = 4$	$\lvert -6 \rvert = 6 \quad \lvert 2 \rvert = 2$
Add the absolute values.	Subtract the lesser absolute value from the greater absolute value.
$3 + 4 = 7$	$6 - 2 = 4$
Use the sign of the addends for the sum.	Use the sign of the addend with the greater absolute value for the sum.
$(-3) + (-4) = -7$	$-6 + 2 = -4$

Subtracting an integer is the same as adding its opposite.

Subtract: $5 - 2$	**Subtract: $6 - (-3)$**	**Subtract: $-4 - 1$**
The opposite of 2 is -2.	The opposite of -3 is 3.	The opposite of 1 is -1.
$5 - 2 = 5 + (-2) = 3$	$6 - (-3) = 6 + 3 = 9$	$-4 - 1 = -4 + (-1) = -5$

Add.

1. $5 + -3 =$ 2. $-4 + -6 =$ 3. $3 + -1 =$ 4. $-7 + 3 =$

_____   _____   _____   _____

5. $-9 + -3 =$ 6. $8 + -1 =$ 7. $4 + -11 =$ 8. $-8 + -10 =$

_____   _____   _____   _____

9. $-1 + -2 =$ 10. $-10 + 2 =$ 11. $12 + -3 =$ 12. $-2 + 15 =$

_____   _____   _____   _____

Rewrite the subtraction problems as addition. Use addition rules to find the answer.

13. $5 - (-3) =$ 14. $-7 - 1 =$ 15. $-9 - (-9) =$ 16. $4 - 8 =$

_____   _____   _____   _____

17. $-8 - (-1) =$ 18. $-6 - (-2) =$ 19. $-12 - (-7) =$ 20. $-9 - 10 =$

_____   _____   _____   _____

19

Name _____   Date _____

Multiplying and Dividing Integers

When multiplying or dividing two integers, first find the product or quotient of their absolute values. Then use the following rules to determine the sign in the product or quotient.

• The product or quotient of two integers with the same sign is positive.

• The product or quotient of two integers with different signs is negative.

Find: -4 × 6	**Find:** -15 ÷ -3
4 × 6 = 24	15 ÷ 3 = 5
The signs of -4 and 6 are different, so the product is negative.	The signs of -15 and -3 are the same, so the quotient is positive.
-4 × 6 = -24	-15 ÷ -3 = 5

Multiply.

1. 3 × -3 =

2. -2 × -2 =

3. -4 × -3 =

4. 7 × -6 =

5. -9 × -3 =

6. 6 × -2 =

7. 2 × -10 =

8. -6 × -3 =

9. -4 × -6 =

10. -8 × 3 =

11. 5 × 6 =

12. -2 × 5 =

13. -1 × 0 =

14 -5 × -4 =

15. -7 × -3 =

16. -4 × -8 =

Divide.

17. 18 ÷ -3 =

18. -4 ÷ 1 =

19. -9 ÷ -3 =

20. 48 ÷ -8 =

21. -8 ÷ -2 =

22. -18 ÷ 9 =

23. -32 ÷ -4 =

24. -90 ÷ 10 =

25. 24 ÷ 4 =

26. 42 ÷ -6 =

27. 0 ÷ -5 =

28. -8 ÷ 8 =

29. -35 ÷ -5 =

30. -28 ÷ -7 =

31. -18 ÷ -2 =

32. -12 ÷ 3 =

Unit 1
Core Skills Math Review

Order of Operations

A **numerical expression** has only numbers and at least one operation.

To simplify such an expression, follow the **order of operations** listed at the right.

Order of Operations:

1. Complete operations within parentheses.
2. Multiply and divide from left to right.
3. Add and subtract from left to right.

Find: 48 ÷ (9 − 3)

$48 ÷ (9 − 3) =$ Complete the operation within the parentheses.

$48 ÷ 6 = 8$ Divide.

Find: 7 + 18 ÷ 6

$7 + 18 ÷ 6 =$ Divide.
$7 + 3 = 10$ Add.

Simplify.

1. $3 × (4 + 6) =$

$3 × 10 = 30$

2. $(18 − 4) ÷ 2 =$

3. $(11 − 7) × \text{-}5 =$

4. $56 ÷ (3 + 4) =$

5. $14 + 16 ÷ 4 =$

6. $20 − 2 × 9 =$

7. $15 + 1 × 6 =$

8. $\text{-}17 − 15 ÷ 5 =$

9. $5 × (12 − 5) =$

10. $36 ÷ (3 + \text{-}6) =$

11. $(8 + 7) × 2 =$

12. $(24 − 12) ÷ 3 =$

13. $36 − 4 × 7 =$

14. $13 + 42 ÷ 6 =$

15. $30 − 20 ÷ 10 =$

16. $3 + 9 × 3 =$

17. $5 × 4 ÷ 2 =$

18. $20 ÷ (2 × 5) =$

19. $(20 ÷ 2) × \text{-}5 =$

20. $(29 − 7) ÷ 2 =$

21. $\text{-}6 + (3 × 3) =$

22. $(16 + \text{-}4) ÷ 6 =$

23. $(9 − 5) × \text{-}2 =$

24. $(35 ÷ \text{-}7) − 8 =$

21

Unit 1 Review

Divide.

1. $32\overline{)7,455}$

2. $48\overline{)5,624}$

3. $401\overline{)92,233}$

4. $225\overline{)87,525}$

Find the GCF of each pair of numbers.

5. 14, 28

6. 36, 40

7. 18, 30

8. 27, 81

Find the LCM of each pair of numbers.

9. 5, 8

10. 6, 10

11. 13, 52

12. 3, 9

Find the absolute value of each number.

13. $|-51|$

14. $|0|$

15. $|16|$

16. $|-43|$

Add, subtract, multiply, or divide.

17. $-3 + {-2} =$

18. $9 - {-1} =$

19. $-3 \times {-1} =$

20. $-64 \div {-8} =$

Evaluate each expression.

21. $9 \div 3 \times 5 =$

22. $4(8 - 1) =$

23. $(5 + 6) \times 3 =$

24. $18 - 8 \div 2 =$

Write in order from least to greatest.

25. $-4, 4, -8$

26. $7, 6, -9$

22

Fraction and Decimal Equivalents

Sometimes you will need to either change a decimal to a fraction or a fraction to a decimal.

To write a decimal as a fraction, identify the value of the last place in the decimal. Use this place value to write the denominator. Simplify if possible.

To write a fraction that has a denominator of 10; 100; or 1,000 as a decimal, write the digits from the numerator. Write the decimal point so that the number of decimal places is the same as the number of zeros in the denominator of the fraction. Write zeros as needed.

Decimal		Fraction or Mixed Number		Fraction or Mixed Number		Decimal
0.9	=	$\frac{9}{10}$		$\frac{3}{10}$	=	0.3
0.01	=	$\frac{1}{100}$		$\frac{15}{100}$	=	0.15
0.045	=	$\frac{45}{1000} = \frac{9}{200}$		$\frac{6}{1000}$	=	0.006
1.74	=	$1\frac{74}{100} = 1\frac{37}{50}$		$\frac{59}{10}$ or $5\frac{9}{10}$	=	5.9

Write each decimal as a fraction. Simplify.

1. 0.4 = _____   **2.** 0.6 = _____   **3.** 0.08 = _____   **4.** 0.002 = _____

5. 0.21 = _____   **6.** 0.083 = _____   **7.** 0.901 = _____   **8.** 0.018 = _____

Write each decimal as a mixed number. Simplify.

9. 4.5 = _____   **10.** 1.62 = _____   **11.** 10.1 = _____   **12.** 1.275 = _____

13. 9.07 = _____   **14.** 38.24 = _____   **15.** 5.46 = _____   **16.** 13.8 = _____

Write each fraction as a decimal.

17. $\frac{1}{10}$ = _____   **18.** $\frac{2}{10}$ = _____   **19.** $\frac{5}{10}$ = _____   **20.** $\frac{7}{10}$ = _____

21. $\frac{6}{100}$ = _____   **22.** $\frac{80}{100}$ = _____   **23.** $\frac{52}{1000}$ = _____   **24.** $\frac{416}{1000}$ = _____

25. $\frac{56}{10}$ = _____   **26.** $\frac{31}{10}$ = _____   **27.** $\frac{76}{10}$ = _____   **28.** $\frac{65}{100}$ = _____

29. $\frac{103}{100}$ = _____   **30.** $\frac{509}{100}$ = _____   **31.** $\frac{1643}{1000}$ = _____   **32.** $\frac{2051}{1000}$ = _____

Name _____ Date _____

More Fraction and Decimal Equivalents

Not all fractions can be changed to decimal form easily. To write fractions that have denominators other than 10; 100; or 1,000 as decimals, first write an equivalent fraction that has a denominator of 10; 100; or 1,000. Then write the equivalent fraction as a decimal.

Some fractions do not have simple decimal equivalents.

Examples: $\frac{2}{3} = 0.666 \ldots$ and $\frac{5}{6} = 0.833 \ldots$

Write $\frac{1}{5}$ as a decimal.

Write $\frac{1}{5}$ with 10 as the denominator.	Write the fraction as a decimal.
$\frac{1}{5} = \frac{1 \times 2}{5 \times 2} = \frac{2}{10}$	$= 0.2$

Write $2\frac{3}{4}$ as a decimal.

Write $2\frac{3}{4}$ as an improper fraction.	Write the new fraction with 100 as the denominator.	Write the fraction as a decimal.
$2\frac{3}{4} = \frac{11}{4}$	$\frac{11}{4} = \frac{11 \times 25}{4 \times 25} = \frac{275}{100}$	$= 2.75$

Write each fraction as a decimal.

1. $\frac{1}{8} = \frac{1 \times 125}{8 \times 125} = \frac{125}{1000} =$ _____

2. $\frac{2}{5} =$ _____

3. $\frac{3}{20} =$ _____

4. $\frac{4}{5} =$ _____

5. $\frac{17}{50} =$ _____

6. $\frac{11}{25} =$ _____

7. $\frac{7}{200} =$ _____

8. $\frac{8}{25} =$ _____

9. $\frac{3}{8} =$ _____

10. $\frac{13}{2} = \frac{13 \times 5}{2 \times 5} = \frac{65}{10} =$ _____

11. $\frac{43}{20} =$ _____

12. $\frac{37}{5} =$ _____

13. $\frac{25}{4} =$ _____

14. $\frac{69}{50} =$ _____

15. $\frac{39}{25} =$ _____

Write each mixed number as a decimal.

16. $1\frac{9}{20} = \frac{29}{20} = \frac{29 \times 5}{20 \times 5} = \frac{145}{100} =$ _____

17. $2\frac{21}{25} =$ _____

18. $6\frac{3}{25} =$ _____

19. $13\frac{1}{50} =$ _____

20. $19\frac{1}{2} =$ _____

21. $4\frac{7}{8} =$ _____

24

Unit 2
Core Skills Math Review

Addition of Decimals

To add decimals, line up the decimal points. Write zeros as needed. Then add as with whole numbers. Be sure to write a decimal point in the sum.

Find: 4.6 + 7.32

Write a zero.

T	O	Ts	Hs
	4	.6	0
+	7	.3	2

Add the hundredths.

T	O	Ts	Hs
	4	.6	0
+	7	.3	2
			2

Add the tenths. Write a decimal point in the sum.

T	O	Ts	Hs
	4	.6	0
+	7	.3	2
		.9	2

Add the ones.

T	O	Ts	Hs
	4	.6	0
+	7	.3	2
1	1	.9	2

Add. Write zeros as needed.

1.

O	Ts	Hs
$3	.1	9
+ 2	.2	2

2.

O	Ts	Hs
$0	.0	2
+ 0	.5	7

3.

T	O	Ts	Hs
$1	4	.9	0
+		1	.9	6

4.

T	O	Ts	Hs
$4	2	.0	8
+		0	.1	6

5.

O	Ts	Hs	Ths
0	.3	0	0
+0	.0	0	6

6.

T	O	Ts	Hs	Ths
2	2	.1	3	
+	7	.0	9	8

7.

H	T	O	Ts
2	3	8	
+	7	7	.3

8.

T	O	Ts	Hs
2	4	.1	5
+3	0	.1	

9.

T	O	Ts	Hs
$	2	.1	0
	4	.0	8
+	5	.2	5

10.

T	O	Ts	Hs	Ths
1	4	.0	0	5
1	6	.1	9	3
+	7	.3	2	7

11.

O	Ts	Hs	Ths
0	.3	5	6
0	.4	3	0
+0	.8	1	7

12.

T	O	Ts	Hs	Ths
1	4	.0	0	5
	0	.0	4	3
+	2	.6	8	9

13.

T	O	Ts	Hs	Ths
1	2	2		
	4	.0	9	0
3	3	.9	8	4
1	0	.4	0	0
+2	3	.7	3	0

14.

T	O	Ts	Hs	Ths
9	.4	5	1	
0	.0	0	7	
7	.3			
+ 6	.5	3	6	

15.

H	T	O	Ts	Hs
$2	3	1	.2	4
	6	1	.6	
1	4	2	.0	5
+1	0	0	.1	1

16.

T	O	Ts	Hs	Ths
5	6	.1	1	2
	4	.2	2	3
2	4	.7	3	6
+1	4			

Practice Addition of Decimals

Add. Write zeros as needed.

1.	5.9 + 3.62	**2.**	7.08 + 3.265	**3.**	14.076 + 8.46	**4.**	17.05 + 3.351

5.	28.009 4.65 + 6.003	**6.**	77.016 4.57 + 0.647	**7.**	84.7 0.403 + 3.08	**8.**	8.23 36.5 + 0.009

9.	$12.20 2.10 4.08 + 5.25	**10.**	8.050 14.005 16.1 + 7.32	**11.**	0.22 0.356 0.439 + 0.8	**12.**	6.126 14.005 0.04 + 2.6

13.	2.005 0.15 0.6 + 3	**14.**	0.009 0.14 0.6 + 2.10	**15.**	0.14 0.060 0.17 + 8.5	**16.**	0.702 0.005 0.034 + 7.16

Line up the decimals. Then find the sums. Write zeros as needed.

17. $9 + 3.4 + 0.7 =$
9.0
3.4
+ 0.7

_____

18. $$6.54 + $10 + $8.35 =$$

_____

19. $6.9 + 12.7 + 38.6 =$

_____

20. $37.5 + 5.3 + 8 + 3.273 =$

_____

Subtraction of Decimals

To subtract decimals, line up the decimal points. Write zeros as needed. Then subtract as with whole numbers. Be sure to write a decimal point in the difference.

Find: 34.3 − 17.94

Write a zero. Regroup to subtract the hundredths.	Regroup to subtract the tenths. Write a decimal point in the difference.	Regroup to subtract the ones.	Subtract the tens.

T	O	Ts	Hs
		2	10
3	4	.3̸	0̸
− 1	7	.9	4
			6

T	O	Ts	Hs
		12	
	3	2̸	10
3	4̸	.3̸	0̸
− 1	7	.9	4
		.3	6

T	O	Ts	Hs
	13	12	
2	3̸	2̸	10
3̸	4̸	.3̸	0̸
− 1	7	.9	4
	6	.3	6

T	O	Ts	Hs
	13	12	
2	3̸	2̸	10
3̸	4̸	.3̸	0̸
− 1	7	.9	4
1	6	.3	6

Subtract. Write zeros as needed.

1.

O	Ts	Hs	Ths
5	.4	9	8
−2	.3	6	2

2.

O	Ts	Hs
7	.5	4
−6	.3	8

3.

T	O	Ts	Hs	Ths
1	5	.0	6	5
−	9	.4	6	6

4.

T	O	Ts	Hs
$4	7	.6	2
−2	3	.8	5

5.

O	Ts	Hs	Ths
7	.0	5	0
−3	.1	3	5

6.

T	O	Ts	Hs
1	2	.5	0
−	7	.7	5

7.

O	Ts	Hs
8	.1	4
−6	.1	0

8.

O	Ts	Hs	Ths
2	.8	7	7
−0	.9	8	0

9.

O	Ts	Hs	Ths
7	.5	8	9
−3	.3	4	7

10.

T	O	Ts	Hs
2	4	.3	6
−	7	.1	6

11.

O	Ts	Hs	Ths
8	.1	1	3
−7	.3	0	5

12.

T	O	Ts	Hs
$2	1	.0	9
−1	6	.9	5

13.

O	Ts	Hs	Ths
8	.0	9	0
−4	.2	5	6

14.

O	Ts	Hs	Ths
1	.5	2	0
−0	.4	0	8

15.

T	O	Ts	Hs
7	5	.1	6
− 5	2	.8	0

16.

T	O	Ts	Hs
4	0	.3	3
−2	9	.7	0

Unit 2
Core Skills Math Review

Practice Subtraction of Decimals

Subtract. Write zeros as needed.

1. 8.325
    − 3.203
    _____

2. 7.278
    − 5.12
    _____

3. 9.068
    − 7.054
    _____

4. 10.399
    − 10.239
    _____

5. $34.95
    − 27.99
    _____

6. $92.00
    − 67.50
    _____

7. $94.78
    − 15.00
    _____

8. $11,532.30
    − 2,500.00
    _____

9. 6.2
    − 4.575
    _____

10. 1.9
    − 0.674
    _____

11. 1.354
    − 0.265
    _____

12. 92.15
    − 84.7
    _____

13. 8.09
    − 4.256
    _____

14. 94.78
    − 15
    _____

15. 19.005
    − 14.5
    _____

16. 1.52
    − 0.408
    _____

Line up the decimals. Then find the difference. Write zeros as needed.

17. 7.05 − 3.035 =

    7.050
    − 3.035
    _____

18. 8.14 − 6.1 =

19. 75.06 − 52.8 =

20. 92.15 − 84.7 =

21. 12.5 − 7.75 =

22. 1.354 − 0.265 =

Write as a decimal.

23. six thousandths _____

24. twelve hundredths _____

25. twenty thousandths _____

26. four hundredths _____

27. nine tenths _____

28. forty thousandths _____

29. three and three tenths _____

30. six and eight thousandths _____

Practice Adding and Subtracting Decimals

Estimate the answer. Then add or subtract. Use your estimate to check your answer.

1.   0.4
    0.2
 + 0.3
	2. 0.02
	    0.05
	 + 0.01
		3. 1.08
		    2.02
		 + 0.45
			4. 4.57
			    2.93
			 + 4.87

5.   3.06
    4.09
    2.08
 + 1.01
	6. 0.08
	    0.03
	    0.02
	 + 0.06
		7. 0.15
		    0.08
		    0.43
		 + 0.17
			8. 0.25
			    0.6
			    0.10
			 + 0.05

9.   2.86
    0.7
    0.12
 + 0.081
	10. 4
	    0.05
	    1.6
	 + 0.003
		11. 2.031
		    4.175
		    3.098
		 + 1.006
			12. 150.48
			    25.98
			    16.50
			 + 250.00

13. 0.8 − 0.2	14. 14.6 − 5.4	15. 0.67 − 0.48	16. 0.86 − 0.79
17. 0.679 − 0.398	18. 15.8 − 3.9	19. 6.504 − 2.8	20. 7.8 − 1.26
21. 0.6593 − 0.4271	22. 1.8531 − 0.9248	23. 84.35 − 36.95	24. 8.000 − 1.742

Line up the decimals. Then find the sum and differences.

25. $1.24 + 0.078 + 2.9 =$

26. $18.4957 - 2.36 =$

_____

27. $324.6 - 75.908 =$

28. $168.95 - 9.36 =$

_____

More Practice Adding and Subtracting Decimals

Add. After you find each answer, check with a calculator.

1.	**2.**	**3.**	**4.**
1.4	8	7.053	1.38
0.7	0.53	0.96	16.48
0.29	2.1	8.524	9.27
+ 2.456	+ 10.68	+ 1.8	+ 0.84

5.	**6.**	**7.**	**8.**
8.3407	3.97	22.95	349.95
0.0038	0.95	5.50	6.50
1.153	8.49	0.98	24.00
+ 7.4619	+ 3.16	+ 16.49	+ 9.99

Line up the decimals. Then find the sums.

9. $3.3 + 0.07 + 6 + 2.63 + 0.174 =$

10. $15.4 + 2.185 + 0.66 + 21.009 =$

11. $0.74 + 1.6 + 0.99 + 4.88 + 0.04 =$

12. $3.42 + 15.98 + 25 + 12.45 =$

Subtract. After you find each answer, check with a calculator.

13.	**14.**	**15.**	**16.**
0.45	23.87	4.2	3.56
− 0.216	− 2.1	− 0.372	− 0.8

17.	**18.**	**19.**	**20.**
12	8.7645	7.0008	56
− 0.743	− 3	− 2.5	− 2.003

Line up the decimals. Then find the differences.

21. $12.54 − 1.054 =$

22. $4 − 0.875 =$

23. $15.42 − 9 =$

24. $27 − 0.0067 =$

25. $0.03 − 0.0034 =$

26. $100 − 84.53 =$

Multiplying Decimals by Whole Numbers

To multiply decimals by whole numbers, multiply the same way you would multiply whole numbers. Place the decimal point in the product by counting the total number of decimal places in the factors. The product will have the same number of decimal places.

Remember, sometimes you might need to write a zero in the product in order to place the decimal point correctly.

Find: 13 × 6.4

Multiply. Write the decimal point in the product.

```
    6.4        1 decimal place
  ×  13      + 0 decimal places
    192      _____
  + 640
   83.2        1 decimal place
```

Find: 0.018 × 5

Multiply. Write the decimal point in the product.

```
   0.018       3 decimal places
  ×    5      + 0 decimal places
   0.090        3 decimal places
     └┘─Write zeros.
```

Multiply. Write zeros as needed.

1.
```
    2
   17
  × 0.3
   5.1
```
__1__ place

2.
```
   24
  × 0.09
```
____ places

3.
```
  0.707
  ×    2
```
____ places

4.
```
    2
  × 0.2
```
____ place

5.
```
  0.105
  ×    8
```
____ places

6.
```
  0.19
  ×   5
```
____ places

7.
```
  0.003
  ×    4
```
____ places

8.
```
    2
  × 0.03
```
____ places

9.
```
  0.006
  ×    9
```
____ places

10.
```
  3.84
  ×  35
```
____ places

11.
```
  0.135
  ×   44
```
____ places

12.
```
  9.28
  × 230
```
____ places

13.
```
   321
  × 1.46
```
____ places

14.
```
  4.53
  × 579
```
____ places

15.
```
  0.692
  ×  168
```
____ places

31

Practice Multiplying Decimals by Whole Numbers

Multiply. Write zeros as needed.

1. 0.862
    × 2

2. 0.084
    × 3

3. 1.63
    × 6

4. 2.34
    × 5

5. 13.6
    × 3

6. 28.52
    × 4

7. 1.3
    × 13

8. 26
    × 1.3

9. 8.2
    × 12

10. 62
    × 0.35

11. 70
    × 5.0

12. 0.90
    × 55

13. 3.07
    × 25

14. 0.048
    × 82

15. 234
    × 0.059

16. 707
    × 0.690

Line up the digits. Then find the products. Write zeros as needed.

17. $15.2 \times 6 =$

    15.2
    × 6

18. $0.908 \times 31 =$

19. $7.85 \times 109 =$

20. $56 \times 0.347 =$

21. $247 \times 0.63 =$

22. $28 \times 0.1279 =$

Multiplying Decimals by Decimals

To multiply decimals by decimals, multiply the same way you would multiply whole numbers. Place the decimal point in the product by counting the total number of decimal places in the factors. The product will have the same number of decimal places. Write zeros as needed.

Find: 0.48×13.7

Multiply. Write the decimal point in the product.

```
      13.7          1 place
  ×   0.48        + 2 places
      1096
  +   548
      6.576          3 places
```

Find: 0.008×0.137

Multiply. Write the decimal point in the product.

```
      0.137          3 places
  ×   0.008        + 3 places
    0.001096          6 places
```
└── Write zeros.

Multiply. Write zeros as needed.

1.
```
      2
      1.6          1 place
  ×   0.4        + 1 place
      0.64          2 places
```

2.
```
      5.3          place
  ×  0.09        + places
                   places
```

3.
```
      0.76          places
  ×   0.5        + place
                   places
```

4.
```
      0.12          places
  ×   0.6        + places
                   places
```

5.
```
      0.09          places
  ×   0.3        + place
                   places
```

6.
```
      0.002          places
  ×   0.4        + place
                   places
```

7.
```
      0.184          places
  ×   0.07        + places
                   places
```

8.
```
      2.04          places
  ×   0.2        + place
                   places
```

9.
```
      5.19          places
  ×   0.03        + places
                   places
```

10.
```
      2.5          place
  ×  0.57        + places
                   places
```

11.
```
      3.47          places
  ×  1.4        + place
                   places
```

12.
```
      16.5          place
  ×  2.8        + place
                   places
```

13.
```
      45.4          place
  ×  4.02        + places
                   places
```

14.
```
      1.54          places
  × 10.6        + place
                   places
```

15.
```
      4.68          places
  ×  3.12        + places
                   places
```

33

Practice Multiplying Decimals by Decimals

Multiply. Write zeros as needed.

1. 0.3
   $\times$ 0.6

2. 0.03
   $\times$ 0.6

3. 9.8
   $\times$ 0.5

4. 6.3
   $\times$ 0.04

5. 0.08
   $\times$ 0.04

6. 0.006
   $\times$ 0.4

7. 1.37
   $\times$ 0.8

8. 1.37
   $\times$ 0.008

9. 0.015
   $\times$ 0.14

10. 0.075
    $\times$ 0.22

11. 15.5
    $\times$ 2.12

12. 7.05
    $\times$ 2.04

Line up the digits. Then find the products. Write zeros as needed.

13. $0.43 \times 0.02 =$
    0.43
    $\times$ 0.02

14. $0.206 \times 0.37 =$

15. $8.79 \times 6.08 =$

16. $5.67 \times 0.003 =$

17. $0.08 \times 0.02 =$

18. $1.17 \times 6.28 =$

19. $10.2 \times 0.102 =$

20. $6.8 \times 0.54 =$

21. $2.4 \times 0.17 =$

34

Dividing Decimals by Whole Numbers

To divide a decimal by a whole number, write the decimal point in the quotient directly above the decimal point in the dividend. Then divide as with whole numbers.

Find: 9.92 ÷ 16

Write a decimal point in the quotient.

$$16\overline{)9.9\,2}$$

Divide.

```
      0.6 2
16)9 9 2
  -9 6↓
      3 2
    -3 2
        0
```

Find: $48.96 ÷ 24

Write a decimal point in the quotient.

$$24\overline{)\$4\,8.9\,6}$$

Divide.

```
       $2.0 4
24)$4 8.9 6
  -4 8 ↓↓
       0 9 6
       -9 6
           0
```

Divide.

1. $8\overline{)65.6}$

2. $5\overline{)\$3.45}$

3. $3\overline{)8.28}$

4. $7\overline{)0.784}$

5. $61\overline{)2.44}$

6. $39\overline{)\$58.50}$

7. $46\overline{)9.338}$

8. $14\overline{)\$43.96}$

9. $7\overline{)29.12}$

10. $4\overline{)\$16.48}$

11. $71\overline{)1.278}$

12. $22\overline{)0.154}$

Set up each problem. Then find the quotient.

13. 22.5 ÷ 15 =

14. $6.03 ÷ 9 =

15. 114.8 ÷ 82 =

Dividing Decimals by Decimals

To divide a decimal by a decimal, change the divisor to a whole number by moving the decimal point. Move the decimal point in the dividend the same number of places. Then divide.

Remember, write a decimal point in the quotient directly above the position of the new decimal point in the dividend.

Find: 4.34 ÷ 0.7

Move each decimal point 1 place.

$0.7\overline{)4.34}$

Divide.

```
    6.2
7)43.4
 -42 ↓
   14
  -14
    0
```

Find: 0.0713 ÷ 0.23

Move each decimal point 2 places.

$0.23\overline{)0.0713}$

Divide.

```
       0.31
23)007.13
   -69 ↓
     23
    -23
      0
```

Divide.

1. $1.7\overline{)8.16}$

2. $0.5\overline{)2.645}$

3. $4.6\overline{)0.0138}$

4. $3.9\overline{)\$53.43}$

5. $0.16\overline{)4.784}$

6. $0.24\overline{)1.488}$

7. $0.08\overline{)\$6.48}$

8. $0.57\overline{)2.565}$

Set up each problem. Then find the quotient.

9. $1.854 \div 0.9 =$

10. $0.91 \div 1.3 =$

11. $\$15.18 \div 0.33 =$

_____   _____   _____

Name _____ Date _____

Dividing Whole Numbers by Decimals

To divide a whole number by a decimal number, change the divisor to a whole number by moving the decimal point. Move the decimal point in the dividend the same number of places by adding one or more zeros. Then divide.

Find: 102 ÷ 1.7

Move each decimal
point 1 place.

1.7)102.0

Divide.

$$\begin{array}{r} 60 \\ 17\overline{)1020} \\ -102\downarrow \\ \hline 00 \end{array}$$

Find: $230 ÷ 0.25

Move each decimal
point 2 places.

0.25)$230.00

Divide.

$$\begin{array}{r} 920 \\ 025\overline{)\$23000} \\ -225\downarrow \\ \hline 50 \\ -50 \\ \hline 00 \end{array}$$

Divide. Write zeros as needed.

1. 0.6)96.0

2. 2.4)72

3. 1.8)9

4. 0.9)$306

5. 0.34)51.00

6. 0.17)85

7. 0.08)$52

8. 0.32)128

9. 0.2)$7

10. 0.5)13

11. 0.14)84

12. 1.6)$224

Set up each problem. Then find the quotient. Write zeros as needed.

13. $117 ÷ 7.8 =

14. 162 ÷ 1.5 =

15. 328 ÷ 0.4 =

_____   _____   _____

Decimal Quotients

Sometimes when you divide, the divisor will be greater than the dividend. To divide, add a decimal point and zeros as needed to the dividend. Continue to divide until the remainder is zero. In some cases, you may never have a remainder of zero. When dividing money, round the quotient to the nearest cent. Remember, zeros may be needed in the quotient also.

You can use this method to change some fractions to decimals by dividing the numerator by the denominator.

Find: $19 ÷ 300

Add a decimal point and zeros to the dividend.

$$300\overline{)\$19.00}$$

Divide. Place a zero in the quotient.

$$\begin{array}{r} \$0.063 \\ 300\overline{)\$19.000} \\ -18\ 00\downarrow \\ \hline 1\ 000 \\ -\ 900 \\ \hline 100 \end{array}$$

Round $0.063 to $0.06.

Change $\frac{8}{125}$ to a decimal.

Divide the numerator by the denominator. Add a decimal point and zeros to the dividend.

$$125\overline{)8.00}$$

Divide until the remainder is zero.

$$\begin{array}{r} 0.064 \\ 125\overline{)8.000} \\ -7\ 50\downarrow \\ \hline 500 \\ -500 \\ \hline 0 \end{array}$$

$$\frac{8}{125} = 0.064$$

Divide. Write zeros as needed.

1. $40\overline{)20.0}$ 2. $100\overline{)\$30}$ 3. $5\overline{)2}$ 4. $20\overline{)\$15}$

5. $50\overline{)1}$ 6. $500\overline{)25}$ 7. $5\overline{)\$4}$ 8. $20\overline{)19}$

Use division to change each fraction to a decimal.

9. $\frac{1}{4}$ 10. $\frac{1}{8}$ 11. $\frac{1}{40}$ 12. $\frac{3}{5}$

13. $\frac{6}{12}$ 14. $\frac{6}{8}$ 15. $\frac{2}{500}$ 16. $\frac{15}{60}$

Unit 2
Core Skills Math Review

Multiplying and Dividing Decimals

Estimate each answer. Then multiply or divide. Use your estimate to check your answer.

1. 0.3
       × 8

2. 4.3
       × 0.24

3. 0.351
       × 86

4. 0.6739
       × 7

5. 75
       × 0.48

6. 0.03
       × 2

7. 14
       × 0.007

8. 0.002
       × 4

9. 3.14
       × 18

10. 0.6
        × 0.3

11. 0.3
        × 0.2

12. 0.58
        × 0.6

13. 4)9.2

14. 0.3)247.8

15. 0.02)521.56

16. 0.006)74.898

17. 7)8.96

18. 0.5)9.25

19. 0.79)4.661

20. 0.018)0.4554

21. 2)5.328

22. 0.8)0.896

23. 0.56)5.0176

24. 0.007)6.53912

Practice Multiplying and Dividing Decimals

Multiply. After you find each answer, check with a calculator.

1. 15.3
    × 8.1

2. 28.7
    × 0.24

3. 12.615
    × 25

4. 8.7
    × 0.48

5. 0.21
    × 0.4

6. 0.56
    × 0.37

7. 0.05
    × 0.01

8. 16.2
    × 0.045

9. 34.89
    × 0.875

10. 0.147
    × 0.03

11. 3.1416
    × 0.75

12. 0.059
    × 0.064

Divide. After you find each answer, check with a calculator.

13. 8)0.736

14. 0.2)0.0034

15. 0.03)0.0009

16. 0.231)0.00924

17. 36)91.44

18. 1.2)108.72

19. 1.44)135.072

20. 0.048)60

21. 8)5.000

22. 0.6)12.0

23. 0.25)50

24. 0.125)53.75

Unit 2 Review

Write each fraction as a decimal.

1. $\frac{1}{10}$ =

2. $\frac{3}{100}$ =

3. $\frac{1}{5}$ =

4. $\frac{3}{4}$ =

_____

_____

_____

_____

5. $\frac{1}{8}$ =

6. $\frac{5}{8}$ =

7. $1\frac{1}{4}$ =

8. $2\frac{3}{5}$ =

_____

_____

_____

_____

Write each decimal as a fraction or a mixed number.

9. 1.1 =

10. 1.5 =

11. 0.75 =

12. 5.50 =

_____

_____

_____

_____

Find each answer.

13. 7.76
    6.67
+ 4.39

14. 1.923
    2.749
+ 1.637

15. 0.09
   0.54
+ 0.978

16. 0.018
   0.209
+ 40.09

17. 7.94
− 4.56

18. 0.506
− 0.1892

19. 306.09
− 46.45

20. 7.4763
− 6.4767

21. 1.25
× 0.04

22. 3.08
× 12

23. 3.5
× 2.4

24. 2.075
× 0.08

25. $6\overline{)0.36}$

26. $12\overline{)1.44}$

27. $0.12\overline{)144}$

28. $0.6\overline{)3.6}$

Division of Fractions by Fractions

To divide a fraction by a fraction, multiply by the **reciprocal** of the second fraction. To find the reciprocal, **invert**, or switch, the second fraction. For example, the reciprocal of $\frac{3}{4}$ is $\frac{4}{3}$. Simplify your answer, if needed. Remember, only the second fraction is inverted.

Find: $\frac{2}{3} \div \frac{5}{12}$

Multiply by the reciprocal of the second fraction.

$$\frac{2}{3} \div \frac{5}{12} = \frac{2}{3} \times \frac{12}{5}$$

Cancel.

$$\frac{2}{\underset{1}{3}} \times \frac{\overset{4}{12}}{5}$$

Multiply the numerators and denominators. Simplify.

$$\frac{2 \times 4}{1 \times 5} = \frac{8}{5} = 1\frac{3}{5}$$

Write the reciprocal.

1. $\frac{2}{9}$ _____

2. $\frac{3}{4}$ _____

3. $\frac{5}{6}$ _____

4. $\frac{7}{10}$ _____

5. $\frac{1}{8}$ _____

6. $\frac{8}{9}$ _____

7. $\frac{1}{7}$ _____

8. $\frac{1}{2}$ _____

9. $\frac{2}{5}$ _____

10. $\frac{5}{11}$ _____

Divide. Simplify.

11. $\frac{4}{9} \div \frac{8}{9} = \frac{\overset{1}{4}}{\underset{1}{9}} \times \frac{\overset{1}{9}}{\underset{2}{8}} = \frac{1 \times 1}{1 \times 2} =$

12. $\frac{5}{6} \div \frac{3}{4} = \frac{5}{6} \times \frac{4}{3} =$

13. $\frac{5}{8} \div \frac{1}{2} = \frac{5}{8} \times \frac{2}{1} =$

14. $\frac{7}{12} \div \frac{7}{8} = \frac{7}{12} \times \frac{8}{7} =$

15. $\frac{2}{8} \div \frac{3}{8} = \frac{2}{8} \times \frac{8}{3} =$

16. $\frac{15}{16} \div \frac{2}{3} = \frac{15}{16} \times \frac{3}{2} =$

17. $\frac{1}{3} \div \frac{1}{16} =$

18. $\frac{4}{5} \div \frac{8}{15} =$

19. $\frac{2}{3} \div \frac{3}{8} =$

20. $\frac{8}{11} \div \frac{1}{2} =$

21. $\frac{3}{4} \div \frac{5}{8} =$

22. $\frac{9}{16} \div \frac{3}{8} =$

Unit 3
Core Skills Math Review

Practice Division of Fractions by Fractions

Divide. Simplify.

1. $\dfrac{1}{8} \div \dfrac{1}{3} =$

2. $\dfrac{5}{12} \div \dfrac{3}{4} =$

3. $\dfrac{9}{16} \div \dfrac{3}{8} =$

4. $\dfrac{1}{3} \div \dfrac{1}{7} =$

5. $\dfrac{7}{8} \div \dfrac{5}{12} =$

6. $\dfrac{4}{6} \div \dfrac{1}{10} =$

7. $\dfrac{1}{3} \div \dfrac{1}{3} =$

8. $\dfrac{10}{64} \div \dfrac{1}{4} =$

9. $\dfrac{2}{9} \div \dfrac{3}{4} =$

10. $\dfrac{3}{7} \div \dfrac{3}{14} =$

11. $\dfrac{3}{5} \div \dfrac{7}{8} =$

12. $\dfrac{4}{9} \div \dfrac{2}{3} =$

13. $\dfrac{5}{6} \div \dfrac{5}{8} =$

14. $\dfrac{1}{8} \div \dfrac{3}{16} =$

15. $\dfrac{5}{16} \div \dfrac{5}{32} =$

16. $\dfrac{1}{3} \div \dfrac{1}{5} =$

17. $\dfrac{5}{12} \div \dfrac{7}{8} =$

18. $\dfrac{3}{4} \div \dfrac{4}{3} =$

19. $\dfrac{1}{10} \div \dfrac{4}{6} =$

20. $\dfrac{6}{7} \div \dfrac{6}{7} =$

21. $\dfrac{2}{3} \div \dfrac{4}{9} =$

22. $\dfrac{3}{5} \div \dfrac{1}{5} =$

Division of Mixed Numbers by Fractions

To divide a mixed number by a fraction, write the mixed number as an improper fraction. Multiply by the reciprocal of the second fraction. Simplify the answer.

Find: $6\frac{5}{6} \div \frac{5}{6}$

Write the mixed number as an improper fraction.	Multiply by the reciprocal of the second fraction.	Cancel.	Multiply. Simplify.
$6\frac{5}{6} \div \frac{5}{6} = \frac{41}{6} \div \frac{5}{6}$	$\frac{41}{6} \times \frac{6}{5}$	$\frac{41}{\cancel{6}_1} \times \frac{\cancel{6}^1}{5}$	$\frac{41 \times 1}{1 \times 5} = \frac{41}{5} = 8\frac{1}{5}$

Divide. Simplify.

1. $2\frac{1}{3} \div \frac{1}{6} = \frac{7}{3} \div \frac{1}{6} = \frac{7}{3} \times \frac{6}{1} = \frac{7 \times 2}{1 \times 1} =$

2. $1\frac{1}{3} \div \frac{2}{3} =$

3. $1\frac{7}{12} \div \frac{3}{4} =$

4. $3\frac{3}{4} \div \frac{1}{2} =$

5. $5\frac{1}{2} \div \frac{1}{2} =$

6. $3\frac{1}{10} \div \frac{2}{5} =$

7. $1\frac{1}{2} \div \frac{3}{4} =$

8. $1\frac{1}{5} \div \frac{4}{5} =$

9. $2\frac{1}{5} \div \frac{4}{5} =$

10. $2\frac{2}{9} \div \frac{4}{5} =$

11. $1\frac{4}{5} \div \frac{2}{3} =$

12. $1\frac{4}{7} \div \frac{1}{7} =$

13. $5\frac{1}{4} \div \frac{1}{3} =$

14. $3\frac{2}{3} \div \frac{11}{12} =$

15. $3\frac{3}{4} \div \frac{5}{8} =$

16. $5\frac{2}{5} \div \frac{3}{5} =$

Unit 3

Core Skills Math Review

Division of Mixed Numbers by Mixed Numbers

To divide a mixed number by a mixed number, write the mixed numbers as improper fractions. Multiply by the reciprocal of the second fraction. Simplify the answer.

Find: $2\frac{1}{4} \div 3\frac{3}{8}$

Write the mixed numbers as improper fractions.	Multiply by the reciprocal of the second fraction.	Cancel.	Multiply.
$2\frac{1}{4} \div 3\frac{3}{8} = \frac{9}{4} \div \frac{27}{8}$	$\frac{9}{4} \times \frac{8}{27}$	$\frac{\overset{1}{9}}{\underset{1}{4}} \times \frac{\overset{2}{8}}{\underset{3}{27}}$	$\frac{1 \times 2}{1 \times 3} = \frac{2}{3}$

Divide. Simplify.

1. $4\frac{1}{4} \div 8\frac{1}{2} = \frac{17}{4} \times \frac{2}{17} = \frac{1 \times 1}{2 \times 1} =$

2. $7\frac{1}{2} \div 4\frac{3}{5} =$

3. $5\frac{1}{2} \div 1\frac{1}{2} =$

4. $3\frac{1}{3} \div 1\frac{20}{21} =$

5. $8\frac{1}{4} \div 2\frac{1}{2} =$

6. $2\frac{1}{3} \div 3\frac{1}{2} =$

7. $6\frac{2}{3} \div 2\frac{1}{5} =$

8. $8\frac{2}{3} \div 1\frac{1}{3} =$

9. $8\frac{1}{2} \div 4\frac{1}{4} =$

10. $6\frac{4}{5} \div 1\frac{1}{5} =$

11. $4\frac{1}{2} \div 1\frac{1}{4} =$

12. $9\frac{7}{9} \div 1\frac{5}{6} =$

13. $2\frac{1}{2} \div 1\frac{1}{3} =$

14. $1\frac{3}{8} \div 3\frac{2}{3} =$

15. $6\frac{2}{3} \div 2\frac{1}{4} =$

16. $4\frac{2}{9} \div 1\frac{7}{12} =$

45

Adding Rational Numbers

Use a number line to find each sum.

1. $5 + (-7) =$ _____

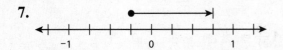

2. $-\frac{1}{2} + (-4\frac{1}{2}) =$ _____

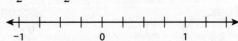

3. $-3 + 8 =$ _____

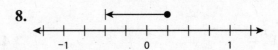

4. $1\frac{1}{2} + (-2\frac{1}{2}) =$ _____

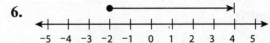

Tell what sum is modeled on each number line. Then find the sum.

5.

_____

6.

_____

7.

_____

8.

_____

Find each sum without using a number line.

9. $-25 + 21 =$

10. $-11.6 + (-17.2) =$

11. $2\frac{1}{3} + (-17\frac{1}{3}) =$

_____   _____   _____

12. $-50 + (-18) + 20 =$

13. $75 + (-85) + 11 =$

14. $-4 + 4 + (-36) =$

_____   _____   _____

15. Describe a real-world situation that can be represented by the expression $-13 + 20$. Then find the sum and explain what it represents in terms of the situation.

_____

16. A player in a video game has 48 points. He makes another 20 points. Then he makes an error and loses 22 points. What is his score then?

_____

17. A student evaluated $-3 + x$ for $x = 18$ and got an answer of 21. What might the student have done wrong?

_____

Name _____   Date _____

Subtracting Rational Numbers

Use a number line to find each difference.

1. $7 - (-5) =$ _____

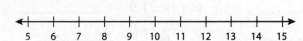

2. $-4\frac{1}{2} - 2\frac{1}{2} =$ _____

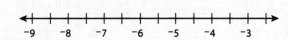

3. $-5 - 8 =$ _____

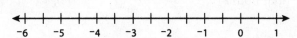

4. $-1 - 2\frac{1}{2} =$ _____

Find each difference.

5. $-25 - 21 =$ _____

6. $-11.6 - (-10.2) =$ _____

7. $2\frac{1}{3} - (-1\frac{1}{3}) =$ _____

8. $-50 - (-18) =$ _____

9. $\frac{2}{7} - (-2) =$ _____

10. $-14\frac{1}{4} - (-4\frac{1}{4}) =$ _____

11. A boy dives 1.5 meters below sea level and then dives down another 1.5 meters. How far below sea level is the boy?

_____

12. A player on a quiz show has 47 points less than 0. She misses the next question and loses another 12 points. What is her total score then?

_____

13. A man lives in a house that is 607 feet above sea level. His brother lives in a house that is 15 feet below sea level. What is the difference in the elevation of the two houses?

_____

14. The temperature on Tuesday was -12 °C. The temperature on Wednesday was 6 degrees less than the day before. What was the temperature on Wednesday?

_____

15. The lowest temperature on Friday was -17 °C. The lowest temperature on Sunday was -8 °C. What was the difference between the lowest temperatures?

_____

16. Tyler withdrew $40.00 from his bank account. Then he used his debit card to buy a shirt for $18.46. What was the total amount Tyler took out of his account?

_____

47

Multiplying Rational Numbers

Find each product.

1. $-1(8) =$ _____

2. $\left(-\frac{1}{3}\right)\left(-\frac{10}{9}\right) =$ _____

3. $(-7)(-3) =$ _____

4. $(-5)(30) =$ _____

5. $(-6)(14) =$ _____

6. $(4)(-21.9) =$ _____

7. $(6)\left(-\frac{3}{13}\right) =$ _____

8. $\left(-\frac{11}{7}\right)(0) =$ _____

9. $(7)(-19) =$ _____

10. In one hour, 17 people each withdrew $50 from a bank. How much money was withdrawn in that hour?

_____

11. Each of a football team's 3 fouls in a game resulted in a loss of 15 yards. How many yards in total did they lose in the game fouls?

_____

12. A mountain climber climbed down a cliff $\frac{1}{3}$ mile at a time. She did this 7 times in one day. How many miles did she climb down?

_____

13. Caleb made 4 withdrawals of $55 each from his bank account. How much did he withdraw in total?

_____

14. The temperature dropped 3 °F every hour for 7 hours. What was the total number of degrees the temperature dropped in the 7 hours?

_____

15. The price of one share of a company declined $4.75 per day for 3 days in a row. How much did the price of one share decline in total after the 3 days?

_____

16. Describe a real-world situation that can be represented by the product $(-12)(2)$.

_____

_____

_____

_____

Dividing Rational Numbers

Find each quotient.

1. $\dfrac{0.64}{-0.8} =$ _____

2. $\left(\dfrac{-\frac{1}{7}}{\frac{8}{7}}\right) =$ _____

3. $\dfrac{42}{-6} =$ _____

4. $\dfrac{116}{3} \div \left(-\dfrac{1}{8}\right) =$ _____

5. $\dfrac{90}{-\frac{1}{6}} =$ _____

6. $\dfrac{-85}{-17} =$ _____

7. $\dfrac{-\frac{3}{7}}{\frac{7}{4}} =$ _____

8. $\dfrac{-20}{0.04} =$ _____

9. $\dfrac{0.65}{-0.5} =$ _____

10. $\dfrac{9}{-\frac{3}{8}} =$ _____

11. $3\frac{1}{3} \div \left(-1\frac{1}{2}\right) =$ _____

12. $\dfrac{-150}{-5} =$ _____

13. A mountain climber explored a cliff that is 175 meters high in 5 equal descents. How many meters was one descent?

_____

14. The price of one share of a company declined a total of \$42 in 6 days. How much did the price of one share decline, on average, per day?

_____

15. Describe a real-world situation that can be represented by the quotient −55 ÷ 13. Then find the quotient and explain what the quotient means in terms of the real-world situation.

_____

_____

_____

16. Divide 7 by 3. Is your answer a rational number? Explain.

_____

_____

17. Is the quotient of an integer divided by zero a rational number? Why or why not?

_____

_____

49

Looking Beyond Rational Numbers

Classify each number as rational or irrational. Use a calculator if necessary.

1. 33

2. $\sqrt{33}$

3. $-\sqrt{259}$

4. $0.\overline{7}$

_____   _____   _____   _____

5. $-\dfrac{5}{16}$

6. $\sqrt{3}$

7. $0.\overline{899}$

8. $\sqrt{121}$

_____   _____   _____   _____

Complete the table. Classify each number by placing an X in each appropriate column.

		Real Number	Rational Number	Whole Number	Integer	Irrational Number
9.	-2					
10.	4.2					
11.	$\sqrt{21}$					
12.	0.8					
13.	$-3.96213\ldots$					

14. A pattern for a dress needs $3\frac{1}{3}$ yd of fabric. If Mary buys $9\frac{1}{3}$ yd and $6\frac{3}{4}$ yd of fabric, will she have enough to make 5 dresses? Explain.

_____

15. Kim has 196 floor tiles. Each tile is 1 square foot. Can he use all the floor tiles to make a square without cutting any of the tiles? Explain.

_____

16. The formula for a falling object is $S = 16t^2$, where S is the distance in feet and t is the time in seconds. About how long will it take an object to fall 96 ft?

_____

Comparing and Ordering Numbers

Use the table below for Exercises 1–3.

City	A	B	C	D	E
Temperature (°F)	-9	10	-2	0	4

1. On the number line, graph a point for the temperature of each of the cities shown above.

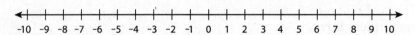

2. Which city was coldest? _____

3. Which city was warmest? _____

List the numbers in order from least to greatest.

4. 4, -6, 0, 8, -9, 1, -3

    _____

5. 31, 5, 7, -0.1, 1, 1.5, -9

    _____

6. -80, 88, 96, -14, 75, 59, -32

    _____

7. -65, 34, 7.6, -13, 55, 62.5, -7.6

    _____

8. Write two inequalities to compare -17 and -22. _____

9. Write two inequalities to compare 16 and -2. _____

Compare. Write < or >.

10. 9 _____ 2   11. 0 _____ 6   12. 3 _____ -7   13. 5 _____ -10

14. -1 _____ -3   15. -8 _____ -4   16. -4.5 _____ 1   17. -2 _____ -2.5

Use the given prices. Express your answer as an inequality.

Fruit cup	$2.49
Veggies and dip	$2.86
Yogurt	$1.97
Fruit smoothie	$3.83
Pretzels	$1.71

18. Which costs more, a fruit cup or veggies and dip? Use the given prices to write an inequality that shows your answer.

    _____

19. Which costs less, pretzels or yogurt? Use the given prices to write an inequality that shows your answer.

    _____

Rational Numbers

Write each fraction as a decimal.

1. $\frac{7}{8}$

2. $\frac{2}{3}$

3. $2\frac{4}{5}$

4. $\frac{23}{24}$

5. $\frac{17}{20}$

6. $\frac{18}{25}$

Write each decimal as a fraction in simplest form.

7. $7.\overline{4}$

8. 0.56

9. 0.45

10. $0.9\overline{3}$

11. $0.\overline{54}$

12. 6.02

Compare. Write <, >, or =.

13. $\frac{4}{7}$ _____ $\frac{3}{8}$

14. $\frac{3}{4}$ _____ 0.75

15. 0.35 _____ $\frac{1}{3}$

16. $0.\overline{5}$ _____ $\frac{5}{9}$

17. 1.5 _____ $1\frac{3}{5}$

18. $\frac{2}{3}$ _____ 0.67

19. The average width of a robin's egg is about 0.015 meter. Write this length as a fraction in simplest form.

20. The weight of an object on the moon is $\frac{1}{6}$ its weight on Earth. Write $\frac{1}{6}$ as a decimal.

21. Oxygen makes up about $\frac{3}{5}$ of the human body. Write $\frac{3}{5}$ as a decimal.

22. The decimal equivalent of $\frac{1}{25}$ is 0.04, and the decimal equivalent of $\frac{2}{25}$ is 0.08. Without dividing, find the decimal equivalent of $\frac{6}{25}$. Explain how you found your answer.

Irrational Numbers

Order $\sqrt{3}$, π, and 1.5 from least to greatest.

1. First approximate $\sqrt{3}$ to the nearest tenth.

   $\sqrt{3}$ is between _____ and _____, so $\sqrt{3} \approx$ _____.

2. You need to find a better estimate for $\sqrt{3}$ so you can compare it to 1.5.

   Approximate $\sqrt{3}$ to the nearest hundredth.

   $\sqrt{3}$ is between _____ and _____, so $\sqrt{3} \approx$ _____.

3. An approximate value of π is 3.14. Plot $\sqrt{3}$, π, and 1.5 on a number line.

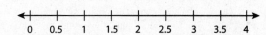

4. Read the numbers from left to right to place them in order from least to greatest.

   From least to greatest, the numbers are _____, _____, _____.

Order the numbers from least to greatest.

5. $\sqrt{5}$, 2.5, $\sqrt{3}$ _____

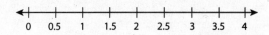

6. π^2, 10, $\sqrt{75}$ _____

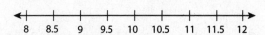

Compare. Write $<$, $>$, or $=$.

7. $\sqrt{2} + 4$ _____ $2 + \sqrt{4}$

8. $\sqrt{12} + 6$ _____ $12 + \sqrt{6}$

53

Unit 3 Review

Divide. Simplify if needed.

1. $\frac{7}{8} \div 7 =$ _____

2. $1\frac{2}{5} \div \frac{7}{10} =$ _____

3. $2\frac{6}{7} \div 3\frac{1}{14} =$ _____

4. $\frac{1}{10} \div \frac{1}{20} =$ _____

5. $5 \div \frac{3}{4} =$ _____

6. $4\frac{1}{4} \div 1\frac{1}{8} =$ _____

7. $15 \div \frac{7}{10} =$ _____

8. $\frac{4}{15} \div \frac{1}{3} =$ _____

Solve each rational expression.

9. $3 + (-8) =$ _____

10. $-6 + 9 =$ _____

11. $10 - (-5) =$ _____

12. $-0.4 - 3.2 =$ _____

13. $(-9)(-7) =$ _____

14. $(3)(-42.3) =$ _____

15. $\frac{0.72}{-0.9} =$ _____

16. $\frac{-120}{-6} =$ _____

Compare. Write < or >.

17. 10 _____ -10 18. -8 _____ -3

19. -2.5 _____ 0 20. 0.4 _____ -1.4

21. A bolt $\frac{5}{16}$ inch long is used in a machine. What is the length of the bolt written as a decimal?

_____

22. Sasha says that $\sqrt{69}$, $\sqrt{117}$, and $-\sqrt{121}$ are irrational numbers. Which of these numbers is rational?

_____

Using Decimals to Find a Percent of a Number

To find a percent of a number, write a percent sentence. Every percent sentence consists of three numbers: the **rate,** the **whole,** and the **part.**

$$20\% \text{ of } 48 = 9.6$$

rate   whole   part

If the part is missing in a percent problem, solve by first changing the rate to a decimal. Then multiply the rate by the whole.

Remember, *of* means multiply.

Find: 25% of 84

$25\% \times 84 = ?$ $0.25 \times 84 = 21$

```
      84
 ×  0.25
   4 20
 +16 8
   21.00
```

Find: 105% of 280

$105\% \times 280 = ?$ $1.05 \times 280 = 294$

```
      280
 ×   1.05
    1400
    000
 +  280
   294.00
```

Change each percent to a decimal. Solve.

1. 50% of 90

_____

2. 300% of 60

_____

3. 80% of 120

_____

4. 75% of 80

_____

5. 40% of 75

_____

6. 90% of 200

_____

7. 250% of 100

_____

8. 99% of 55

_____

Solve.

9. Rachel decided to save 15% of the money she earned. In one month, Rachel earned $1,584. How much money did she save?

_____

10. Walter read an advertisement for a 30%-off sale on stereo equipment. How much money would Walter save if he bought a CD player that normally sold for $219?

_____

55

Using Fractions to Find a Percent of a Number

Another way to find the missing part in a percent problem is to use fractions rather than decimals. Change the rate and the whole to fractions. Multiply the fractions. Simplify.

Find: 20% of 50

$20\% \times 50 = ?$

$\frac{1}{\cancel{5}} \times \frac{\cancel{50}^{10}}{1} = \frac{10}{1} = 10$

Find: 75% of $1\frac{3}{4}$

$75\% \times 1\frac{3}{4} = ?$

$\frac{3}{4} \times \frac{7}{4} = \frac{21}{16} = 1\frac{5}{16}$

Change each percent to a fraction. Solve. Simplify.

1. 25% of 16

_____

2. 50% of $1\frac{1}{3}$

_____

3. 85% of 40

_____

4. 40% of $3\frac{1}{3}$

_____

5. 60% of 55

_____

6. 80% of $3\frac{3}{4}$

_____

7. 6% of 20

_____

8. 70% of $6\frac{2}{3}$

_____

Solve.

9. A sweater that normally sells for $66 was on sale for $33\frac{1}{3}$% off. How much would a customer save by paying the sale price? (Hint: $33\frac{1}{3}\% = \frac{1}{3}$.)

_____

10. A survey of college students showed that $66\frac{2}{3}$% of the 600 students studied a foreign language. How many students studied a foreign language? (Hint: $66\frac{2}{3}\% = \frac{2}{3}$.)

_____

Finding a Number When a Percent of It Is Known

To find the whole in a percent problem, write a percent sentence. Change the rate to a decimal.
Divide the part by the decimal.

12% of what number is 18?
$12\% \times ? = 18$

$? = 18 \div 0.12$
$150 = 18 \div 0.12$

30% of what number is 180?
$30\% \times ? = 180$

$? = 180 \div 0.30$
$600 = 180 \div 0.30$

Change each percent to a decimal. Solve.

1. 25% of what number is 17?

_____

2. 32% of what number is 40?

_____

3. 80% of what number is 64?

_____

4. 135% of what number is 270?

_____

5. 60% of what number is 33?

_____

6. 45% of what number is 90?

_____

7. 10% of what number is 73?

_____

8. 75% of what number is 120?

_____

Solve.

9. Peter bought a sweater for $32. This was
80% of the original price. What was the
original price?

_____

10. Katie got a 5% discount for paying cash for
her furniture purchase. She paid $2,850 for
the furniture. What would the price have
been if she had charged her purchase?

_____

11. The distance by boat from New York City to
San Francisco is 5,200 miles by way of the
Panama Canal. This is 40% of the distance by
way of the Strait of Magellan. How far is it
by way of the Strait of Magellan?

_____

12. Adelena got a score of 90% on a true-false
test. She answered 36 questions correctly.
How many questions were on the test?

_____

Simple Interest

Interest is a charge that is paid for borrowing money. To find the **simple interest** on a loan, multiply the amount borrowed, or **principal,** times the annual rate of interest (a percent) times the number of years the loan is for. Change part of a year to a decimal.

Find the simple interest on a loan of $2,000 for 3 years at a rate of 6% per year.

Interest = Principal × Rate × Time
$$I = prt$$
$$I = \$2{,}000 \times 0.06 \times 3$$
$$I = \$360$$

Find the simple interest for each loan. Round to the nearest cent.

1. $500 at 5.5% for 6 months
   I = $500 × 0.055 × 0.5

2. $225 at $6\frac{1}{2}$% for 1 year
   I = $225 × 0.065 × 1

3. $800 at 18% for 1 year
   I = $800 × 0.18 × 1

4. $1,000 at 5% for 2 years
   I = $1,000 × 0.05 × 2

5. $400 at 8.25% for 3 months

6. $150 at 12% for 2 years

7. $2,000 at 7% for 5 years

8. $850 at 4% for 6 months

Practice Simple Interest

Find the simple interest for each loan. Round to the nearest cent as needed.

1. $3,460 at 6.5% for 6 months
(Hint: Change 6 months to 0.5 year.)

2. $75 at 5.25% for 1 year

_____

3. $225 at 4.75% for $1\frac{1}{4}$ years
(Hint: Change $1\frac{1}{4}$ years to 1.25 years.)

4. $3,210 at 6% for 3 years

_____

5. $615 at 6.5% for 2 years

6. $4,000 at $6\frac{7}{10}$% for 4 years

_____

7. $3,750 at $6\frac{1}{4}$% for 3 months

8. $525 at 5% for 15 months

_____

9. $2,940 at 4.8% for 2.25 years

10. $465 at 4.75% for $1\frac{1}{2}$ years

_____

11. $3,500 at 5.75% for 6 years

12. $11,500 at 8.25% for 3 years

_____

59

Percent of Increase

To find the **current value** or amount, first multiply the original amount by the **percent of increase**. Then add.

The rent for a 1-bedroom apartment was $425 per month. This year the rent went up 4%. For how much will the apartment rent each month this year?

original amount	$425		original amount	$425
percent of increase	× 0.04		amount of increase	+ $ 17
amount of increase	$17		current rent	$442

The apartment will rent for $442 this year.

Solve.

1. Rajeev's dog weighed 60 pounds 4 months ago. Since then his weight has increased by 6%. How much does Rajeev's dog weigh now?

   $$\begin{array}{r} 60 \\ \times\ 0.06 \\ \hline 3.6 \end{array} \qquad \begin{array}{r} 60.0 \\ +\ 3.6 \end{array}$$

   _____

2. A local movie theater increased the price of admission by 20%. Tickets had sold for $6.50. What is the current ticket price?

   _____

3. Lawrence bought his condominium for $100,900. During the past 2 years, its value increased 8%. What is the current value of Lawrence's condominium?

   _____

4. A university's enrollment is up 4% from last year. Last year's enrollment was 19,050 students. How many students are attending the university this year?

   _____

5. The price of a mid-size car went up 7% from last year. The car sold for $22,000 last year. What is the price for the same car this year?

   _____

6. The Steak House increased its menu prices by 10%. A complete dinner had been $22.50. What is the new price for the dinner?

   _____

Name _____   Date _____

Percent of Decrease

To find the current value or amount, first multiply the original amount by the **percent of decrease**. Then subtract.

Last year's total sales figure for The Clothier Chain was $950,000. This year the total sales figure decreased by 3%. What is this year's sales figure?

original figure	$950,000		original figure	$950,000
percent of decrease	× 0.03		amount of decrease	− $ 28,500
amount of decrease	$ 28,500		new sales figure	$921,500

This year's total sales figure at The Clothier Chain is $921,500.

Solve.

1. A school had 500 students last year. This year the enrollment decreased by 5%. How many students are attending the school this year?

   500   500
   × 0.05   − 25
   ─────   ─────
    25   475

2. A store decreased the price of its best shirts by 20%. If the shirts normally sold for $30, what was the reduced price?

3. The value of a car that cost $16,000 decreased by 20% the first year. What was the value of the car after the first year?

4. The average number of points scored by the Ridgeview basketball team decreased by 8%. They had been averaging 75 points per game. What is their new average?

5. A city had a population of 560,000 in 2002. In 2003, its population had decreased by 2%. How many people were living in the city in 2003?

6. The Rinallis' average gas bill decreased by 4.5% after they moved. They had been spending about $125 per month for gas. How much are they now spending for gas? Round to the nearest cent.

Unit 4
Core Skills Math Review

Name _____   Date _____

Percent Applications

Fill in the numbered circles to show the answers.

1. The selling price of athletic shoes is a 65% increase over the store's cost. Run-Fast running shoes cost the store $60. What is the selling price of the shoes?

⑨ ⑨
⑧ ⑧
⑦ ⑦
⑥ ⑥
⑤ ⑤
④ ④
③ ③
② ②
① ①
⓪ ⓪

2. A customer saved $135 by buying a dishwasher on sale for 30% off the regular price. What was the regular price?

⑨ ⑨ ⑨
⑧ ⑧ ⑧
⑦ ⑦ ⑦
⑥ ⑥ ⑥
⑤ ⑤ ⑤
④ ④ ④
③ ③ ③
② ② ②
① ① ①
⓪ ⓪ ⓪

3. A 300-seat theater has 25% of the seats reserved. How many seats are reserved?

⑨ ⑨
⑧ ⑧
⑦ ⑦
⑥ ⑥
⑤ ⑤
④ ④
③ ③
② ②
① ①
⓪ ⓪

4. Sonya's TV and Appliance requires a 20% down payment to hold a purchase. If a down payment is $172, what is the total cost of the item?

⑨ ⑨ ⑨
⑧ ⑧ ⑧
⑦ ⑦ ⑦
⑥ ⑥ ⑥
⑤ ⑤ ⑤
④ ④ ④
③ ③ ③
② ② ②
① ① ①
⓪ ⓪ ⓪

5. Several years ago, a desk sold for $120. Now the same desk sells for $150. What is the percent of increase in the price?

⑨ ⑨
⑧ ⑧
⑦ ⑦
⑥ ⑥
⑤ ⑤
④ ④
③ ③
② ②
① ①
⓪ ⓪

6. Lin bought a new television. The sales tax on the television was $16.00. The sales tax rate was 5%. What was the selling price of the television?

⑨ ⑨ ⑨
⑧ ⑧ ⑧
⑦ ⑦ ⑦
⑥ ⑥ ⑥
⑤ ⑤ ⑤
④ ④ ④
③ ③ ③
② ② ②
① ① ①
⓪ ⓪ ⓪

7. In an order of 60 lamps, 12 were broken when the clerk unpacked them. What percent of the lamps were broken?

⑨ ⑨
⑧ ⑧
⑦ ⑦
⑥ ⑥
⑤ ⑤
④ ④
③ ③
② ②
① ①
⓪ ⓪

8. A leather coat that regularly sells for $400 is on sale for 20% off. What is the sale price of the coat?

⑨ ⑨ ⑨
⑧ ⑧ ⑧
⑦ ⑦ ⑦
⑥ ⑥ ⑥
⑤ ⑤ ⑤
④ ④ ④
③ ③ ③
② ② ②
① ① ①
⓪ ⓪ ⓪

62

Using Percents to Solve Problems

1. A ticket to a play costs $50. There is a 5% transaction fee. What is the total cost of the ticket?

_____

2. A taxi ride costs $32. Paulie gives the driver a 15% tip. What is the total amount Paulie gives the driver?

_____

3. Emily earns $75 per day plus a commission on all sales. Her commission is 15%. She sells $600 worth of furniture. How much does she earn for the day?

_____

4. Martin finds a shirt for $20 at a store. The sign says it is 10% off the marked price. Martin must also pay 8.5% sales tax. What is the cost of the shirt before and after the sales tax?

_____

5. Joe borrowed $2,000 from the bank at a rate of 7% simple interest per year. How much interest did he pay in 5 years?

_____

6. You have $550 in a savings account that earns 3% simple interest each year. How much will be in your account in 10 years?

_____

7. **Error Analysis** A store makes a profit of $1,000 in January. In February sales are up 25%, but in March sales are down 25%. The store manager says that the profit for March is still $1,000. What is his error? What is the actual profit for March?

_____

8. Percent error calculations are used to determine how close to the true values, or how accurate, experimental values really are. The formula is similar to finding percent of change.

$$\text{percent error} = \frac{\text{amount of change}}{\text{actual value}} \times 100$$

In chemistry, Bob records the volume of a liquid as 13.3 ml. The actual volume is 13.6 ml. What is his percent error? Round to the nearest percent.

_____

9. Complete the table. Round to the nearest percent.

Item	Scooter	Bike
Original Price	$45	$110
New Price	$56	$96
Percent Change		
Increase or Decrease		

Unit 4 Review

Find the percent or number.

1. 54% of 75

    _____

2. 0.9% of 200

    _____

3. 35% of 100

    _____

4. 50% of $2\frac{1}{4}$

    _____

5. What percent of 60 is 9?

    _____

6. What percent of 18 is 36?

    _____

7. 70% of what number is 21?

    _____

8. 34% of what number is 17?

    _____

Find the simple interest for each loan. Round to the nearest cent.

9. $1,590 at 7% for 4 years

    _____

10. $940 at 8% for 3 months

    _____

11. $1,100 at 3% for 9 months

    _____

12. $150 at 8% for 2 years

    _____

13. $630 at 4% for 3 years

    _____

14. $1,050 at 2% for $1\frac{1}{2}$ years

    _____

Solve.

15. The selling price on toys at Toy City is a 40% increase over the store's cost. What is the selling price of a doll that costs the store $16.50?

    _____

16. Last year the cost of a Quick-Calc computer was $1,200. This year the cost dropped by 15%. What is this year's cost of a Quick-Calc computer?

    _____

17. Last year Carlos built a gymnastics set for $50. This year it cost him $75 to build one. What is the percent of increase?

    _____

18. Last week an almanac cost $3.50. This week it is on sale for $2.80. What is the percent of decrease?

    _____

Name _____ Date _____

Exponents

Write each power.

1. the 10th power of 8

_____

2. the 8th power of 10

_____

3. the 11th power of $\frac{1}{2}$

_____

4. the 6th power of $\frac{2}{3}$

_____

Use exponents to write each expression.

5. $6 \times 6 \times 6$

_____

6. $10 \times 10 \times 10 \times 10 \times 10 \times 10 \times 10$

_____

7. $\frac{3}{4} \times \frac{3}{4} \times \frac{3}{4} \times \frac{3}{4} \times \frac{3}{4}$

_____

8. $\frac{7}{9} \times \frac{7}{9} \times \frac{7}{9} \times \frac{7}{9} \times \frac{7}{9} \times \frac{7}{9} \times \frac{7}{9} \times \frac{7}{9}$

_____

Find the value of each power.

9. 8^3 _____   10. 7^4 _____   11. 5^3 _____   12. 4^2 _____

13. $\left(\frac{1}{4}\right)^2$ _____   14. $\left(\frac{1}{3}\right)^3$ _____   15. $\left(\frac{6}{7}\right)^2$ _____   16. $\left(\frac{9}{10}\right)^1$ _____

Write the missing exponent.

17. $100 = 10$ 18. $8 = 2$ 19. $25 = 5$ 20. $27 = 3$

21. $\frac{1}{169} = \left(\frac{1}{13}\right)$ 22. $14 = 14$ 23. $32 = 2$ 24. $\frac{64}{81} = \left(\frac{8}{9}\right)$

Write the missing base.

25. $1,000 = \quad^3$ 26. $256 = \quad^4$ 27. $16 = \quad^4$ 28. $9 = \quad^2$

29. $\frac{1}{9} = \left(\quad\right)^2$ 30. $64 = \quad^2$ 31. $\frac{9}{16} = \left(\quad\right)^2$ 32. $729 = \quad^3$

33. Hadley's softball team has a phone tree in case a game is cancelled. The coach calls 3 players. Then each of those players calls 3 players, and so on. How many players will be notified during the 3rd round of calls?

_____

34. **Reasoning** What is the value of 1 raised to any power? Explain.

_____

65

© Houghton Mifflin Harcourt Publishing Company

Unit 5
Core Skills Math Review

Exponents in Expressions

A numerical expression with exponents can be evaluated using the order of operations or the **rules of exponents.**

When adding or subtracting exponential numbers, use the order of operations. First, evaluate each number with the exponent. Then add or subtract.

$3^2 + 3^4$

$9 + 81$

90

$4^5 - 4^3$

$1,024 - 64$

960

When multiplying two numbers with the same base, add their exponents. When dividing two numbers with the same base, subtract their exponents.

$2^2 \times 2^6$

$2^{2 + 6}$

2^8

256

$3^4 \div 3^2$

$3^{4 - 2}$

3^2

9

To evaluate a number with an exponent raised to an exponent, multiply the exponents.

$$(5^2)^2 = 5^{2 \times 2} = 5^4 = 625$$

Evaluate each expression.

1. $7^4 - 7^2 =$

2. $(9^2)^2 =$

3. $(2^5)^3 =$

4. $4^4 + 4^5 =$

5. $3^3 \times 3^4 =$

6. $2^8 - 2^4 =$

7. $(7^3)^2 =$

8. $(4^2)^4 =$

9. $(8^3)^2 =$

10. $(2^4)^3 =$

11. $4^9 \div 4^7 =$

12. $5^4 - 5^2 =$

13. $2^8 \div 2^5 =$

14. $(2^3)^2 \times 2^4 =$

15. $3^6 - 3^2 =$

16. $(8^4)^2 \div 8^7 =$

17. $(3^4)^2 + 3^3 =$

18. $8^5 - 8^3 =$

19. $(5^4)^2 \times 5^2 =$

20. $9^7 \div 9^4 =$

Practice Exponents in Expressions

Evaluate each expression.

1. $6^2 + 6^5 =$

2. $10^7 \div 10^5 =$

3. $4^2 \times (4^2)^2 =$

_____   _____   _____

4. $3^4 - (3^4)^3 =$

5. $7^9 \div (7^4)^2 =$

6. $5^3 \times 5^1 =$

_____   _____   _____

7. $8^4 + 8^2 =$

8. $9^2 \times 9^2 =$

9. $2^8 \div (2^3)^2 =$

_____   _____   _____

10. $7^3 + 7^2 =$

11. $6^9 \div (6^2)^2 =$

12. $6^3 \times 6^4 =$

_____   _____   _____

13. $10^2 \times 10^4 =$

14. $(8^3)^4 \div 8^8 =$

15. $5^3 + 5^5 =$

_____   _____   _____

16. $(4^4)^2 - 4^7 =$

17. $7^7 \div 7^4 =$

18. $(9^6)^4 \div (9^3)^5 =$

_____   _____   _____

19. $10^3 \times 10^6 =$

20. $(2^3)^2 + (2^2)^4 =$

21. $6^5 - 6^3 =$

_____   _____   _____

22. $(10^3)^7 \div (10^4)^5 =$

23. $8^9 \div 8^6 =$

24. $2^4 + 2^5 =$

_____   _____   _____

Integer Exponents

Find the value of each power.

1. 7^{-2}

2. 20^0

3. 10^{-3}

_____ _____ _____

4. 2^{-5}

5. 5^{-3}

6. 7^3

_____ _____ _____

Use properties of integers to write an equivalent expression.

7. $15^2 \cdot 15^{-5}$

8. $\dfrac{20^{10}}{20^7}$

9. $\dfrac{14^4}{14^9}$

_____ _____ _____

10. $(8^4)^{12}$

11. $(12^{-5})^3$

12. $4^{-3} \cdot 4^{-21}$

_____ _____ _____

13. $m \cdot m^4$

14. $\dfrac{r^5}{r^2}$

15. $(a^3)^{-3}$

_____ _____ _____

Find the missing exponent.

16. $b^{\boxed{}} \cdot b^2 = b^8$

17. $\dfrac{x^5}{x^{\boxed{}}} = x^{-2}$

18. $\left(n^{\boxed{}}\right)^4 = n^0$

_____ _____ _____

Simplify each expression.

19. $(2 + 4)^2 + 8^{-6} \times (12 - 4)^{10}$ _____

20. $(3^3)^2 \times \left(\dfrac{(5 - 2)^3}{3^4}\right) + (10 - 4)^2 \times 6^{10}$ _____

21. Error Analysis A student simplified the expression $\dfrac{4^3}{16^3}$ as $\dfrac{1}{4}$. Do you agree with the student? Justify your answer.

_____

22. Find the values of $x^5 \cdot x^{-3}$ and $\dfrac{x^5}{x^3}$. What do you notice about the two values? Explain why your results make sense based on the properties you know.

_____

Exploring Scientific Notation

Large numbers are sometimes easier to read and understand when they are written in **scientific notation.** A number written in scientific notation has two factors: a number between 1 and 10 and a power of 10.

For example, 40,000 written in scientific notation is 4.0×10^4. The **standard form** of the number is 40,000.

Write 2,190,000 in scientific notation.

2,190,000 — Move the decimal point to the left until it is behind the 2.

2.190000 — Count the number of places the decimal point moved. The decimal moved 6 places to the left.

Use 6 as the exponent for the power.

$2,190,000 = 2.19 \times 10^6$

Write 5.2×10^6 in standard form.

5.2×10^6 — The exponent 6 tells you to move the decimal point 6 places to the right. Fill in zeros to make enough places.

$5.2 \times 10^6 = 5,200,000$

In standard form
$5.2 \times 10^6 = 5,200,000$

Write the following numbers in scientific notation.

1. 5,600,000 =

2. 6,040,000 =

3. 6,700 =

4. 1,013,000 =

5. 330,000 =

6. 716,000,000 =

7. 2,021,000,000 =

8. 2,070,000 =

Write the following numbers in standard form.

9. $4.1 \times 10^5 =$

10. $5.99 \times 10^2 =$

11. $1.1 \times 10^5 =$

12. $2.23 \times 10^4 =$

13. $8.9 \times 10^3 =$

14. $5.03 \times 10^7 =$

15. $3.12 \times 10^9 =$

16. $7.5 \times 10^4 =$

17. $1.011 \times 10^5 =$

18. $6.0 \times 10^8 =$

19. $3.14 \times 10^4 =$

20. $1.0 \times 10^1 =$

Unit 5
Core Skills Math Review

Using Scientific Notation

Write each number in scientific notation.

1. 58,927

2. 1,304,000,000

3. 0.000487

4. 0.000028

5. 0.000059

6. 6,730,000

7. 13,300

8. 0.0417

Write each number in standard notation.

9. 4×10^5

10. 1.8499×10^9

11. 8.3×10^{-4}

12. 3.582×10^{-6}

13. 2.97×10^{-2}

14. 6.41×10^3

15. 8.456×10^7

16. 9.06×10^{-5}

Circle the correct answer.

17. 8×10^5 is 2 / 20 / 200 / 2,000 times as great as 4×10^2.

18. 9×10^{10} is 30 / 300 / 3,000 / 30,000 times as great as 3×10^7.

19. 4×10^{-5} is 0.02 / 0.2 / 2 / 20 times as great as 2×10^{-4}.

20. 4×10^{-12} is 0.00001 / 0.0001 / 10 / 1000 times as great as 4×10^{-8}.

21. The air distance between Los Angeles, California, and New York City, New York, is about 3.9×10^3 units. Circle the best choice for the units this measurement is given in: cm / m / km.

Adding and Subtracting Scientific Notation

The table below shows the population of the three largest countries in North America. **Find the total population of the three countries.**

Country	United States	Canada	Mexico
Population	3.1×10^8	3.38×10^7	1.1×10^8

Use powers of 10 to solve.

1. First write each population with the same power of 10.

   United States: _____ $\times 10^{\square}$

   Canada: _____ $\times 10^{\square}$

   Mexico: _____ $\times 10^{\square}$

2. Add the multipliers for each population. $3.1 +$ _____ $+ 1.1 =$ _____

3. Write the final answer in scientific notation.

   _____

Use standard notation to solve.

4. First write each number in standard notation.

   United States: _____

   Canada: _____

   Mexico: _____

5. Find the sum of the numbers in standard notation.

   $310,000,000 +$ _____ $+$ _____ $=$ _____

6. Write the answer in scientific notation.

   _____

7. Using the population table above, tell how many more people live in Mexico than in Canada.

   _____

Multiplying and Dividing Scientific Notation

When the sun makes an orbit around the center of the Milky Way, it travels 2.025 3 10^{14} kilometers. The orbit takes 225 million years. At what rate does the sun travel around the Milky Way? Write your answer in scientific notation.

1. Set up a division problem to represent the situation.

   $\text{Rate} = \dfrac{\text{Distance}}{\text{Time}}$ $\text{Rate} = \dfrac{\boxed{}\text{kilometers}}{\boxed{}\text{years}}$

2. Write 225 million years in scientific notation.

   _____

3. Write the expression for rate with years in scientific notation.

   $\text{Rate} = \dfrac{\boxed{}\text{kilometers}}{\boxed{}\text{years}}$

4. Find the quotient by dividing the multipliers.

   $2.025 \div \boxed{} = \boxed{}$

5. Use the laws of exponents to divide the powers of 10.

   $\dfrac{10^{14}}{10^{8}} = 10^{\boxed{}} = 10^{\boxed{}}$

6. Combine the answers from 4 and 5 to write the rate in scientific notation.

   _____

7. Light from the sun travels at a speed of 1.86×10^5 miles per second. It takes sunlight about 4.8×10^3 seconds to reach Saturn. Find the approximate distance from the sun to Saturn. Write your answer in scientific notation.

   $d = rt$

   $= \left(\boxed{} \times 10^5\right)\left(\boxed{} \times 10^3\right)$

   $= \left(\boxed{}\right)(4.8) \times \left(\boxed{}\right)(10^3)$

   $= \boxed{} \times 10^{\boxed{}}$

   $= \boxed{} \times 10^{\boxed{}} \text{ miles}$

Square Roots

When you square a number, you multiply the number by itself. To find the **square root** of a number n, ask the following question: What number when multiplied by itself gives the number n as a result?

$9 \times 9 = 81$ $\sqrt{81} = 9$ The square root of 81 is 9 because $9 \times 9 = 81$.

$7 \times 7 = 49$ $\sqrt{49} = 7$ The square root of 49 is 7 because $7 \times 7 = 49$.

The root of a number is called the **radical**, and the number under the radical sign ($\sqrt{}$) is called the **radicand**.

Square each number. Then find the square root ($\sqrt{}$) of the product.

1. 8

2. 15

_____

3. 1

4. 6

_____

Find the square root ($\sqrt{}$) of each number.

5. 25

6. 9

_____

7. 100

8. 4

_____

9. 144

10. 16

_____

Square Roots and Cube Roots

Find the square roots of each number.

1. 144 _____

2. 256 _____

3. $\dfrac{1}{81}$ _____

4. $\dfrac{49}{900}$ _____

5. 400 _____

6. $\dfrac{1}{100}$ _____

Find the cube root of each number.

7. 216 _____

8. 8,000 _____

9. $\dfrac{27}{125}$ _____

10. $\dfrac{1}{27}$ _____

11. $\dfrac{27}{64}$ _____

12. 512 _____

Simplify each expression.

13. $\sqrt{16} + \sqrt{25}$ _____

14. $\sqrt[3]{125} + 10$ _____

15. $\sqrt{25} + 10$ _____

16. $8 - \sqrt{64}$ _____

17. $\sqrt[3]{\dfrac{16}{2}} + 1$ _____

18. $\sqrt{\dfrac{16}{4}} + \sqrt{4}$ _____

19. The foyer of Ann's house is a square with an area of 36 square feet. What is the length of each side of the foyer?

_____

20. A chessboard has 32 black squares and 32 white squares arranged in a square. How many squares are along each side of the chessboard?

_____

21. A cubic aquarium holds 27 cubic feet of water. What is the length of each edge of the cube?

_____

22. **Reasoning** How can you check your answer when you find the square root(s) of a number?

_____

_____

23. **Reasoning** Can you arrange 12 small squares to make a larger square? Can you arrange 20 small cubes to make a larger cube? Explain how this relates to perfect squares and perfect cubes.

_____

_____

Unit 5 Review

Find the value of each power.

1. $7^3 =$

2. $9^2 =$

3. $\left(\dfrac{1}{5}\right)^3 =$

4. $\left(\dfrac{5}{7}\right)^1 =$

_____

5. $4^{-2} =$

6. $15^{-1} =$

7. $17^{-2} =$

8. $2^{-4} =$

_____

Evaluate each expression.

9. $6^2 + 6^4 =$

10. $(3^2)^2 + (2^3)^3 =$

11. $7^2 - 2^4 =$

12. $5^2 \times 4^1 =$

_____

13. $9^2 \div 3^3 =$

14. $6^3 - 6^0 =$

15. $10^3 \times 10^2 =$

16. $(4^3)^2 \div (2^3)^1 =$

_____

Change each number to scientific notation or standard form.

17. $215,000,000 =$

18. $56,200 =$

19. $8.9 \times 10^4 =$

20. $9.4 \times 10^6 =$

_____

21. $\sqrt{25} - \sqrt{16} =$

22. $\sqrt{36} + \sqrt{4} =$

23. $\sqrt[3]{27} \div 3 =$

24. $\sqrt[3]{216} \times 4 =$

_____

Solve.

25. The population of Maysville is 2.6×10^4 and the population of Westin is 1.7×10^3. How many more people live in Maysville than in Westin?

26. Store A made a yearly profit of 7.5×10^7 dollars. Store B made a yearly profit of 8.2×10^5 dollars. Which store had more profit? How much more?

Name _____ Date _____

Ratios as Fractions

> A **ratio** is a fraction used to compare two quantities. For example, if a baseball player gets 3 hits for every 6 times at bat, the ratio of hits to times at bat is $\frac{3}{6}$ or $\frac{1}{2}$. The ratio of times at bat to hits is $\frac{6}{3}$ or $\frac{2}{1}$.

Write a fraction for each ratio. Simplify.

1. the ratio of inches in a foot to inches in a yard

   Ratio: _____

2. the ratio of hours in a day to hours in a week

   Ratio: _____

3. the ratio of cups in a pint to cups in a quart

   Ratio: _____

4. the ratio of 3 apples on a table to 6 apples in a bowl

   Ratio: _____

5. the ratio of cents in a quarter to cents in a dollar

   Ratio: _____

6. the ratio of 8 men to 10 women

   Ratio: _____

7. the ratio of cents in a half dollar to cents in a dime

   Ratio: _____

8. the ratio of 10 women to 8 men

   Ratio: _____

9. the ratio of 17 "yes" votes to 20 "no" votes

   Ratio: _____

10. the ratio of 5 wall outlets to 3 wall switches

    Ratio: _____

11. the ratio of the number of days in December to the number of days in January

    Ratio: _____

12. the ratio of 8 hours asleep to 16 hours awake

    Ratio: _____

13. the ratio of minutes in an hour to minutes in a half hour

    Ratio: _____

14. the ratio of 8 computers to 8 desks

    Ratio: _____

Unit 6
Core Skills Math Review

Name _____ Date _____

Ratios

The contents of Dean's pencil box are shown. Write each ratio in three different ways.

1. pencils to pens _____

2. total items to crayons _____

3. erasers to pencils _____

4. markers to total items _____

Dean's Pencil Box
5 pencils
2 erasers
3 pens
12 markers
24 crayons

Write three ratios equivalent to the given ratio.

5. $\frac{12}{28}$

6. $\frac{5}{2}$

7. $\frac{10}{3}$

_____ _____ _____

8. Aaron's math homework includes the following problem: $\frac{15}{25} = \frac{9}{\square}$

   How is this problem different from the problems involving equivalent ratios in this lesson?

   _____

9. You can use a table to solve the problem in Exercise 8. Complete the table to find the answer to Aaron's homework problem.

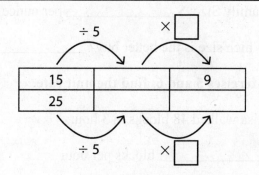

10. Why can you multiply or divide both terms of a ratio by the same number without changing the value of the ratio?

    _____

    _____

77

Unit Rate and Unit Price

The sizes and prices of three brands of laundry detergent are shown in the table. Use the table for Exercises 1 and 2.

Brand	Size (oz)	Price ($)
A	32	4.80
B	48	5.76
C	128	17.92

1. What is the unit price for each detergent?

   Brand A: $ _____ per ounce

   Brand B: $ _____ per ounce

   Brand C: $ _____ per ounce

2. Which detergent is the best buy? _____

Mason's favorite brand of peanut butter is available in two sizes. Each size and its price are shown in the table. Use the table for Exercises 3 and 4.

	Size (oz)	Price ($)
Regular	16	3.36
Family Size	40	7.60

3. What is the unit rate for each size of peanut butter?

   Regular: $ _____ per ounce

   Family Size: $ _____ per ounce

4. Which size is the better buy? _____

For Exercises 5 and 6, find the unit rate.

5. Lisa walked 48 blocks in 3 hours.

   _____ blocks per hour

6. Gordon can type 1,800 words in 25 minutes.

   _____ words per minute

7. A particular frozen yogurt has 75 calories in 2 ounces. How many calories are in 8 ounces

   of the yogurt? _____ calories

8. The cost of 10 oranges is $1.00. What is the cost of 5 dozen oranges? $ _____

9. A carpenter installed 10 windows in 4 hours. Another carpenter installed 50 windows in 20 hours. Are the two carpenters working at the same rate? Explain.

   _____

   _____

78

Using Unit Rates

1. Brandon enters bike races. He bikes $8\frac{1}{2}$ miles every $\frac{1}{2}$ hour. Complete the table to find how far Brandon bikes for each time interval.

Distance (mi)	$8\frac{1}{2}$				
Time (h)	$\frac{1}{2}$	1	$1\frac{1}{2}$	2	$2\frac{1}{2}$

Simplify each complex fraction.

2. $\dfrac{\frac{3}{4}}{\frac{2}{3}} =$

3. $\dfrac{\frac{1}{2}}{\frac{5}{8}} =$

4. $\dfrac{\frac{4}{5}}{\frac{2}{3}} =$

5. $\dfrac{\frac{6}{7}}{\frac{1}{7}} =$

_____   _____   _____   _____

Find each unit rate.

6. Julio walks $3\frac{1}{2}$ miles in $1\frac{1}{4}$ hours.

_____

7. Kenny reads $\frac{5}{8}$ page in $\frac{2}{3}$ minute.

_____

8. Marcia uses $\frac{3}{4}$ cup sugar when she halves the recipe.

_____

9. Sandra tiles $\frac{5}{4}$ square yards in $\frac{1}{3}$ hour.

_____

The information for two cell phone companies is given.

10. What is the unit rate for On Call?

_____

On Call	Talk Time
3.5 hours: $10	$\frac{1}{2}$ hour: $1.25

11. What is the unit rate for Talk Time?

_____

12. Determine which of the companies offers the best deal. Explain your answer.

_____

13. Another company offers a rate of $0.05 per minute. How would you find the unit rate per hour?

_____

79

Ratios in Measurement

Here you will form ratios using what you know about finding areas of squares and rectangles and volumes of rectangular prisms.

$$A = lw$$

$$V = lwh$$

The ratio of the sides of two squares is $\frac{1}{2}$. What is the ratio of the areas?

$$\frac{\text{Area A}}{\text{Area B}} = \frac{lw}{lw} = \frac{1 \times 1}{2 \times 2} = \frac{1}{4}$$

square A ⬜ $\Big\}1$ square B $\Big\}2$

The ratio of the two areas is $\frac{1}{4}$.

The area of square B is 4 times as great as the area of square A.

Or, the area of square A is $\frac{1}{4}$ the area of square B.

Solve.

1. The ratio of the sides of two squares is $\frac{1}{3}$. What is the ratio of the areas?

2. The ratio of the sides of two squares is $\frac{1}{4}$. What is the ratio of the areas?

3. The ratio of the edges of two cubes is $\frac{1}{5}$. What is the ratio of the volumes?

4. The ratio of the edges of two cubes is $\frac{3}{4}$. What is the ratio of the volumes?

5. The ratio of the edges of two cubes is $\frac{2}{3}$. What is the ratio of the volumes?

6. The ratio of the sides of two squares is $\frac{10}{1}$. What is the ratio of the areas

Proportions

A **proportion** is an equation stating that two ratios are equal. For example, if you mix 2 gallons of red paint with 3 gallons of white, the ratio of red to white is $\frac{2}{3}$. If you mix 4 gallons of red paint with 6 gallons of white, the ratio of red to white is $\frac{4}{6}$. The shades of pink for the two mixtures are the same, because $\frac{2}{3} = \frac{4}{6}$ is a true proportion.

A quick way to check that two ratios are equal is to **cross-multiply.** Write the ratios side by side and draw double-pointed arrows that cross. Multiply the pairs of numbers and see if you get the same result both times. It does not matter which pair of numbers is multiplied first. Look at this example.

Is $\frac{2}{3} = \frac{4}{6}$ a true proportion? $\frac{2}{3} \diagdown\!\!\!\!\!\diagup \frac{4}{6}$ Cross-multiply.

$$(2)(6) = 12 \text{ and } (3)(4) = 12$$

Since you get the same result (12), then $\frac{2}{3} = \frac{4}{6}$ is a true proportion. If you get different results when you cross-multiply, the ratios are not equal.

Use cross-multiplying to tell whether the proportion is true or false. Write *true* or *false*.

1. $\frac{8}{12} = \frac{6}{9}$ _____

$\frac{8}{12} \diagdown\!\!\!\!\!\diagup \frac{6}{9}$ $72 = 72$

2. $\frac{4}{5} = \frac{9}{10}$ _____

3. $\frac{16}{24} = \frac{2}{3}$ _____

4. $\frac{8}{10} = \frac{11}{15}$ _____

5. $\frac{6}{10} = \frac{12}{20}$ _____

6. $\frac{7}{8} = \frac{21}{24}$ _____

7. $\frac{18}{20} = \frac{9}{10}$ _____

8. $\frac{8}{16} = \frac{10}{20}$ _____

9. $\frac{8}{27} = \frac{2}{6}$ _____

Using Proportions to Solve Problems

There are many problems that you can solve by setting up and solving proportions.

If Paul can walk 15 miles in 6 hours, how far can he walk, at the same rate, in 8 hours?

Let x = number of miles he can walk in 8 hours.

$\frac{15}{6} = \frac{x}{8}$

$6x = 120$

$x = 20$ He can walk 20 miles in 8 hours.

Check: $\frac{15}{16} = \frac{x}{8}$

$\frac{15}{6} = \frac{20}{8}$

$8(15) = 6(20)$

$120 = 120$

Solve.

1. Martina bought 6 feet of wire for $21.66. How much would 10 feet of the same wire have cost?

Let x = the cost of 10 feet of wire.

$\frac{21.66}{6} = \frac{x}{10}$

_____

2. Kristen bought a 14-ounce bottle of catsup for 91¢. At the same rate, how much would a 20-ounce bottle cost?

_____

3. Carlos used $3.20 worth of gasoline to drive 68 miles. How many dollars worth of gas will he use to drive 85 miles?

_____

4. The tax on a piece of property valued at $20,000 was $264. At the same rate, what would be the tax on a piece of property valued at $22,000?

_____

5. A train is traveling at the rate of 75 miles per hour. At this speed, how far will it travel in 40 minutes? (Hint: Change 1 hour to minutes.)

_____

6. Clint bought 3 yards of fabric for $15.75. How much would 5 yards of the same fabric have cost?

_____

Direct Variation

In the formula $D = rt$, distance equals the rate times the time. If a car travels at a constant rate of r miles per hour for 3 hours, the distance D that it travels can be found by using the equation $D = r \times 3$. If the car doubles its time, it will double its distance. If the car triples its time, it will triple its distance. The distance traveled **varies directly** as the time varies. This is an example of **direct variation.**

Complete the tables.

1. $D = rt$

r	50	50	50	50	50
t	1	2	3	4	5
D	50				

Distance varies directly as the time varies.

2. $A = lw$

w	10	10	10	10	10	10	10
l	2	4	6	8	10	12	14
A	20						

Area varies directly as the length varies.

3. $A = \frac{1}{2}bh$

b	6	6	6	6	6	6	6
h	2	4	6	8	10	12	14
A	6						

Area varies directly as the height varies.

Ratios, Tables, and Graphs

The Webster family is taking a train to Washington, D.C. The train travels at a constant speed.
The table shows the distance that the train travels in various amounts of time.

Distance (mi)	120	150		240	
Time (h)	2		3		5

1. Use the numbers in the first column of the table to write a ratio of distance to time.

_____

2. How far does the train travel in one hour?

_____

3. Use your answer from Exercise 2 to write another ratio of distance to time.

_____

4. The ratios in Exercises 1 and 3 are

_____

5. How can you use your answer to Exercise 1 to find the distance the train travels in a given number of hours?

_____

6. Complete the table. What are the equivalent ratios shown in the table?

$$\frac{120}{2} = \frac{150}{\boxed{}} = \frac{\boxed{}}{\boxed{}} = \frac{\boxed{}}{\boxed{}} = \frac{\boxed{}}{\boxed{}}$$

7. Write the information in the table as ordered pairs.
   Use Time as the x-coordinates and Distance as the
   y-coordinates. (2, 120) $\left(\boxed{}, 150\right)$ $\left(3, \boxed{}\right)$ $\left(\boxed{}, 240\right)$ $\left(5, \boxed{}\right)$
   Graph the ordered pairs and connect the points.
   Describe your graph.

_____

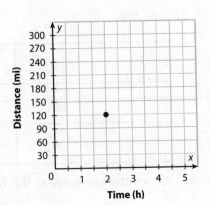

Proportional Relationships, Tables, and Equations

Tell whether the relationship is a proportional relationship. Write *yes* or *no*. If so, give the constant of proportionality.

1.

Number of Minutes	3	4	5	6	7
Number of Seconds	180	240	300	360	420

_____

2.

Time (h)	1	2	3	4	5
Biking Distance (mi)	12	26	36	44	50

_____

3. Naomi reads 9 pages in 27 minutes, 12 pages in 36 minutes, 15 pages in 45 minutes, and 50 pages in 150 minutes.

_____

4. A scuba diver descends at a constant rate of 8 feet per minute.

_____

Write an equation for the relationship. Tell what the variables represent.

5. It takes Li 1 hour to drive 65 miles, 2 hours to drive 130 miles, and 3 hours to drive 195 miles.

_____

6.

Cups of Batter	2	6	8	12
Number of Muffins	5	15	20	30

_____

Information on three car rental companies is given.

7. Write an equation that gives the cost, *y*, of renting a car for, *x*, days from Rent-All.

_____

8. What is the cost per day of renting a car from A-1?

_____

9. Which company offers the best deal? Why?

_____

Rent-All				
Days	3	4	5	6
Total Cost ($)	55.50	74.00	92.50	111.00

A-1 Rentals	**Car Town**
The cost *y* of renting a car for *x* days is given by $y = 22.5x$.	The cost of renting a car from us is just $19.25 per day!

Proportional Relationships and Graphs

Tell whether the relationship is a proportional relationship. Explain why or why not.

1. A student reads 65 pages per hour.

Time (h)	3	5	9	10
Pages	195	325	585	650

_____

_____

2. A babysitter makes $7.50 per hour.

Time (h)	2	3	5	8
Earnings	15	22.50	37.50	60

_____

_____

3.

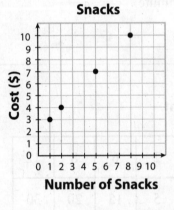

Snacks

_____

_____

4.

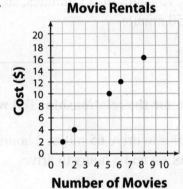

Movie Rentals

_____

_____

The graph shows the relationship between time and the distance run by two horses.

5. How long does it take each horse to run 1 mile?

_____

6. What does the point (0, 0) represent?

_____

_____

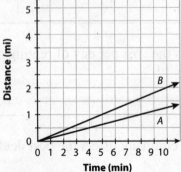

Horse Training

7. Write an equation for the relationship between time and distance for each horse.

_____

_____

Scale Drawings

The scale of a room in a blueprint is 3 in:5 ft.

1. Complete the table.

Blueprint length (in.)	3	6	9	12	15	18
Actual length (ft)						

2. A wall in the blueprint is 18 inches. How long is the actual wall?

_____

3. A window in the room has an actual width of 2.5 feet. Find the width of the window in the blueprint.

_____

4. The scale in the drawing is 2 in:4 ft. What are the length and width of the actual room? Find the area of the actual room.

_____

_____

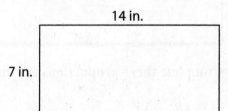

5. The scale in the drawing is 2 cm:5 m. What are the length and width of the actual room? Find the area of the actual room.

_____

_____

6. In the scale drawing below, assume the rectangle is drawn on centimeter grid paper. The scale is 1 cm:4 m. Redraw the rectangle on centimeter grid paper using a scale of 1 cm:6 m.

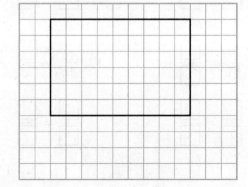 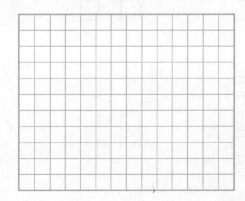

Similar Triangles

Two triangles are **similar** if the **corresponding** angles
are the same size and if the ratios of the lengths of the
corresponding sides are equal. Since the ratios are equal,
they form a proportion.

Find the length of side *YZ*.

$$\frac{\text{side } AB}{\text{side } XY} = \frac{\text{side } BC}{\text{side } YZ}$$

$$\frac{AB}{XY} = \frac{BC}{YZ}$$

$$\frac{1}{2} = \frac{1.5}{x}$$

$$1(x) = 2(1.5)$$

$$x = 3$$

Check: $1(3) = 2(1.5)$

$$3 = 3$$

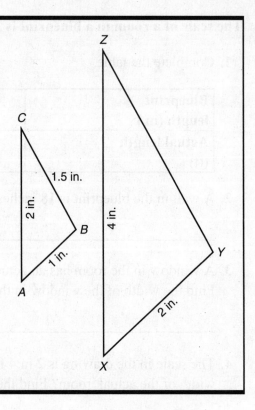

The length of *YZ* is 3 in.

Complete these proportions for the similar triangles above.

1. $\dfrac{AB}{BC} = \dfrac{XY}{\boxed{YZ}}$

$\dfrac{1}{1.5} = \dfrac{2}{\boxed{3}}$

2. $\dfrac{BC}{YZ} = \dfrac{AC}{\Box}$

$\dfrac{1.5}{3} = \dfrac{2}{\Box}$

3. $\dfrac{XY}{AB} = \dfrac{\Box}{BC}$

$\dfrac{2}{1} = \dfrac{\Box}{1.5}$

4. $\dfrac{AB}{BC} = \dfrac{XY}{\Box}$

$\dfrac{1}{2} = \dfrac{2}{\Box}$

5. $\dfrac{AC}{XZ} = \dfrac{\Box}{XY}$

$\dfrac{\Box}{\Box} = \dfrac{\Box}{\Box}$

6. $\dfrac{BC}{\Box} = \dfrac{YZ}{XY}$

$\dfrac{\Box}{\Box} = \dfrac{\Box}{\Box}$

7. $\dfrac{YZ}{BC} = \dfrac{\Box}{AC}$

$\dfrac{\Box}{\Box} = \dfrac{\Box}{\Box}$

8. $\dfrac{XY}{AB} = \dfrac{\Box}{AC}$

$\dfrac{\Box}{\Box} = \dfrac{\Box}{\Box}$

9. $\dfrac{XY}{XZ} = \dfrac{\Box}{\Box}$

$\dfrac{\Box}{\Box} = \dfrac{\Box}{\Box}$

10. $\dfrac{YZ}{XZ} = \dfrac{\Box}{\Box}$

$\dfrac{\Box}{\Box} = \dfrac{\Box}{\Box}$

11. $\dfrac{AC}{BC} = \dfrac{\Box}{\Box}$

$\dfrac{\Box}{\Box} = \dfrac{\Box}{\Box}$

12. $\dfrac{AC}{AB} = \dfrac{\Box}{\Box}$

$\dfrac{\Box}{\Box} = \dfrac{\Box}{\Box}$

Using Similar Triangles

Proportions can help you solve for the lengths of sides in similar triangles.

Triangles *ABC* and *XYZ* are similar. What is the length of side *YZ*?

You can solve this using two methods.

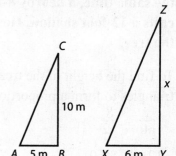

$$\frac{AB}{XY} = \frac{BC}{YZ}$$

$$\frac{5}{6} = \frac{10}{x}$$

$$5x = 60$$

$$x = 12$$

or

$$\frac{AB}{BC} = \frac{XY}{YZ}$$

$$\frac{5}{10} = \frac{6}{x}$$

$$5x = 60$$

$$x = 12$$

Set up and solve a proportion to solve each problem.

1. Triangles *ABC* and *XYZ* are similar. What is the length of side *XY*?

$$\frac{7}{z} = \frac{6}{18}$$

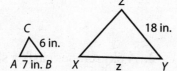

_____

2. Triangles *ABC* and *XYZ* are similar. What is the length of side *YZ*?

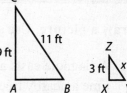

_____

3. Triangles *ABC* and *XYZ* are similar. What is the length of side *BC*?

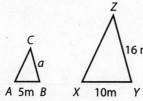

_____

4. Triangles *ABC* and *XYZ* are similar. What is the length of side *BC*?

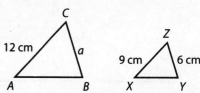

_____

5. Triangles *ABC* and *XYZ* are similar. What is the length of side *XY*?

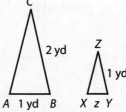

_____

6. Triangles *ABC* and *XYZ* are similar. What is the length of side *YZ*?

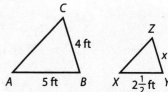

_____

89

Using Proportions in Similar Figures

You can use proportions to solve problems about similar figures.

A tree casts a shadow 60 feet long. At the same time, a nearby 8-foot post casts a 12-foot shadow. How tall is the tree?

To find the height of the tree, use similar triangles to form a proportion. Then solve.

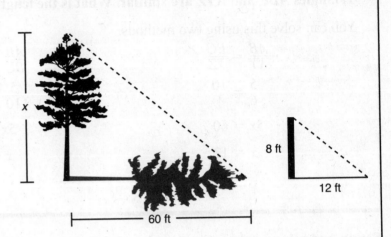

$$\frac{x}{60} = \frac{8}{12}$$

$$12x = 8(60)$$

$$x = \frac{8(60)}{12}$$

$$x = 40 \quad \text{The tree is 40 feet tall.}$$

Draw a picture. Use a proportion. Solve.

1. A flagpole casts a 75-foot shadow at the same time a nearby tree 20 feet tall casts a shadow of 30 feet. How tall is the flagpole?

2. A skyscraper casts a shadow 111 feet long at the same time a nearby 50-foot telephone pole casts a shadow 10 feet long. How high is the skyscraper?

3. A telephone pole casts a shadow 30 feet long, while a nearby fence post 4 feet high casts a shadow 3 feet long. How high is the pole?

4. A grain silo casts a shadow of 40 feet, while a nearby fence post casts a shadow of 2 feet. The fence post is 5 feet high. How tall is the grain silo?

Name _____ Date _____

Unit 6 Review

Write a fraction for each ratio.

1. the ratio of seconds in one minute to minutes in two hours

_____

2. the ratio of 7 pencils to 13 erasers

_____

Find the unit rate for each situation.

3. Cameron walked 12 miles in 3 hours.

_____ miles per hour

4. Shania climbed 560 feet up in 4 hours.

_____ feet per hour

Use cross-multiplication to tell whether the proportion is true or false. Write *true* or *false*.

5. $\frac{2}{6} = \frac{5}{15}$

_____

6. $\frac{4}{7} = \frac{12}{14}$

_____

7. $\frac{3}{12} = \frac{10}{40}$

_____

Solve.

8. A tree cast a 24-foot shadow at the same time a fence post 5 feet high cast a 4-foot shadow. How tall is the tree?

_____

9. The table below shows a proportional relationship. Fill in the missing value.

Time (sec)	3	5	11	17
Distance (ft)	10.2	17		57.8

10. What is the constant of proportionality for the proportional relationship shown in the graph?

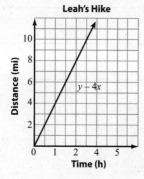

11. The figure is a scale drawing of a rectangular room. The scale is 2 cm:4 m. What is the length of the actual room?

12 cm

6 cm

_____

_____

Unit 6
Core Skills Math Review

What Is Algebra?

Study the following number sentences to find a pattern.

$1 \times 2 = 2$ $1 \times 29 = 29$ $1 \times 3.45 = 3.45$

You can write a general statement about the three number sentences: if a number is multiplied by 1, the product is the number. Here is a way to describe the pattern using a **variable.** Variables are letters or symbols used to represent numbers. The number is represented by the variable n.

$1 \times n = n$ where n represents any number

Algebra is the study of variables and operations with variables. Sometimes more than one variable is needed to describe a pattern.

Describe the pattern using two variables, a and b.	**Write three number sentences that fit the pattern $\frac{p}{p} = 1$.**
$3 + 5 = 5 + 3$	Choose any number for p. Here are three possible number sentences.
$10 + 12 = 12 + 10$	
$9.8 + 3.4 = 3.4 + 9.8$	
The pattern is $a + b = b + a$.	$\frac{2}{2} = \frac{4.5}{4.5} = \frac{78}{78} =$

Describe each pattern using one or two variables.

1. $1 \times 4 = 4 \times 1$
$3 \times 4 = 4 \times 3$
$10 \times 4 = 4 \times 10$

_____

2. $2 - 2 = 0$
$46 - 46 = 0$
$1.5 - 1.5 = 0$

_____

3. $3 + 3 = 2 \times 3$
$10 + 10 = 2 \times 10$
$25 + 25 = 2 \times 25$

_____

4. $0 \times 6 = 0$
$0 \times 8 = 0$
$0 \times 42 = 0$

_____

Write three number sentences that fit the pattern.

5. $0 + q = q$

_____

_____

_____

6. $s \div 2 = t$

_____

_____

_____

Evaluating Numerical Expressions

To **evaluate** an expression means to find a single value for it. Use the order of operations to evaluate expressions the same way you simplified numerical expressions on page 21.

If you are given an expression consisting of a numerator and a denominator that each have an operation, evaluate the numerator and the denominator separately. Then divide.

Evaluate:	**Evaluate:**	**Evaluate:**	**Evaluate:**
$16 + 8 \div 2$	$(10 - 8) \cdot 2$	$\frac{1}{4}(20 - 4)$	$\frac{8 - 2}{2 + 1}$
$16 + 4 = 20$	$2 \cdot 2 = 4$	$\frac{1}{4}(16) = 4$	$\frac{6}{3} = 2$

Evaluate each expression.

1. $7 + 10 \div 5 =$

2. $3(2 + 8) =$

3. $8 \cdot 2 - 3 =$

4. $(5 - 1)(4) =$

_____

5. $2(11 - 3) =$

6. $4 \cdot 5 + 6 =$

7. $18 - (6 \div 3) =$

8. $2 \cdot (15 - 3) =$

_____

9. $8 + 18 \div 3 =$

10. $(21 + 4) \div 5 =$

11. $(10 - 2) \cdot 7 =$

12. $7 + 9 \div 3 =$

_____

13. $\frac{1}{3}(6 + 3) =$

14. $\frac{3}{4}(12) - \frac{1}{2}(2) =$

15. $\frac{1}{5}(10) + \frac{1}{4}(12) =$

16. $\frac{1}{2}(8 - 3) =$

_____

17. $\frac{2}{3 - 1} =$

18. $\frac{20 - 10}{2 \cdot 5} =$

19. $\frac{9 - 5}{4 + 4} =$

20. $\frac{17 + 2(2)}{3} =$

_____

21. $\frac{15 \div 5}{1 + 2} =$

22. $\frac{2(9 + 6)}{3 \cdot 6} =$

23. $\frac{7 + 5}{2(5) - 6} =$

24. $\frac{12(2) \div 3}{11 - 9} =$

_____

Exploring Expressions

An **algebraic expression** consists of at least one of each of the following: a variable, a number, and an operation. Remember, a variable is a symbol or a letter used to represent a number.

The following are examples of algebraic expressions:

$9n \qquad a + 4 \qquad d - 18 \qquad \dfrac{x}{2}$

Use these examples to help you write algebraic expressions.

Verbal Expression	Operation	Algebraic Expression
the product of 9 and n, 9 times n	multiplication	$9n$, $9(n)$, $9 \cdot n$, or $9 \times n$
4 more than a, a increased by 4	addition	$a + 4$
18 less than d, d decreased by 18	subtraction	$d - 18$
x separated into 2 equal parts	division	$\dfrac{x}{2}$ or $x \div 2$

Write an algebraic expression for each verbal expression.

1. r more than 10

2. 9 less than t

3. the product of 7 and s

4. a number, w, divided by 3

5. the sum of m and 12

6. h multiplied by $2x$

7. a number, n, subtracted from 25

8. the difference between p and g

9. 24 divided by k

10. 13 increased by b

11. c decreased by 7

12. y separated into 5 equal parts

Writing Expressions

1. Identify the constant(s) and variable(s) in the algebraic expression $t - 4n + 2$.

   Constant(s) _____   Variable(s) _____

2. Circle the algebraic expression(s) in the list below.

   $180 + 25$ $x - 79$ $7(12)$ $a + b$ -220 $13t$ $\frac{n}{16}$ $24 - 3h$ $\frac{4}{7}$ r

Write each phrase as an algebraic expression.

3. n divided by 8 _____   4. p multiplied by 4 _____

5. b plus 14 _____   6. 90 times x _____

7. a take away 16 _____   8. k less than 24 _____

9. 3 groups of w _____   10. the sum of 1 and q _____

11. the quotient of 13 and z _____   12. c added to 45 _____

Write a phrase in words for each algebraic expression.

13. $m + 83$ _____   14. $42s$ _____

15. $\frac{9}{d}$ _____   16. $t - 29$ _____

17. $2 + g$ _____   18. $11x$ _____

19. $\frac{h}{12}$ _____   20. $5 - k$ _____

21. Kayla's score on yesterday's math test was 12 points greater than Julianne's score. Let k represent Kayla's score. Write an algebraic expression to represent Julianne's score.   _____

22. The town of Rayburn received 6 more inches of snow than the town of Greenville. Let g represent the amount of snow in Greenville. Write an algebraic expression to represent the amount of snow in Rayburn.   _____

23. Abby baked 48 cookies and divided them evenly into bags. Let b represent the number of bags. Write an algebraic expression to represent the number of cookies in each bag.   _____

Parts of an Expression

Use words from the box to complete each sentence.

factor	product	quotient	sum	difference

1. $15 + x$ represents a _____ of two terms.

2. $9a$ represents the _____ of 9 and a.

3. $p \div 3$ represents a _____.

4. $12 - x$ is a _____ of two terms.

There may be several different ways to describe a given expression. Use the following terms to describe each expression.

algebraic expression	sum of two terms	product of two factors	sum of a quotient and a constant	product of a coefficient and a variable

5. $\frac{9a}{5} + 32$ _____

_____

6. $3(m + 1)$ _____

_____

7. $7c$ _____

_____

8. $5 + 9$ _____

_____

Write an algebraic expression that matches each description.

9. A product of two variables _____

10. A sum of a product and a constant _____

11. An expression with 3 terms _____

Evaluating Expressions with Variables

A number in an expression is either a constant or a coefficient. In the expression $4x - 7$, 4 is a coefficient because it is a multiplier of the variable; -7 is a constant because it appears alone.

A term in an expression is either a single number or the product of numbers and variables. There are two terms in the expression $3 \div 8xy$. The term 3 is a constant. The term $8xy$ has a coefficient of 8 and two variables.

To evaluate an expression containing one or more variables, substitute a value for each variable. Then simplify the expression.

Evaluate:

$2t - 8$ if $t = 5$

$2(5) - 8 = 10 - 8$

$\qquad = 2$

Evaluate:

$\frac{1}{3}(q + 3)$ if $q = 6$

$\frac{1}{3}(6 + 3) = \frac{1}{3}(9)$

$\qquad = 3$

Evaluate:

$x(7 + s)$ if $x = 2$ and $s = 3$

$2(7 + 3) = 2(10)$

$\qquad = 20$

Identify each number in the expression as a constant or a coefficient.

1. $5m + 9$

5 is a coefficient.
9 is a constant.

2. $3q - t$

3. $6s - 2y$

4. $10x - 7$

Evaluate each expression if $p = 8$, $k = 2$, and $n = 4$.

5. $pk + n =$

6. $kp - kn =$

7. $n(5 + n) =$

8. $pn - k =$

9. $\frac{k}{p} =$

10. $\frac{n}{k} + p =$

11. $\frac{3n + 3}{5} =$

12. $\frac{2k + 2p}{n} =$

Evaluate each expression if $s = 15$, $d = 20$, and $u = 5$.

13. $du - s =$

$20 \times 5 - 15 =$
$100 - 15 = 85$

14. $u(d - s) =$

15. $2ds =$

16. $(d - u)(s + u) =$

17. $\frac{1}{u}(s + d) =$

18. $\frac{1}{5}s + u =$

19. $\frac{u}{d - s} =$

20. $\frac{d(s - u)}{5} =$

© Houghton Mifflin Harcourt Publishing Company

Unit 7
Core Skills Math Review

Name _____ Date _____

Evaluating Algebraic Expressions

Evaluate each expression for the given value(s) of the variable(s).

1. $x - 7$; $x = 23$ _____

2. $3r$; $r = 6$ _____

3. $\frac{8}{t}$; $t = 4$ _____

4. $9 + m$; $m = 1.5$ _____

5. $p - 2$; $p = 19$ _____

6. $3h$; $h = \frac{1}{6}$ _____

7. $2.5 - n$; $n = 1.8$ _____

8. k^2; $k = 4$ _____

9. $4(b - 4)$; $b = 5$ _____

10. $38 - \frac{x}{2}$; $x = 12$ _____

11. $\frac{30}{d} - 2$; $d = 6$ _____

12. $x^2 - 34$; $x = 10$ _____

13. $\frac{1}{2}w + 2$; $w = \frac{1}{9}$ _____

14. $5(6.2 + z)$; $z = 3.8$ _____

15. $2a^2 + a$; $a = 8$ _____

16. $7y + 32$; $y = 9$ _____

17. xy; $x = 8$ and $y = 6$

18. $x + y - 1$; $x = 12$ and $y = 4$

_____   _____

19. $3x + 4y$; $x = 4$ and $y = 5$

20. $4x + 1 + 3y$; $x = 6$ and $y = 8$

_____   _____

21. The expression lwh gives the volume of a rectangular prism with length l, width w, and height h. Find the volume of the rectangular prism. _____ in^3

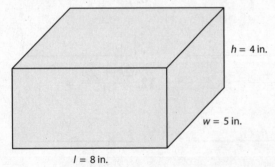

h = 4 in.

w = 5 in.

l = 8 in.

22. The expression $1.8c + 32$ gives the temperature in degrees Fahrenheit for a given temperature in degrees Celsius, c. Find the temperature in degrees Fahrenheit that is equivalent to 30 °C. _____ °F

23. **Error Analysis** Marjorie evaluated the expression $3x + 2$ for $x = 5$ as shown: $35 + 2 = 37$ What was Marjorie's mistake? What is the correct value of $3x + 2$ for $x = 5$?

_____

Equivalent Expressions

1. Draw lines to match the expressions in List A with their equivalent expressions in List B.

List A	List B
$4 + 4b$	$4b - 4$
$4(b - 1)$	$4(b + 1)$
$4b + 1$	$1 + 4b$

For each expression, use a property to write an equivalent expression. Tell which property you used.

2. $ab =$ _____

3. $x + 13 =$ _____

4. $5(3x - 2) =$ _____

5. $2 + (a + b) =$ _____

Circle the like terms in each list.

6. $3a$ $16a$ 5 y $2a^2$

7. $5x^3$ $3y$ $7x^3$ $4x$ 21

8. $6b^2$ $2a^2$ $4a^3$ b^2 b

9. $12t^2$ $4x^3$ a $4t^2$ 1 $2t^2$

10. $32y$ 5 $3y^2$ 17 y^3 6

11. $10k^2$ m 9 $2m$ $10k$

Combine like terms.

12. $7x^4 - 5x^4 =$

13. $2x + 3x + 4 =$

14. $6b + 7b - 10 =$

15. $32y + 5y =$

16. $y + 4 + 3(y + 2) =$

17. $7a^2 - a^2 + 16 =$

18. $8y - 3y =$

19. $6x^2 + 4(x^2 - 1) =$

20. $4a^5 - 2a^5 + 4b + b =$

21. $8m + 14 - 12 + 4n =$

22. $3a + 2(b + 5a) = 3a + 2b + 2(5a)$ *Distributive Property*

$= 3a + 2b + (2 \cdot 5)a$ *Associative Property of Multiplication*

$= 3a + 2b + \square a$ *Multiply 2 and 5.*

$= 3a + 10a + 2b$ _____ *Property of Addition*

$= (3 + 10)a + 2b$ *Distributive Property*

$= \square a + 2b$ *Add inside the parentheses.*

$3a + 2(b + 5a) =$ _____

Unit 7
Core Skills Math Review

Algebraic Expressions

Add or subtract each expression.

1. $(4.8x + 15.5) + (2.1x - 12.2)$ **2.** $(7x + 8) - (3x + 12)$ **3.** $\left(\frac{1}{2}x + \frac{3}{4}\right) + \left(\frac{1}{2}x - \frac{1}{4}\right)$

_____   _____   _____

4. Each week, Joey gets paid $10 plus $2 for each chore he does. His sister Julie gets paid $5 plus $3 per chore. Write an expression for how much their parents pay Joey and Julie each week if they do the same amount of chores.

_____

5. If Joey and Julie each do 5 chores, how much do they get paid individually? How much do their parents pay all together?

_____

6. A company sets up a food booth and a game booth at the county fair. The fee for the food booth is $100 plus $5 per day. The fee for the game booth is $50 plus $7 per day. How much does the company pay for both booths for 5 days?

_____

7. A group of 4 people go out to eat. They decide to split the bill so each person pays $\frac{1}{4}$ of the total price. Appetizers are $6 and main dishes are $9. Each person orders 1 appetizer and 1 main dish. Write an expression to show how much each person pays.

_____

Factor each expression by finding the GCF.

8. $24 + 36x$ **9.** $5x - 25$ **10.** $12x + 10$ **11.** $10x - 60$

GCF: _____   GCF: _____   GCF: _____   GCF: _____

_____   _____   _____   _____

12. How could you use the Distributive Property to check your factoring?

_____

Name _____ Date _____

Rewriting Expressions

A sports store buys skateboards from a supplier for *s* dollars. The store's manager decides to mark up the price for retail sale by 42%. Find the retail price as a single term.

1. The markup is _____% of the price, *s*.

2. Find the amount of the markup.
   Use a bar model.

   The unshaded bar represents the cost of

   the skateboard, _____.

   The shaded section is _____ % of _____. This can be written as a decimal, _____.

3. Add _____ to the cost of the skateboard to find the retail price.

   Retail price = _____ + _____
               Original cost   Markup

4. You can combine like terms in the expression and write the retail price as a single term.

   Retail price = _____

Keeley is selling bicycles. For the holiday sale, she will mark down each bike's selling price by 24%. Find the sales price as a single term.

5. The markdown is _____ % of the price, *b*.

6. Find the amount of the markdown.
   Use a bar model.

   The unshaded bar represents the current price of the bike, _____.

   The shaded section is _____ % of _____. This can be written as a decimal, _____.

7. Subtract _____ from the price of the bike to find the sales price.

   Sales price = _____ – _____
              Price of bike   Markdown

8. You can combine like terms in the expression and write the sales price as a single term.

   Sales price = _____

Unit 7 Review

Name the property shown.

1. $3(x + 2) = 3x + 6$ 2. $0 \times 67 = 0$ 3. $3.8 - 3.8 = 0$ 4. $28 \times 13 = 13 \times 28$

_____ _____   _____   _____

Evaluate each expression.

5. $(9 \div 3) \times 5 =$ 6. $4(8 - 1) =$ 7. $\dfrac{18 + 2}{5(4 - 3)}$ 8. $\dfrac{24 \div 3}{2(2)}$

_____ _____   _____   _____

Write an algebraic expression for each verbal expression.

9. a number, n, divided by $4m$ 10. a sum of a product and a constant

_____   _____

Evaluate each expression if $a = 3$, $b = 4$, and $c = (\text{-}2)$.

11. $a(2b - c) =$ 12. $\dfrac{3}{4}b + ac =$ 13. $\dfrac{6ac}{5b} =$

_____   _____   _____

Write an equivalent expression.

14. $4(8 + d) =$ 15. $15s + 10t =$ 16. $g + g + g =$

_____   _____   _____

Add or subtract each expression.

17. $(3x + 9) + (21x - 8)$ 18. $(6x + 11) - (5x + 1)$ 19. $(10x - 4) - (2x + 7)$

_____   _____   _____

Solve.

20. Rick buys remote control cars to resell. He applies a markup of 10%. Write two expressions that represent the price of the cars.

21. Jane sells pillows. For a sale she marks them down 5%. Write two expressions that represent the sale price of the pillows.

_____   _____

Equations and Solutions

Determine whether the given value is a solution of the equation. Write *yes* or *no*.

1. $23 = x - 9$; $x = 14$ _____

2. $\frac{n}{13} = 4$; $n = 52$ _____

3. $14 + x = 46$; $x = 32$ _____

4. $17y = 85$; $y = 5$ _____

5. $25 = \frac{k}{5}$; $k = 5$ _____

6. $2.5n = 45$; $n = 18$ _____

7. $21 = m + 9$; $m = 11$ _____

8. $21 - h = 15$; $h = 6$ _____

9. $d - 4 = 19$; $d = 15$ _____

10. $5 + x = 47$; $x = 52$ _____

11. $w - 9 = 0$; $w = 9$ _____

12. $5q = 31$; $q = 13$ _____

13. $7a = 126$; $a = 18$ _____

14. $3.6 = 3c$; $c = 1.2$ _____

15. $\frac{1}{2}r = 8$; $r = 4$ _____

16. $9x = 117$; $x = 12$ _____

For Exercises 17–19, write an equation to represent the situation.

17. Each floor of a hotel has r rooms. On 8 floors, there are a total of 256 rooms.

_____

18. Mario had b books. After receiving 5 new books for his birthday, he had 18 books.

_____

19. In the school band, there are 5 trumpet players and f flute players. There are twice as many flute players as there are trumpet players.

_____

20. Halfway through a bus route, 48 students remain on the bus, and 23 students have already been dropped off. Write an equation to determine whether there are 61 or 71 students on the bus at the beginning of the route.

_____

21. The high temperature was 92°F. This was 24°F higher than the overnight low temperature. Write an equation to determine whether the low temperature was 62°F or 68°F.

_____

Name _____ Date _____

Finding Missing Addends and Missing Factors

When you add two numbers, the numbers that you add are called addends. When you multiply two numbers, the numbers you multiply are called factors. An equation is a statement that two quantities are equal. Variables are often used to stand for unknown, or missing, addends or factors. For example, in the equation $x + 3 = 11$, the variable x stands for the missing addend that you would add to 3 to get 11. In the equation $3a = 27$, the variable a stands for the missing factor you would multiply by 3 to get 27.

Remember, $3a$, $3 \cdot a$, and $3(a)$ all mean 3 times a.

To find a missing addend, subtract the known addend from both sides of the equation. To find a missing factor, divide both sides of the equation by the known factor. Check by substituting the answer into the original equation.

Solve for the missing addend: $x + 3 = 11$

$x + 3 = 11$

$x + 3 - 3 = 11 - 3$ Subtract 3.

$x = 8$

Check: $x + 3 = 11$

      $8 + 3 = 11$

Solve for the missing factor: $3a = 27$

$3a = 27$

$\dfrac{3a}{3} = \dfrac{27}{3}$ Divide by 3.

$a = 9$

Check: $3a = 27$

      $3(9) = 27$

Solve. Check.

1. $x + 7 = 10$

    $x + 7 - 7 = 10 - 7$

2. $5x = 20$

    $\dfrac{5x}{5} = \dfrac{20}{5}$

3. $y + 5 = 15$

    $y + 5 - 5 = 15 - 5$

_____

4. $10m = 80$

_____

5. $n + 12 = 29$

_____

6. $8x = 96$

_____

7. $9\frac{1}{3} + x = 30\frac{2}{3}$

_____

8. $7k = 91$

_____

9. $40 + x = 93$

104

Practice Finding Missing Addends and Missing Factors

Solve. Simplify.

1. $x + \frac{1}{4} = \frac{3}{4}$

2. $9n = 315$

3. $3x = 7$

4. $1\frac{2}{3} + x = 5$

5. $k + 15 = 40$

6. $16x = 90$

7. $m + 6 = 7\frac{3}{8}$

8. $12k = 156$

9. $5x = 37$

10. $81 + k = 92$

11. $x + 1\frac{1}{2} = 2\frac{1}{4}$

12. $11x = 572$

13. $6k = 70$

14. $x + 46 = 75$

15. $3x = 261$

16. $1\frac{1}{8} + x = 6\frac{1}{4}$

17. $21n = 105$

18. $21n = 45$

19. $63 + x = 79$

20. $n + 7\frac{1}{2} = 15$

21. $13 + x = 81$

22. $5x = 43$

23. $12x = 144$

24. $x + 102 = 200$

Addition and Subtraction Equations

Solve each equation.

1. $t + 6 = 10$

_____

2. $a + 7 = 15$

_____

3. $x - 16 = 72$

_____

4. $d - 125 = 55$

_____

5. $w + 87 = 102$

_____

6. $k + 13 = 61$

_____

7. $h + 6.9 = 11.4$

_____

8. $y + 2.3 = 10.5$

_____

9. $82 + p = 122$

_____

10. $n + \frac{1}{2} = \frac{7}{4}$

_____

11. $z - \frac{2}{3} = \frac{3}{5}$

_____

12. $19 + m = 29$

_____

13. $16 = q - 125$

_____

14. $9.6 = 5.6 + g$

_____

15. $r - 8 = 56$

_____

For Exercises 16–18, write and solve an equation to answer each question.

16. Kim bought a poster that cost $8.95 and some colored pencils. The total cost was $21.35. How much did the colored pencils cost?

_____

17. The Acme Car Company sold 37 vehicles in June. How many compact cars were sold in June?

_____

Acme Car Company - June Sales	
Type of Car	Number Sold
SUV	8
Compact	?

18. Lindsey finished a race in 58.4 seconds. This was 2.6 seconds faster than her practice time. What was Lindsey's practice time?

_____

19. How do you know whether to add or subtract on both sides when solving an equation?

_____

_____

Multiplication and Division Equations

Solve each equation.

1. $6c = 18$

_____

2. $2a = 14$

_____

3. $75 = 15x$

_____

4. $25d = 350$

_____

5. $9.5w = 76$

_____

6. $2.5k = 17.5$

_____

7. $805 = 7h$

_____

8. $9y = 81$

_____

9. $\dfrac{n}{4} = 68$

_____

10. $12 = \dfrac{m}{9}$

_____

11. $\dfrac{n}{2.4} = 15$

_____

12. $\dfrac{z}{64} = 8$

_____

13. $\dfrac{y}{9} = 12$

_____

14. $\dfrac{x}{4} = 24$

_____

15. $9 = \dfrac{w}{9}$

_____

For Exercises 16–19, write and solve an equation to answer each question.

16. Carmen participated in a read-a-thon. Mr. Cole pledged $4.00 per book and gave Carmen $44. How many books did Carmen read?

_____

17. Lee drove 420 miles and used 15 gallons of gasoline. How many miles did Lee's car travel per gallon of gasoline?

_____

18. Last week Tina worked 38 hours in 5 days. How many hours did she work each day?

_____

19. On some days, Melvin commutes 3.5 hours per day to the city for business meetings. Last week he commuted for a total of 14 hours. How many days did he commute to the city?

_____

20. One way to solve the equation $4x = 32$ is to divide both sides by 4.

Another way to solve this equation is to multiply both sides by _____.

Solving Multi-Step Equations

Some equations require two or more operations to solve for the unknown.

Remember:
- Add, subtract, multiply, or divide the same number on both sides of the equal sign.
- You cannot divide by zero.

Solve: $5x - 2 = 38$

$5x - 2 = 38$

$5x - 2 + 2 = 38 + 2$ Add 2.

$5x = 40$

$\dfrac{5x}{5} = \dfrac{40}{5}$ Divide by 5.

$x = 8$

Check: $5x - 2 = 38$

$5(8) - 2 = 38$

$40 - 2 = 38$

$38 = 38$

Solve. Check.

1. $7x + 9 = 51$

$7x + 9 - 9 = 51 - 9$

2. $3x - 6 = 30$

$3x - 6 + 6 = 30 + 6$

3. $6x + \dfrac{1}{5} = 65$

$6x + \dfrac{1}{5} - \dfrac{1}{5} = 65 - \dfrac{1}{5}$

4. $10x + 9 = 59$

5. $4x - \dfrac{1}{2} = 270$

6. $5x - 10 = 60$

7. $8x + 32 = 200$

8. $9x + 11 = 74$

9. $13x + 13 = 143$

Name _____ Date _____

Practice Solving Multi-Step Equations

Solve. Check.

1. $12x + 7 = 67$

2. $6x + 1 = 4$

3. $2x + 16 = 32$

4. $7x - 5\frac{1}{2} = 12$

5. $2x + 19 = 29$

6. $4x + 7 = 10$

7. $9x + 92 = 128$

8. $8x - 35 = 37$

9. $5x - \frac{1}{2} = \frac{1}{2}$

10. $8x + \frac{1}{3} = \frac{2}{3}$

11. $2x - \frac{1}{5} = \frac{2}{5}$

12. $10x - 8 = 32$

13. $10x - 29 = 11$

14. $17x + 2 = 49$

15. $7x - \frac{4}{7} = \frac{3}{7}$

16. $6x + \frac{1}{4} = \frac{3}{4}$

17. $11x - 8 = 69$

18. $13x + 8 = 86$

Name _____ Date _____

Collecting Like Terms in Equations

In the equation $2x + 3x = 15$, the two addends, called terms, both contain the unknown x as a factor. They are **like terms**. These two terms, $2x$ and $3x$, can be added to get the single term $5x$ because they are like terms. Check the solution to the equation by substitution.

Collect like terms and solve: $2x + 3x = 15$

$$2x + 3x = 15$$
$$5x = 15 \text{ Collect like terms.}$$
$$\frac{5x}{5} = \frac{15}{5} \text{ Divide by 5.}$$
$$x = 3$$

Check: $2(3) + 3(3) = 15$
$$6 + 9 = 15$$
$$15 = 15$$

Collect like terms and solve: $9x - 3x = 24$

$$9x - 3x = 24$$
$$6x = 24 \text{ Collect like terms.}$$
$$\frac{6x}{6} = \frac{24}{6} \text{ Divide by 6.}$$
$$x = 4$$

Check: $9(4) - 3(4) = 24$
$$36 - 12 = 24$$
$$24 = 24$$

Solve. Check.

1. $\frac{1}{2}x + 4x = 45$

$4\frac{1}{2}x = 45$

2. $6x + 5x = 55$

$11x = 55$

3. $23x + 27x = 100$

$50x = 100$

4. $19x - 7x = 84$

5. $16x + 12x = 84$

6. $35x - 2\frac{1}{2}x = 65$

7. $10x + \frac{2}{5}x = 156$

8. $17x + 12x = 87$

9. $12x + 5x = 51$

Unit 8
Core Skills Math Review

Practice Collecting Like Terms in Equations

Collect like terms. Then solve. Check.

1. $6x - 2x = 4$

2. $7x - 3x = 20$

3. $9x + 11x = 80$

_____

_____

_____

4. $15x - 3x = 144$

5. $20x - 9x = 77$

6. $5x + 3x = 6$

_____

_____

_____

7. $2x + 14x = 8$

8. $5x - x = 24$

9. $7x + 7x = 70$

_____

_____

_____

10. $2x + 5x = 1\frac{1}{2}$

11. $9x - 4x = 5$

12. $30x - 10x = 1\frac{1}{3}$

_____

_____

_____

13. $18x - 15x = 39$

14. $3\frac{1}{2}x - 1\frac{1}{2}x = 18$

15. $\frac{1}{3}x + \frac{2}{3}x = 10$

_____

_____

_____

16. $7x + x = 72$

17. $15x - 5x = 20$

18. $13x - x = 28$

_____

_____

_____

111

Solving Equations

Solve each equation.

1. $3x + 4 + 2x + 5 = 34$

   _____

2. $2.5x - 5 + 3x + 8 = 19.5$

   _____

3. $\frac{1}{2}x + 6 - 2x + \frac{1}{2} = \frac{7}{2}$

   _____

4. $-10x - 3 - 2.5x + 20 = 67$

   _____

5. $2(x + 1) + 4 = 12$

   _____

6. $-3(x + 4) + 15 = -12$

   _____

7. $15 - 3(x - 1) = 12$

   _____

8. $3(x - 2) + 2(x + 1) = -14$

   _____

9. $\frac{1}{2}(x + 8) - 15 = -3$

   _____

10. $2.5(x + 2) + 4.5 + 1.5(x - 3) = 15$

    _____

The monthly membership dues and private lesson fees at three tennis clubs are shown in the table.

	Club A	Club B	Club C
Monthly Membership Dues	$25	$55	$15
Private Lesson Fee	$30	$20	$40

11. After how many private lessons in one month is the total monthly cost of Club A equal to the total monthly cost at Club B?

    _____

12. After how many private lessons in one month is the total monthly cost of Club A equal to the total monthly cost at Club C?

    _____

13. After how many private lessons in one month is the total monthly cost of Club B equal to the total monthly cost at Club C?

    _____

Solving Equations with an Unknown on Both Sides

To solve an equation in which an unknown is on both sides of the equation, use the methods you have learned to move all the unknowns to the same side of the equation. Combine like terms and solve. Check by substitution.

Solve: $7x + 3 = 15 + 5x$

$7x + 3 = 15 + 5x$

$7x + 3 - 3 = 15 + 5x - 3$ Subtract 3 from both sides.

$7x = 12 + 5x$

$7x - 5x = 12 + 5x - 5x$ Subtract $5x$ from both sides.

$2x = 12$

$\dfrac{2x}{2} = \dfrac{12}{2}$ Divide both sides by 2.

$x = 6$

Check: $7(6) + 3 = 15 + 5(6)$

$42 + 3 = 15 + 30$

$45 = 45$

Solve.

1. $9x + 6 = 4x + 36$

$9x + 6 - 6 = 4x + 36 - 6$

$9x = 4x + 30$

$9x - 4x = 4x + 30 - 4x$

_____

2. $5x - 9 = 1 + 3x$

$5x - 9 + 9 = 1 + 3x + 9$

$5x - 3x = 10 + 3x - 3x$

_____

3. $10x = 8 + 2x$

$10x - 2x = 8 + 2x - 2x$

_____

4. $5x - 3 = 17 - 5x$

_____

5. $3x + 1 = 41 - 2x$

_____

6. $11x - 5 = 45 + 6x$

_____

7. $7x + 16 = 32 - x$

_____

8. $2x = 7 + x$

_____

9. $20x - 13 = 15x + 62$

_____

Practice Solving Equations with an Unknown on Both Sides

Solve.

1. $25x + 9 = 209 + 5x$

2. $7x - 10 = 14 - x$

3. $16x + 5 = 59 + 7x$

_____

4. $3x - 12 = 2x + 5$

5. $10x + 6 = 7 + 9x$

6. $23x + 100 = 725 - 2x$

_____

7. $15x + 3 = 13x + 13$

8. $6x + 8 = 98 + 3x$

9. $3x + 2 = 50 - 3x$

_____

10. $15x + 7 = 107 + 5x$

11. $8x - 6 = 42 + 6x$

12. $6x = 27 + 3x$

_____

13. $20x - 9 = 13x - 7$

14. $16x - 10 = 89 + 7x$

15. $25x + 24 = 13x$

_____

16. $17x - 7 = 3x$

17. $19x + 6 = 31 + 4x$

18. $22x = 100 + 18x$

_____

Using Equations to Solve Problems

Many kinds of problems can be solved by deciding what is unknown, writing an equation, and solving. Check your answer in the original problem.

Jack and Lisa together have $250. Jack has $10 more than 3 times as much as Lisa. How much does each have?

Decide what is unknown.

Let x = Lisa's money.

$3x + 10$ = Jack's money

Write an equation.

Lisa's money + Jack's money = $250

$x + 3x + 10 = 250$

Solve.

$x + 3x + 10 = 250$

$4x + 10 = 250$

$4x + 10 - 10 = 250 - 10$

$4x = 240$

$$\frac{4x}{4} = \frac{240}{4}$$

$x = 60$

Answer:

$x = \$60$ Lisa's money

$3x + 10 = \$190$ Jack's money

Check: $x + 3x + 10 = 250$

$(60) + 3(60) + 10 = 250$

$60 + 180 + 10 = 250$

$60 + 190 = 250$

$250 = 250$

Write an equation for each problem and solve.

1. If 24 is added to a certain number, the result is 52. What is the number?

Let n = the number.
$n + 24 = 52$

_____

2. Arsenio has $25 more than twice as much money as Malik has. Together they have $145. How much money does each have?

Let x = Malik's money.
$2x + 25$ = Arsenio's money
$x + 2x + 25 = 145$

Malik _____

Arsenio _____

3. Pat has three times as much money as does Jerry. Together they have $12.80. How much does each have?

Let x = Jerry's money.
$3x$ = Pat's money

Jerry _____

Pat _____

4. Louisa is thinking of a number. Five times that number equals 240. What is the number?

Let n = the number.

115

Practice Using Equations to Solve Problems

Write an equation for each problem and solve.

1. Elena has five times as much money as Tori does. Together they have $42. How much does each have?

   Elena _____

   Tori _____

2. DeWayne has $15 more than Hakeem. Together they have $55. How much does each have?

   DeWayne _____

   Hakeem _____

3. One package contains 20 more envelopes than a second package does. Together they contain 80 envelopes. How many envelopes does each package contain?

   1st package _____

   2nd package _____

4. One parking lot contains 50 fewer cars than a second lot. Together the lots contain 200 cars. How many cars are there in each parking lot?

   1st lot _____

   2nd lot _____

5. Ricardo's mother is 3 times as old as Ricardo. The sum of their ages is 72. How old is each?

   Mother _____

   Ricardo _____

6. Natasha's father is 2 years less than three times as old as Natasha. The sum of their ages is 78 years. How old is each?

   Father _____

   Natasha _____

7. Three numbers add up to 180. The second number is twice the first, and the third is three times the first. What is each number? Let n = the first number.

   1st _____

   2nd _____

   3rd _____

8. Three numbers add up to 140. The second number is twice the first, and the third number is twice the second. What are the three numbers?

   1st _____

   2nd _____

   3rd _____

Equations with Two Variables

An equation such as $x + y = 4$ has many solutions. Each solution is an ordered pair. To find a solution, choose a value to substitute for one of the variables, and then solve the equation for the other variable. Study the following examples.

EXAMPLE 1

Solve: $x + y = 4$ when $x = 1$

$$1 + y = 4$$
$$y = 3$$

The equation $x + y = 4$ is true when $x = 1$ and $y = 3$.

(1, 3) is a solution.

EXAMPLE 2

Solve: $x + y = 4$ when $y = -2$

$$x + (-2) = 4$$
$$x = 6$$

The equation $x + y = 4$ is true when $x = 6$ and $y = -2$.

(6, -2) is a solution.

Solve each equation using the given value of x or y. Write the ordered pair that makes the equation true.

1. $x + 2y = 7$ when $x = -1$

$$-1 + 2y = 7$$
$$2y = 8$$
$$y = 4$$

Ordered pair _____

2. $x + 2y = 7$ when $x = -3$

Ordered pair _____

3. $x + 2y = 7$ when $x = 5$

Ordered pair _____

4. $2x + y = 11$ when $x = 3$

$$2(3) + y = 11$$
$$6 + y = 11$$
$$y =$$

Ordered pair _____

5. $2x + y = 11$ when $x = 0$

Ordered pair _____

6. $2x + y = 11$ when $x = -1$

Ordered pair _____

7. $x + y = -6$ when $y = -2$

Ordered pair _____

8. $x + y = -6$ when $y = -1$

Ordered pair _____

9. $x + y = -6$ when $y = 3$

Ordered pair _____

Analyzing Solutions

So far, when you solved a linear equation in one variable, you found one value of x that makes the equation a true statement. When you simplify some equations, you may find that they have 1, 0, or infinitely many solutions.

Use the properties of equality to simplify each equation. Tell whether the final equation is a true statement. Write *true* or *false*.

1. $4x - 5 = 2(2x - 1) - 3$

$4x - 5 = \boxed{}x - \boxed{} - 3$

$4x - 5 = 4x - \boxed{}$

$\underline{-4x \qquad -4x}$

$-5 = \boxed{}$

The statement is _____.

Since the statement is always true, this equation has infinitely many solutions.

2. $4x + 2 = 4x - 5$

_____ _____

$4x = 4x - 7$

_____ _____

$\boxed{} = \boxed{}$

The statement is _____.

Since the statement is always false, this equation has no solution.

3. What happens when you substitute any value for x in the original equation in problem 1? In the original equation in problem 2?

_____

Tell whether each equation has one, zero, or infinitely many solutions.

4. $6 + 3x = x - 8$ _____

5. $8x + 4 = 4(2x + 1)$ _____

Complete each equation so that it has the indicated number of solutions.

6. No solutions: $3x + 1 = 3x +$ _____

7. Infinitely many: $2x - 4 = 2x -$ _____

Name _____ Date _____

Solving Systems Algebraically

Systems of equations can be solved algebraically using a method called substitution. On page 139, you will learn how to solve a system of equations by graphing.

Solve each system algebraically.

1. $y = 7x + 10$
$y = 9x + 38$

$7x + 10 = 9x + 38$

Substitute the expression for y given in the first equation for the value of y in the second equation.

Then use properties of equality to solve the equation for x.

Substitute the value of x into one of the original equations to solve for y.

$x =$ _____ $y =$ _____

The solution of the system is (_____, _____).

2. $3x + 4y = 31$
$2x - y = 6$

$2x - y = 6$

_____ _____

$-y = \boxed{} - 2x$

$-y\,(-1) = \left(6 - \boxed{}\right)(-1)$

$\boxed{} = -6 + \boxed{}$

Solve one equation for one of the variables. Because y is by itself in the second equation, solving that equation for y is a good place to start.

$3x + 4y = 31$

$3x + 4\left(\boxed{}\right) = 31$

$3x + (-24) + \boxed{} = 31$

$11x - 24 = 31$

Substitute the expression for y into the first equation and solve for x.

Substitute the value of x into one of the original equations to solve for y.

$x =$ _____ $y =$ _____

The solution of the system is (_____, _____).

119

Unit 8 Review

Determine whether the given value is a solution of the equation.

1. $24 - s = 16; s = -8$

2. $\frac{t}{35} = 3; t = 105$

Solve for the unknown addend or factor.

3. $n + 5\frac{1}{2} = 16$

4. $8a = 104$

5. $3.5p = 8.75$

Solve.

6. $5x - 2 = 48$

7. $10x + 6.2 = 112$

8. $7x - 3x = 60$

9. $\frac{1}{4}x + \frac{1}{2}x = 18$

10. $20x + 4 = 4x + 16$

11. $11x - 10 = 2x + 8$

Solve each equation for y when $x = -2$. Write the answer as an ordered pair.

12. $3x + y = 12$

13. $13y - x = 15$

14. $x + y = -4$

Tell whether each equation has one, zero, or infinitely many solutions.

15. $9x + 4 = 3(3x + 4)$

16. $14x + 7 = 35$

17. $18 \cdot x = 2x \cdot 9$

Solve each system algebraically.

18. $-4x + 5y = 14$
$7x + 3y = -1$

19. $7x - y = 7$
$-3x + 2y = 8$

20. $8x + 2y = 26$
$2x - 3y = -25$

Write an equation for each problem and solve.

21. Logan is thinking of a number. Six times that number equals four more than 80. What is the number?

22. One plane has 40 passengers fewer than a second plane. Together the planes have 358 passengers. How many passengers are there on each plane?

Graphing Ordered Pairs

Write the coordinates of the point.

1. B _____ 2. H _____ 3. A _____

4. I _____ 5. D _____ 6. F _____

7. C _____ 8. E _____ 9. L _____

10. G _____ 11. J _____ 12. O _____

Name the point given by the coordinates.

13. (3, 2) _____ 14. (–2, 5) _____ 15. (6, –4) _____

16. (–1, –3) _____ 17. (–5, 3) _____ 18. (7, 0) _____

Draw a coordinate plane. Graph and label these points.

19. A (–4, 2) 20. B (6, 8) 21. C (–6, –2)

22. D (1, –4) 23. E (7, –1) 24. F (–1, 8)

25. G (1, 4) 26. H (5, 1) 27. I (0, –3)

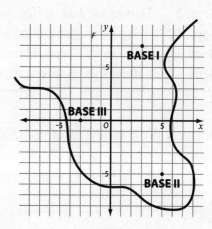

28. A bus drove 3 blocks south, 5 blocks east, 7 blocks north, and 10 blocks west. How many blocks south would the bus need to drive in order to be directly west of where it started?

_____

29. In Exercise 28, how many blocks east would the bus need to drive in order to be directly north of where it started?

_____

30. A pilot has to land at Base 1, Base 2, and Base 3 on the map. Give the coordinates for each base.

_____

_____

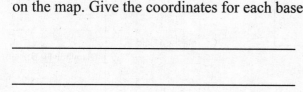

121

The Coordinate Plane

Use the coordinate plane for Exercises 1–10.

Identify the coordinates of each point and name the quadrant in which it is located.

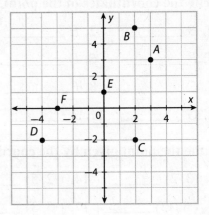

1. A _____   2. B _____

3. C _____   4. D _____

5. E _____   6. F _____

Graph each point on the coordinate plane.

7. (2, -4)   8. (-4, 4)

9. (3, 0)   10. (0, -5)

11. Circle the point(s) located in Quadrant III.

   (6, 4)   (-5, -1)   (3.5, -7)   (-1, 0)   (-2, -4)   (-2, 9.1)

12. **a.** Choose a point located in Quadrant IV and give its coordinates. _____

   b. Choose a point that is not located in any quadrant and give its coordinates. _____

13. The September game schedule for Justin's soccer team is shown. The location of each game is graphed on the coordinate plane.

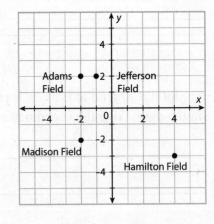

HAWKS' GAME SCHEDULE

September
Sept. 3 — Hawks vs. Jets, Jefferson Field
Sept. 10 — Hawks vs. Mustangs, Madison Field
Sept. 17 — Hawks vs. Lions, Hamilton Field
Sept. 24 — Hawks vs. Arrows, Adams Field

a. Identify the coordinates of each location.

Jefferson Field _____   Madison Field _____

Hamilton Field _____   Adams Field _____

b. On October 1, the team has a game scheduled at Lincoln Field. The coordinates for Lincoln Field are (4, 4). Graph and label this point on the coordinate plane. What quadrant is Lincoln Field located in?

_____

Distance in the Coordinate Plane

Use the coordinate plane for Exercises 1–4.

1. What are the coordinates of point P? _____

2. What are the coordinates of point Q? _____

3. What is the distance between P and Q? _____ units

4. What is the distance between (-4, -4) and (-4, 7)?

   _____ units

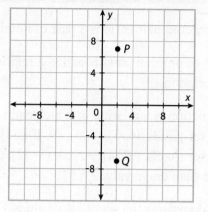

The coordinate plane represents a map. Each grid unit represents one mile. A retail company has warehouses at $M(-7, 1)$ and $N(5, 1)$. The company also has two stores along the straight road between the two warehouses. Use the coordinate plane for Exercises 5–8.

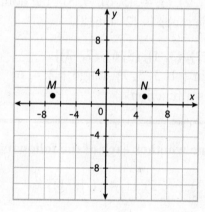

5. What is the distance between the warehouses?

   _____

6. Each store is the same distance from a warehouse. Also, the distance between the stores is half the distance between the warehouses. The nearest warehouse to store 1 is warehouse M, and the nearest warehouse to store 2 is warehouse N. What is the distance between the two stores?

   _____

7. What are the coordinates of store 1's location? Graph and label this point on the map. What is the distance from store 1 to the nearest warehouse?

   _____

   _____

8. What are the coordinates of store 2's location? Graph and label this point on the map. What is the distance from store 2 to the nearest warehouse?

   _____

Functions and Relations

An ordered pair (x, y) is a pair of numbers. For example, (2, 3) is an ordered pair.

A set of ordered pairs is called a relation. The set {(-2, 4), (-2, 5), (6, 9), (9, 10), (11, 12)} is a relation.

A function is a relation in which each x value has only one y value.
The set {(2, 3), (4, 5), (6, 5), (9, 10), (11, 12)} is a function.
The set {(6, 9), (-2, 4), (-2, 5), (8, 12), (11, 13)} is not a function because the x value -2 has more than one y value.

The domain is the set of all x values.
The range is the set of all y values.
For {(1, 2), (3, 4), (5, 6), (7, 8)}, the domain is {1, 3, 5, 7},
and the range is {2, 4, 6, 8}.

{(-1, -2), (3, 4), (5, 6), (7, -2)}
domain {-1, 3, 5, 7}, range {-2, 4, 6}
This is a function.

{(-1, -2), (4, 5), (4, 6), (7, 8)}
domain {-1, 4, 7}, range {-2, 5, 6, 8}
This is not a function.

Determine whether each of the following relations is a function.

1. {(0, 3), (-5, 5), (1, 4), (-1, -1)}

_____

2. {(2, 1), (-6, 1), (1, 8), (-6, -7)}

_____

3. {(-4, 3), (-3, 3), (1, 3)}

_____

4. {(3, 3), (-2, 5), (2, 4), (0, 0)}

_____

Find the domain and range for each relation.

5. {(1, 3), (-2, 5), (9, 4), (-10, -1)}

Domain: _____

Range: _____

6. {(-2, 6), (7, 8), (1, -3)}

Domain: _____

Range: _____

7. {(4, 9), (4, -5), (0, -6), (-1, 0)}

Domain: _____

Range: _____

8. {(2, 9), (5, -2), (1, 1)}

Domain: _____

Range: _____

124

Name _____ Date _____

Equations, Tables, and Graphs

Ship to Shore rents paddleboats for a fee of $10 plus an additional $5 per hour that the boat is rented.

1. Let x represent the number of hours a paddleboat is rented, and let y represent the total cost of the rental. Complete the equation to show the relationship between x and y.

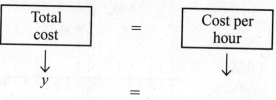
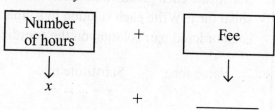

$$\begin{array}{ccccccc} \boxed{\text{Total cost}} & = & \boxed{\text{Cost per hour}} & \cdot & \boxed{\text{Number of hours}} & + & \boxed{\text{Fee}} \\ \downarrow & & \downarrow & & \downarrow & & \downarrow \\ y & & & & x & & \end{array}$$

$$y = \underline{\hspace{1cm}} \cdot x + \underline{\hspace{1cm}}$$

2. What is the input?

   _____

3. What is the output?

   _____

4. What are the two quantities in this situation?

   _____

5. Which of these quantities depends on the other?

   _____

6. What is the independent variable?

   _____

7. What is the dependent variable?

   _____

8. Complete the table.

Time Rented (h), x	1	2	3	4	5	6
Total Cost ($), y						

9. Write the ordered pairs from the table.

   _____

10. Graph the ordered pairs on the coordinate plane. Connect the points and extend the line to the right.

11. What is the cost to rent a paddleboat for 8 hours?

   _____

12. The cost to rent a paddleboat for 8 hours is represented on the graph by the point _____.

13. The cost to rent a paddleboat for _____ hours is $60. This is represented on the graph by the point _____.

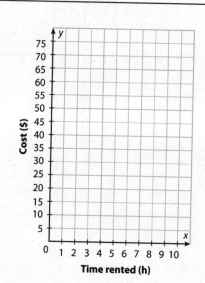

125

Graphing Solutions

Remember, an equation with two variables has many solutions. Each solution is an ordered pair.

Graph the solutions to $x + y = 4$ when $x = -2, 0,$ and 1.

Substitute each given value for x into the equation. Then solve for y. Write each solution in a table. Finally, plot each ordered pair solution on the coordinate graph.

Value for x	Substitute into $x + y = 4$.	Solve for y.	Table of solutions	
			x	y
-2	$-2 + y = 4$	6	-2	6
0	$0 + y = 4$	4	0	4
1	$1 + y = 4$	3	1	3

These solutions are plotted on the graph.

Find the values for y using the given values of x. Graph each solution.

1. $2x + y = 5$

x	y
0	
1	
3	

2. $x + y = -4$

x	y
-2	
0	
3	

3. $-3x + y = 2$

x	y
-1	
0	
1	

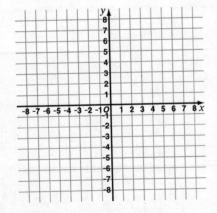

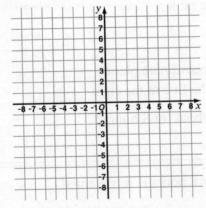

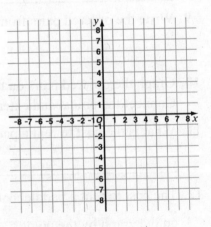

Name _____ Date _____

Graphing Linear Equations

For the 2-variable equations that we have studied, the graphs of all the solutions lie on a line. For this reason, equations of this type are called linear equations. To graph a linear equation, begin by choosing a value to substitute for either x or y. Then solve for the other variable. Repeat this process to find three or more ordered pair solutions. Finally, graph the solutions and draw the line through those points.

Graph the equation $2x - 2y = 4$.

Choose a value.	Solve for the other variable.	Write the solution.
$x = 0$	$2(0) - 2y = 4$ $0 - 2y = 4$ $-2y = 4$ $y = -2$	$(0, -2)$
$y = 0$	$2x - 2(0) = 4$ $2x - 0 = 4$ $2x = 4$ $x = 2$	$(2, 0)$
$x = 4$	$2(4) - 2y = 4$ $8 - 2y = 4$ $-2y = -4$ $y = 2$	$(4, 2)$

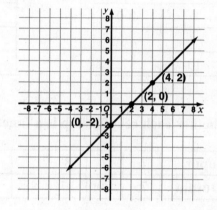

Now plot the points and draw a straight line through them.

For each equation, find and graph three solutions. Draw a straight line through those points.

1. $3x - y = 2$

(—, —) (—, —) (—, —)

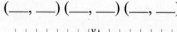

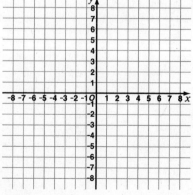

2. $-x + y = 6$

(—, —) (—, —) (—, —)

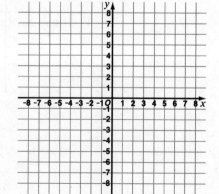

3. $x - 2y = 4$

(—, —) (—, —) (—, —)

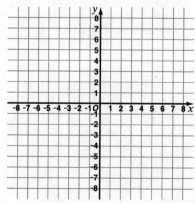

127

Functions, Tables, and Graphs

Fill in each table. In the row with *x* as the input, write a rule as an algebraic expression for the output. Then complete the last row of the table using the rule.

1.

Input	Output
Tickets	Cost ($)
2	40
5	100
7	140
8	160
x	
10	

2.

Input	Output
Minutes	Pages Read
2	1
10	5
20	10
30	15
x	
60	

3.

Input	Output
Muffins	Cost ($)
1	2.25
3	6.75
6	13.50
12	27.00
x	
18	

Tell whether each relationship is a function. Write *yes* or *no*.

4.

Input	6	7	8	7	9
Output	75	80	87	88	95

5.

Input	1	2	3	4	5
Output	4	8	12	16	20

_____

_____

6. (1, 3), (2, 5), (3, 0), (4, −1), (5, 5)

7. (2, 7), (6, 4), (0, 3), (2, 6), (1, 5)

_____

_____

Graph each function on the coordinate plane.

8. $y = -2x$

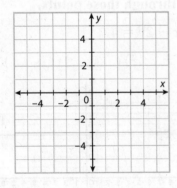

9. $y = x - 3$

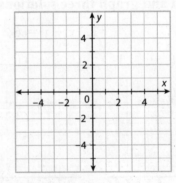

Exploring Linear Equations

Use the table and graph for Exercises 1–6.

1. Complete the table.

2. What pattern do you see for the value of *y* in each ordered pair?

   _____

3. State a rule to find the ordered pairs of the table.

   _____

4. Represent your rule with an equation.

   _____

5. Graph the set of ordered pairs.

6. Draw a line through the ordered pairs.

x	y
-2	1
-1	2
0	3
1	☐
2	☐
3	☐

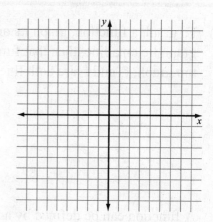

Use the table and graph for Exercises 7–10.

7. Write a rule that describes the pattern you see in the ordered pairs shown at the right.

   _____

8. Write a linear equation for the rule you described in Exercise 7.

   _____

x	y
-2	-6
-1	-3
0	0
1	3
2	6

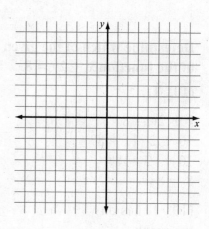

9. Graph the points that represent the ordered pairs in this table.

10. Draw a line through the ordered pairs.

11. Write a linear equation for a graph that has the ordered pairs (-3, 1), (1, 1), and (3, 1).

    _____

12. Write a linear equation for a graph that has the ordered pairs (2, -1), (2, 0), and (2, 1).

    _____

129

Linear Functions

To graph a function, graph its ordered pairs. If all the points in the graph lie on a line, then that function is a **linear function.** In the top graph, f_1 and f_2 are both linear functions.

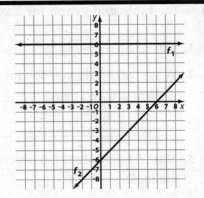

A function can be defined by an equation. Some of the ordered pairs in the linear function defined by $x + y = 3$ are shown in the graph to the right. To determine whether a point lies on the graph of the function, substitute the first coordinate for x and the second coordinate for y. If these substitutions make the equation true, then that point lies on the line. For example, $(4, -1)$ lies on the line, since $4 + (-1) = 3$. $(1, 5)$ does not lie on the line, since $1 + 5 \neq 3$.

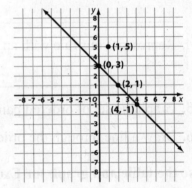

Determine which of the given points lies on the graph of the function $x + 2y = 8$.

(10, -1)

$x + 2y = 8$
$10 + 2(-1) = 8?$
$10 + -2 = 8?$
$8 = 8$

(10, -1) lies on the graph.

(3, -4)

$x + 2y = 8$
$3 + 2(-4) = 8?$
$3 + -8 = 8?$
$-5 \neq 8$

(3, -4) does not lie on the graph.

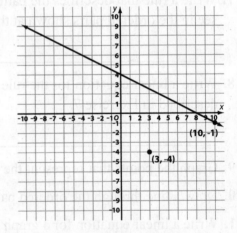

Determine if the given points lie on the graph of the given function. Write *yes* or *no*.

1. $2x + y = 26$ (3, -12) _____   (0, 6) _____   (-4, 1) _____

2. $-3x + y = 9$ (3, 0) _____   (-2, 3) _____   (4, 3) _____

3. $x - 4y = 10$ (6, -1) _____   (12, 1) _____   (14, 1) _____

4. $x + 2y = 25$ (-5, 0) _____   (1, -3) _____   (-9, 2) _____

Graphing Linear Functions

Graph solutions of each equation and tell whether the equation is *linear* or *non-linear*.

1. $y = 5 - 2x$

Input, x	-1	1	3	5
Output, y				

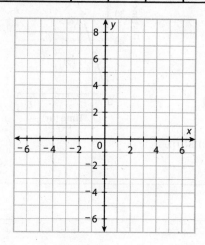

2. $y = 2 - x^2$

Input, x	-2	-1	0	1	2
Output, y					

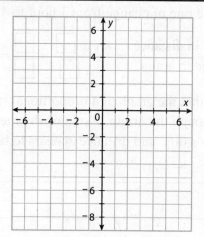

_____

_____

3. Olivia measured several rooms in her house in feet. She wants to express the measurements in inches. Write an equation relating feet, x, and inches, y. Tell whether it is linear or non-linear.

_____

4. Seth receives $100 from his grandmother for his birthday. He also saves $20 every month. Write an equation relating months, x, and total savings y. Tell whether the equation is linear or non-linear.

_____

Explain why each equation is or is not a linear equation.

5. $y = x^2 - 1$

_____

_____

_____

6. $y = 1 - 1$

_____

_____

_____

7. A student claims that the equation $y = 7$ is not a linear equation because it does not have the form $y = mx + b$. Do you agree or disagree? Why?

_____

_____

131

Rate of Change and Slope

The graph shows the distance Nathan bicycled over time. Use the graph to complete Exercises 1–5.

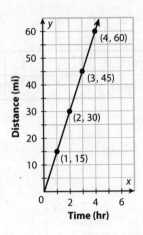

1. Find the rate of change from 1 hour to 2 hours.

$$\frac{\text{change in distance}}{\text{change in hours}} = \frac{30 - \square}{2 - 1} = \frac{\square}{1} = \square \text{ miles per hour}$$

2. Find the rate of change from 1 hour to 4 hours.

$$\frac{\text{change in distance}}{\text{change in hours}} = \frac{60 - \square}{4 - \square} = \frac{\square}{\square} = \square \text{ miles per hour}$$

3. Recall that the graph of a proportional relationship is a straight line through the origin. Explain why the relationship between Nathan's time and distance appears to be a proportional relationship.

_____

_____

4. Find Nathan's unit rate.

_____

5. Compare the rate of change to the unit rate.

_____

6. Does it matter what interval you use when you find the rate of change of a proportional relationship? Explain.

_____

_____

7. Do you think that the value of r in the point $(1, r)$ is always the unit rate for any situation? Explain.

_____

_____

_____

Core Skills Math Review

Slope

The slope of a line tells how steep the line is. The slope is the ratio of the vertical change, or **rise,** to the horizontal change, or **run,** from one point to another point on a line.

$$\text{slope} = \frac{\text{change in } y \text{ (rise)}}{\text{change in } x \text{ (run)}}$$

The vertical change, or rise, of the line at right is 3. The horizontal change, or run, of the line is 4. This line has a slope of $\frac{3}{4}$.

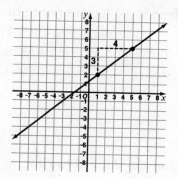

The slope of a line can be positive or negative.

When a line slants upward from left to right, it has a **positive slope**.

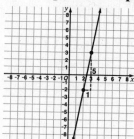

$$\text{slope} = \frac{\text{rise}}{\text{run}} = \frac{5}{1}$$

When a line slants downward from left to right, it has a **negative slope**.

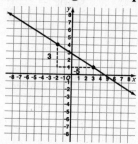

$$\text{slope} = \frac{\text{rise}}{\text{run}} = \frac{3}{-5}$$

Identify the slope of each line. Write whether the slope is positive or negative.

1.

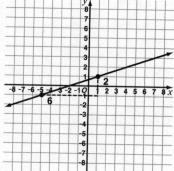

$$\text{slope} = \frac{\text{rise}}{\text{run}} =$$

_____

2.

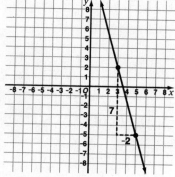

$$\text{slope} =$$

_____

3.

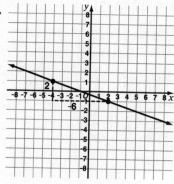

$$\text{slope} =$$

_____

133

Name _____   Date _____

The Slope Formula

Slope is the ratio of rise to run from one point to another point on a line. If you know two points on a line, you can find its slope by using a formula.

Find the slope of the line.

Write the formula. $\text{slope} = \dfrac{(y_2 - y_1)}{(x_2 - x_1)}$

Substitute the coordinates. $\text{slope} = \dfrac{(5 - 2)}{(7 - 1)}$

Use (7, 5) and (1, 2).

Simplify. $\text{slope} = \dfrac{3}{6} = \dfrac{1}{2}$

The slope of this line is $\frac{1}{2}$.

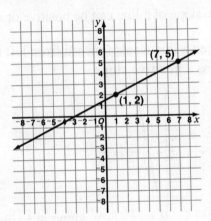

Find the slope of each line that passes through the given points.

1. (-2, 4), (4, 2)

$$\frac{(2 - 4)}{(4 - -2)} =$$

2. (3, 5), (4, 7)

3. (6, 2), (8, 0)

4. (-2, -2), (1, 4)

5. (-5, 3), (7, -6)

6. (-3, 2), (1, 4)

7. (1, 1), (-4, 7)

8. (0, -2), (9, 3)

9. (1, 1), (4, 10)

Slope-Intercept Form

> The graph of every non-vertical line crosses the y-axis. The **y-intercept** is the y-coordinate of the point where the graph intersects the y-axis. The x-coordinate of this point is always 0.

1. Let L be a line with slope m and y-intercept b. Circle the point that must be on the line. Justify your choice.

   $(b, 0)$ $(0, b)$ $(0, m)$ $(m, 0)$

   _____

Let (x, y) be a point on line L other than the point containing the y-intercept.

2. Write an expression for the change in y values between the point that includes the y-intercept and the point (x, y). _____

3. Write an expression for the change in x values between the point that includes the y-intercept and the point (x, y). _____

4. Recall that slope is the ratio of change in y to change in x. Complete the equation for the slope m of the line.

$$m = \frac{y - \Box}{\Box - 0}$$

5. In an equation of a line, we often want y by itself on one side of the equation. Solve the equation from Exercise 4 for y.

   $m = \dfrac{y - b}{x}$ *Simplify the denominator.*

   $m \cdot x = \dfrac{y - b}{x} \cdot x$ *Multiply both sides of the equation by x.*

   _____   *Add b to both sides of the equation.*

   _____   *Write the equation with y on the left side.*

To write the equation of a line or to graph a line, you just need to know its slope (m) and y-intercept (b). Write an equation for the line with the given slope and y-intercept.

6. slope: –4; y-intercept: 6

   _____

7. slope: $\dfrac{5}{2}$; y-intercept: –3

   _____

135

Writing Equations to Describe Functions

The table shows the temperature at different altitudes. The temperature is a linear function of the altitude.

Altitude (ft), x	0	2,000	4,000	6,000	8,000	10,000	12,000
Temperature (°F), y	59	51	43	35	27	19	11

1. Find the slope of the function.

   _____

2. Find the y-intercept of the function.

   _____

3. Write an equation in slope-intercept form that represents the function.

   _____

4. Use your equation to determine the temperature at an altitude of 5,000 feet.

   _____

The graph shows a scuba diver's ascent over time.

5. Use the graph to find the slope of the line. Tell what the slope means in this context.

   _____

   _____

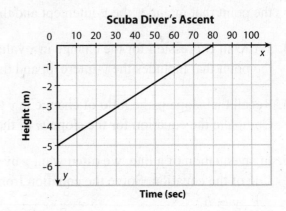

6. Identify the y-intercept. Tell what the y-intercept means in this context.

   _____

7. Write an equation in slope-intercept form that represents the function.

   _____

The formula for converting Celsius temperatures to Fahrenheit temperatures is a linear function. Water freezes at 0 °C, or 32 °F, and it boils at 100 °C, or 212 °F.

8. Find the slope and y-intercept. Then write an equation in slope-intercept form that represents the function.

   _____

9. Average human body temperature is 37 °C. What is this temperature in degrees Fahrenheit?

   _____

Name _____ Date _____

Comparing Functions

The table and graph show how many words Morgan and Brian typed correctly on a typing test. For both students, the relationship between words typed correctly and time is linear.

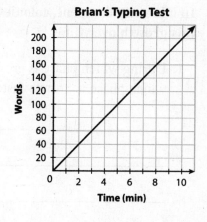

Brian's Typing Test

Morgan's Typing Test					
Time (min)	2	4	6	8	10
Words	30	60	90	120	150

1. Find Morgan's unit rate.

_____

2. Find Brian's unit rate.

_____

3. Which student types more correct words per minute?

_____

4. Sketch a graph of Morgan's test results on the same coordinate grid as Brian's results. How are the graphs similar? How are they different?

_____

_____

5. Katie types 17 correct words per minute. Explain how a graph of Katie's test results would compare to Morgan's and Brian's.

_____

_____

6. The equation that describes Jen's test results is $y = 24x$. Explain how a graph of Jen's test results would compare to Morgan's and Brian's.

_____

_____

Analyzing Graphs

In a lab environment, colonies of bacteria follow a predictable pattern of growth. The graph shows this growth over time.

1. During which phase is growth slowest? During which phase is growth fastest? Explain.

    _____

    _____

    _____

    _____

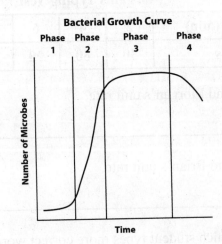

Bacterial Growth Curve

2. What is happening to the population during Phase 3?

    _____

    _____

    _____

3. What is happening to the population during Phase 4?

    _____

    _____

A woodland area on an island contains a population of foxes. The graph describes the changes in the fox population over time.

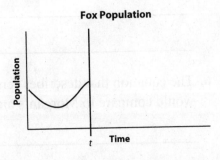

Fox Population

4. At time *t*, a conservation organization moves a large group of foxes to the island. Sketch a graph to show how this action might affect the population on the island after time *t*.

5. At some point after time *t*, a forest fire destroys part of the woodland area on the island. Describe how your graph from Exercise 4 might change.

    _____

    _____

Solving Systems Graphically

An ordered pair (x, y) is a solution of an equation in two variables if substituting the x- and y-values into the equation results in a true statement. A **system of equations** is a set of equations that have the same variables. An ordered pair is a solution of a system of equations if it is a solution of every equation in the system. Since the graph of a function represents all ordered pairs that are solutions of the related equation, a point that lies on the graphs of two functions is a solution of both related equations.

Solve each system by graphing.

1. $y = -x + 4$
   $y = 3x$

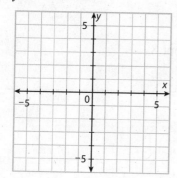

Start by graphing each function.
The solution of the system appears to be

_____ .

To check your answer, you can substitute the values for x and y into each equation and make sure the equations are true statements.

2. $y = 2x - 2$
   $y = 2x + 4$

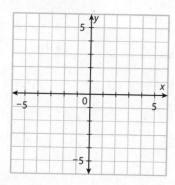

Start by graphing each function.

The graphs are _____, so there is no ordered pair that is a solution of both equations. The system has

_____ .

3. $y = 3x - 3$
   $y = 3(x - 1)$

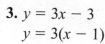

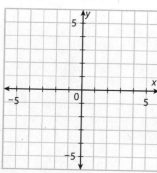

Start by graphing each function.
The graphs overlap, so every ordered pair that is a solution of one equation is also a solution of the other equation. The system has

_____ .

139

Unit 9 Review

Determine whether each of the following relations is a function.

1. $\{(2, 2), (1, 4), (3, 6), (-1, 2)\}$

2. $\{(-4, 6), (5, -3), (1, 1), (-4, 7)\}$

_____   _____

Find the slope of the line that passes through the given points.

3. $(0, 2)$ and $(9, -3)$

4. $(2, 3)$ and $(-4, 1)$

_____   _____

Write an equation for the line with the given slope and _y_-intercept.

5. slope: 5; _y_-intercept 2

6. slope: -7; _y_-intercept 8

_____   _____

Graph each equation.

7. $y = -3x + 4$

8. $y = \frac{1}{2}x + 1$

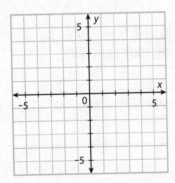   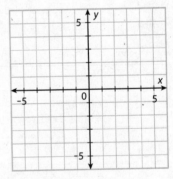

9. Solve the system by graphing.
   $y = 4x$
   $y = -x + 5$

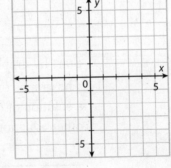

Exploring Stretching, Shrinking, and Twisting

Use a geoboard and rubber bands. Begin with a 2-by-3 rectangle. Make changes as directed. Name the new shape. Return to the original rectangle before each exercise.

1. Stretch both bases the same amount. _____

2. Stretch both ends of one base the same amount. _____

3. Shrink one base to a point. _____

4. Move one base to the left or right without stretching or shrinking. _____

Begin with an isosceles right triangle whose congruent sides have lengths of 2. Make changes as directed. Name the new shape. Return to the original triangle before each exercise.

5. Stretch both congruent sides by the same amount and keep the right angle. _____

6. Stretch one of the congruent sides and keep the right angle. _____

7. Stretch the other congruent side and keep the right angle. _____

8. Move the vertex of the right angle to the left. _____

9. Move the vertex of the right angle to the right. _____

10. Stretch both congruent sides the same amount by changing the right angle. _____

11. Stretch one of the congruent sides by changing the right angle. _____

12. Stretch the other congruent side by changing the right angle. _____

13. Name a way that stretching, shrinking, and twisting might be used in everyday life.

_____

_____

Name _____   Date _____

Translations and Reflections

Determine whether each pair of figures represents a *translation* or a *reflection*.

1.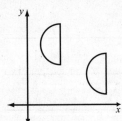

2.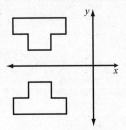

3.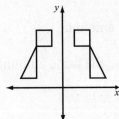

4.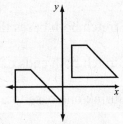

_____ _____ _____ _____

5. Draw the translation image 6 units right and 2 units down.

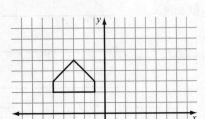

6. Draw the reflection image over the *y*-axis.

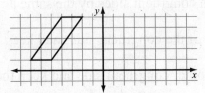

Triangle *ABC* is formed by connecting points (1, 2), (3, 4), and (6, 1).

7. Draw △*ABC* and its reflection over the *y*-axis.

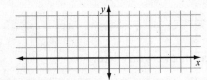

8. Draw △*ABC* and its translation 7 units left and 1 unit down.

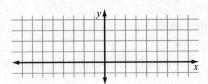

9. Draw the next line of reflection and the fifth triangle.

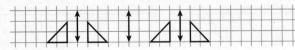

Unit 10
Core Skills Math Review

Rotations and Congruent Figures

The flag at the right is rotated clockwise in each figure below. The new image is unshaded. Write the number of degrees in the turn angle.

1.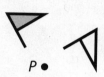

_____

2.

_____

3.

_____

4.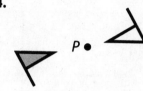

_____

5. On the coordinate grid, plot the points (0, 3), (-2, 1), (-4, 1), and (-6, 3). Connect the points in turn and then rotate the figure 180° about the origin. Write the coordinate pairs of the new image.

_____

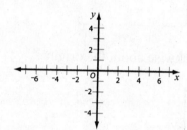

Draw the rotation image of each figure about the origin.

6. 180° turn

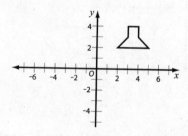

7. 90° turn

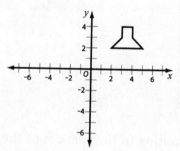

8. If A is rotated to B about point P, what is the measure of the turn angle?

_____

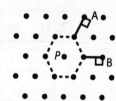

Translations, Reflections, and Rotations

Sketch the image of the figure after the given transformation. Label each vertex.

1. Translation: $(x, y) \rightarrow (x - 3, y + 1)$

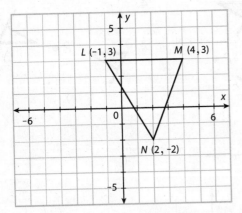

2. Reflection: $(x, y) \rightarrow (x, ^-y)$

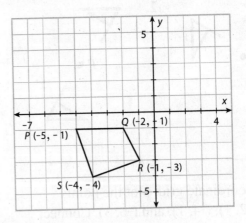

3. Rotation: 90° clockwise about the origin

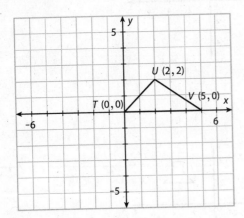

4. Reflection: $(x, y) \rightarrow (^-x, y)$

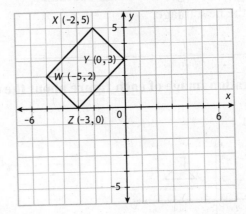

Apply each transformation to the vertices of the original rectangle and give the coordinates of each vertex of the image.

Vertices of Rectangle	(2, 2)	(2, 4)	(−3, 4)	(−3, 2)
5. $(x, y) \rightarrow (x, ^-y)$				
6. $(x, y) \rightarrow (x + 2, y - 5)$				
7. $(x, y) \rightarrow (^-x, y)$				
8. $(x, y) \rightarrow (^-x, ^-y)$				
9. $(x, y) \rightarrow (x - 3, y + 1)$				

Properties of Transformations

Trace the rectangle and triangle on a piece of paper. Then cut out your traced figures.

1. Place your copy of the rectangle on top of the rectangle in the figure. Then translate the rectangle by sliding your copy 6 units to the right and 1 unit down. Draw the new location of the rectangle on the coordinate plane and label the vertices A', B', C', and D'.

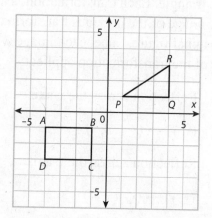

2. Place your copy of the triangle on top of the triangle in the figure. Then translate the triangle by sliding your copy 5 units to the left and 2 units up. Draw the new location of the triangle on the coordinate plane and label the vertices P', Q', and R'.

3. Does a translation change the length of line segments or the angle measures? Explain how to find out.

_____

_____

Trace the rectangle and triangle on a piece of paper. Then cut out your traced figures.

4. Place your copy of the rectangle on top of the rectangle in the figure. Then reflect the rectangle across the x-axis by flipping your copy across the x-axis. Draw the new location of the rectangle on the coordinate plane and label the vertices A', B', C', and D'.

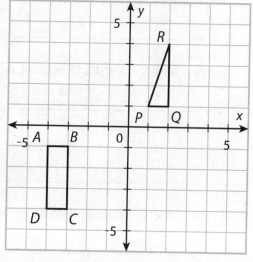

5. Place your copy of the triangle on top of the triangle in the figure. Then reflect the triangle across the y-axis by flipping your copy across the y-axis. Draw the new location of the triangle on the coordinate plane and label the vertices P', Q', and R'.

6. A reflection does not change the length of line segments or the angle measures. How do you think a rotation changes a figure?

_____

_____

145

Name _____   Date _____

Transformations and Congruence

1. Apply the indicated series of transformations to the triangle. Each transformation is applied to the image of the previous transformation, not the original figure. Label each image with the letter of the transformation applied.

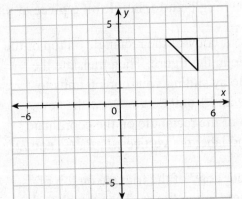

   a. Reflection across the x-axis

   b. $(x, y) \rightarrow (x - 3, y)$

   c. Reflection across the y-axis

   d. $(x, y) \rightarrow (x, y + 4)$

   e. Rotation 90° clockwise around the origin

2. Two figures are said to be **congruent** if one can be obtained from the other by a sequence of translations, reflections, and rotations. Congruent figures have the same size and shape.

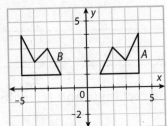

   a. Identify a sequence of transformations that will transform figure A into figure B.

   _____

   b. Identify another sequence of transformations that transforms figure A into figure B.

   _____

3. Are figures A and B congruent? Why or why not?

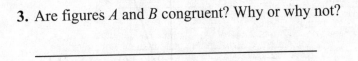

4. Are figures F and G congruent? Why or why not?

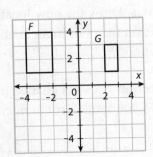

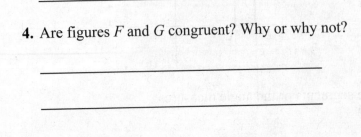

Dilations

1. The square is the preimage. The center of dilation is the origin. Write the coordinates of the vertices of the preimage in the first column of the table. Then apply the dilation $(x, y) \rightarrow (\frac{3}{2}x, \frac{3}{2}y)$ and write the coordinates of the vertices of the image in the second column. Sketch the image of the figure under the dilation.

Preimage	Image
(2, 0)	**(3, 0)**

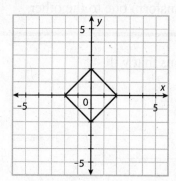

Sketch the image of the figure under the given dilation.

2. $(x, y) \rightarrow (2x, 2y)$

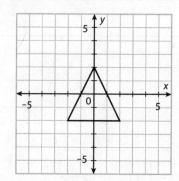

3. $(x, y) \rightarrow (\frac{2}{3}x, \frac{2}{3}y)$

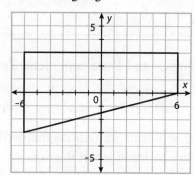

Identify the scale factor of the dilations shown.

4. scale factor = _____

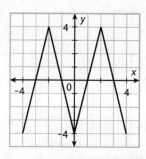 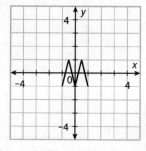

5. scale factor = _____

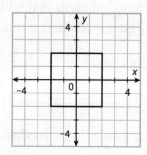 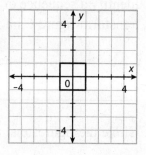

147

Transformations and Similarity

Two figures are **similar** if one can be obtained from the other by a sequence of translations, reflections, rotations, and dilations. Similar figures have the same shape but may be different sizes.

When you are told that two figures are similar, there must be a sequence of translations, reflections, rotations, and/or dilations that can transform one to the other.

1. Identify a sequence of transformations that will transform figure *A* into figure *B*.

   _____

   _____

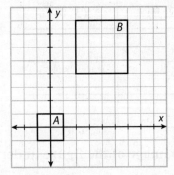

2. What happens if you reverse the order of the sequence you defined in problem 1?

   _____

   _____

3. Tell whether figures *A* and *B* are congruent. Tell whether they are similar.

   _____

4. Identify a sequence of transformations that will transform figure *C* into figure *D*. Include a reflection.

   _____

   _____

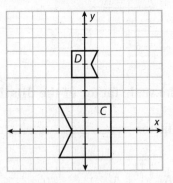

5. Identify a sequence of transformations that will transform figure *C* into figure *D*. Include a rotation.

   _____

   _____

6. Circle the figures that are similar to each other.

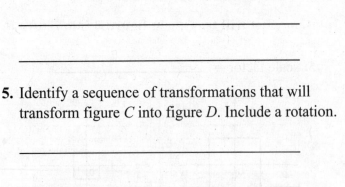

Name _____ Date _____

Unit 10 Review

Apply the indicated series of transformations to the triangle. Each transformation is applied to the image of the previous transformation, not the original figure. Label each image with the number of the transformation applied.

1. Reflection across the *x*-axis.

2. $(x, y) \rightarrow (x - 3, y)$

3. Reflection across the *y*-axis.

4. $(x, y) \rightarrow (x, y - 2)$

5. Rotation 90° clockwise around the origin.

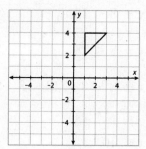

6. Sketch the image of the figure under the given dilation.
   $(x, y) \rightarrow (3x, 3y)$

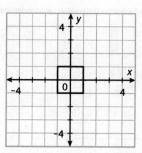

7. Does a reflection change the length of line segments or angle measures? Explain your reasoning.

_____

8. Does a dilation change the length of line segments or angle measures? Explain your reasoning.

_____

Give a sequence of translations, reflections, or rotations that will transform figure *A* into figure *B*.

9.

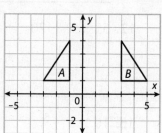

10.

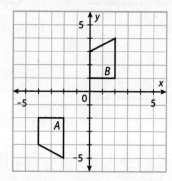

_____   _____

_____   _____

Solving Inequalities with Addition and Subtraction

Many inequalities are solved in much the same way equations are. To solve an inequality, you can add or subtract the same amount from both sides without changing its solution.

Solve: $x + 8 < 18$

$x + 8 < 18$

$x + 8 - 8 < 18 - 8$ Subtract 8 from both sides.

$x < 10$

Solve: $15 \geq x - 5$

$15 \geq x - 5$

$15 + 5 \geq x - 5 + 5$ Add 5 to both sides.

$20 \geq x$

Solve.

1. $x - 4 > 12$
$x - 4 + 4 > 12 + 4$

_____

2. $x - 9 \leq 6$

_____

3. $17 > x - 8$

_____

4. $x + 3 \leq 10$

_____

5. $16 < x + 13$

_____

6. $11 \leq x + 5$

_____

7. $5 < x - 10$

_____

8. $36 \geq 12 + x$

_____

9. $x - 9 > 14$

_____

10. $16 + x > 40$

_____

11. $x - 6 \geq 19$

_____

12. $55 \leq x + 20$

_____

13. $x + 7 < 5$

_____

14. $x + 6 \geq 2$

_____

15. $10 > x + 1$

_____

16. $10 \geq 8 + x$

_____

17. $14 > 6 + x$

_____

18. $x + 8 \leq 3$

_____

Solving Inequalities with Multiplication and Division

As with equations, you can multiply or divide both sides of an inequality by the same number without changing the solution. However, if you multiply or divide by a negative number, you must change the direction of the inequality symbol.

Solve: $\frac{x}{2} \leq 4$

$\frac{x}{2} \leq 4$

Multiply both sides by 2.

$2\left(\frac{x}{2}\right) \leq 2(4)$

$x \leq 8$

Check (using any number $\leq$ 8):

$\frac{6}{2} \leq 4?$

$3 \leq 4$

Solve: $-3x < 12$

$-3x < 12$

Divide both sides by -3.

Reverse the sign.

$\frac{-3x}{-3} > \frac{12}{-3}$

$x > -4$

Check (using any number > -4):

$-3(-1) < 12?$

$3 < 12$

Solve: $-2x + 3 < 5x + 10$

$-2x + 3 < 5x + 10$

First, subtract 3 from both sides.

$-2x + 3 - 3 < 5x + 10 - 3$

$-2x < 5x + 7$

Subtract $5x$ from both sides.

$-2x - 5x < 5x + 7 - 5x$

$-7x < 7$

Divide by -7. Reverse the sign.

$\frac{-7x}{-7} > \frac{7}{-7}$

$x > -1$

Check (using any number > -1):

$-2(0) + 3 < 5(0) + 10?$

$3 < 10$

Solve.

1. $\frac{x}{4} < 5$

2. $\frac{x}{2} \geq -8$

3. $6 \leq \frac{x}{-3}$

_____

4. $2x > 10$

5. $-15 \leq 3x$

6. $-6x > -24$

_____

7. $2x + 1 < 7$

8. $43 > 5x + 8$

9. $-4x + 3 \geq 19$

_____

10. $14 > 3x - 4$

11. $54 \leq 8x - 2$

12. $6x - 9 > 21$

_____

13. $4x - 2 \geq 6x + 8$

14. $9x + 3 < 12x + 30$

15. $8x + 6 < 10x - 12$

_____

151

Solving Problems with Inequalities

Some problems can be solved using inequalities.

Michael has 20 cups of flour to complete his baking for the annual family reunion picnic. If he uses 8 cups of flour to make his famous brownies, what is the greatest number of cups of flour that will be left over for making cookies?

$$\text{Let } x = \text{cups of flour for cookies}$$

$$8 \text{ cups for brownies} + x \le 20 \text{ total cups of flour}$$

$$8 + x \le 20$$

$$8 + x - 8 \le 20 - 8$$

$$x \le 12$$

Michael can use no more than 12 cups of flour to make his cookies for the family reunion.

Solve using inequalities.

1. Holly has 12 feet of ribbon. If she uses 3.5 feet to wrap one gift, what is the maximum length of ribbon Holly can use to wrap the rest of her gifts?

2. Drew runs fewer than 30 miles in a week. If he runs 5 miles a day, what is the maximum number of days Drew will run that week?

3. The Hobbs family has a fixed income of $4,500 per month. Their fixed expenses are $2,200 per month. What is the maximum amount the Hobbs family could save each month?

4. Sylvia saved $800 to buy furnishings for the living room of her new apartment. She spent $480 on a sofa. If Sylvia buys an antique chair for $80, what is the most she can spend on other items for her living room?

© Houghton Mifflin Harcourt Publishing Company   Core Skills Math Review

Name _____   Date _____

Solutions to Inequalities

1. Which numbers in the set {-5, 0.03, -1, 0, 1.5, -6, $\frac{1}{2}$} are solutions of $x \geq 0$?

_____

Graph each inequality.

2. $t \leq 8$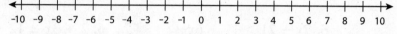

3. $-7 < h$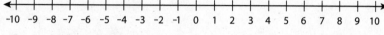

4. $x \geq -9$

5. A child must be at least 48 inches tall to ride a roller coaster.

   a. Write and graph an inequality to represent this situation. _____

      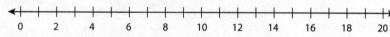

   b. Can a child who is 46 inches tall ride the roller coaster? Explain.

   _____

Write and graph an inequality to represent each situation.

6. There are fewer than 15 students in the cafeteria. _____

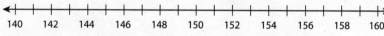

7. No more than 150 people can be seated at the restaurant. _____

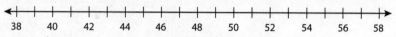

8. At least 20 students must sign up for the field trip. _____

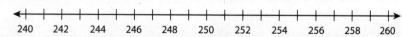

9. Shaun can pay at most $50 to have his computer repaired. _____

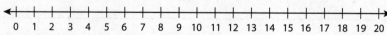

10. The goal of the fundraiser is to raise more than $250. _____

11. Megan must run a mile in 6 minutes or less to beat her best time. _____

12. The temperature today will rise above 2 °F. _____

Unit 11 Review

Solve each inequality.

1. $x + 13 > 45$

2. $49 \geq x - 17$

3. $-3x \leq 15$

_____

_____

_____

4. $6 + 5x < 8 + 4x$

5. $2x - 21 > 11 - 6x$

6. $2 + 3x \geq 12 - 2x$

_____

_____

_____

7. $4x \leq 40$

8. $\frac{x}{2} > 18$

9. $5x + 8 \leq -2x + 3x$

_____

_____

_____

Graph each inequality.

10. $p \geq 5$

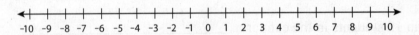

11. $q < 7$

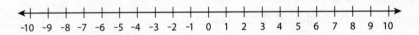

12. $r \leq -1$

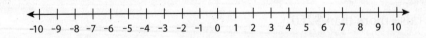

Write and graph an inequality to represent each situation.

13. Today's high temperature will be less than 2 °F.

_____

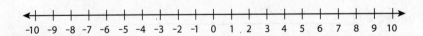

14. Today's temperature will be higher than -4 °F.

_____

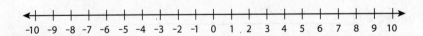

Angle Pairs

Use the diagram below.

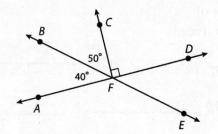

1. Name a pair of adjacent angles. _____

2. Name a pair of vertical angles. _____

3. Name a pair of complementary angles. _____

4. Name an angle that is supplementary to ∠CFE. _____

5. Name an angle that is supplementary to ∠BFD. _____

6. Name an angle that is supplementary to ∠CFD. _____

7. Name a pair of non-adjacent angles that are complementary.

_____

8. What is the measure of ∠DFE? Explain how you found the measure.

_____

_____

9. Are ∠CFB and ∠DFE vertical angles? Why or why not?

_____

_____

10. Are ∠BFD and ∠AFE vertical angles? Why or why not?

_____

_____

Parallel Lines Cut by a Transversal

Lines *a* and *b* are parallel.

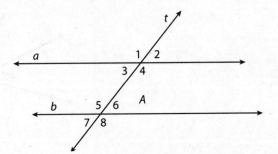

1. Trace line *a* and line *t* on a piece of paper. Label ∠1. Translate your traced angle down so that line *a* aligns with line *b* and line *t* aligns with itself.

   Which angle does ∠1 align with? _____

2. Because there is a translation that

   transforms ∠1 to_____, ∠1 and _____ are congruent.

3. Name a pair of alternate interior angles. What transformation(s) could you use to show that that those angles are congruent?

   _____

   _____

Find each angle measure.

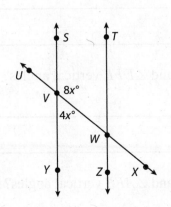

4. $m\angle 5$ when $m\angle 4 = 55°$
   $m\angle 5 =$ _____ °
   ∠4 is congruent to ∠5 because they are

   _____.

5. $m\angle SVW$

   ∠*SVW* is _____ to ∠*YVW*
   because they are a linear pair.

   $\angle SVW + \angle YVW = 180°$

   $8x° +$ _____° $= 180°$

   _____ $x = 180°$

   $\dfrac{x}{\boxed{}} = \dfrac{180}{12}$

   $x = 15$

   $\angle SVW = \angle 8x° = (8 \cdot 15)° =$ _____

Name _____ Date _____

Triangle Angle Theorems

Find the missing angle measure.

1.

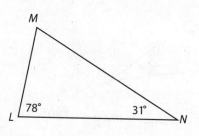

$m\angle M =$ _____

2.

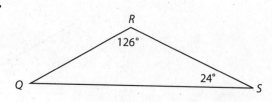

$m\angle Q =$ _____

Use the Triangle Sum Theorem to find the measure of each angle in degrees.

3.

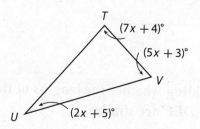

$m\angle T =$ _____

$m\angle U =$ _____

$m\angle V =$ _____

4.

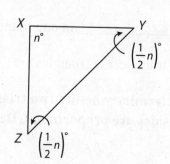

$m\angle X =$ _____

$m\angle Y =$ _____

$m\angle Z =$ _____

Use the Exterior Angles Theorem to find the measure of each angle in degrees.

5.

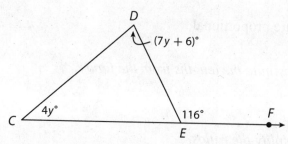

$m\angle C =$ _____

$m\angle D =$ _____

$m\angle DEC =$ _____

6.

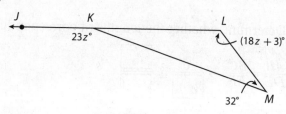

$m\angle L =$ _____

$m\angle MKL =$ _____

$m\angle MKJ =$ _____

157

Name _____ Date _____

Angles and Triangles

1. The figure shows only one pair of congruent angles. Find the measure of the third angle in each triangle. Label the angle measures in the figure.

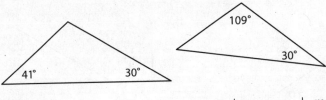

$41° + 30° + m\angle 3 = 180°$

$71° + m\angle 3 = 180°$

$71° + m\angle 3 - $ _____ $= 180° - $ _____

$m\angle 3 = $ _____

_____ $+ $ _____ $+ m\angle 3 = 180°$

_____ $+ m\angle 3 = 180°$

_____ $+ m\angle 3 - $ _____ $= 180° - $ _____

$m\angle 3 = $ _____

2. Because _____ in one triangle are congruent to _____

in the other triangle, the triangles are _____.

You can also determine whether two triangles are similar by deciding whether the lengths of the corresponding sides are proportional. Determine if $\angle ABC$ and $\angle DEF$ are similar.

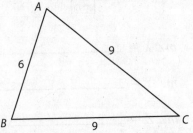
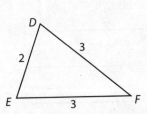

3. Corresponding parts of triangles are listed in the same order, so $\overline{AB}$ corresponds to $\overline{DE}$, $\overline{BC}$

corresponds to _____, and $\overline{AC}$ corresponds to _____.

4. Determine whether the lengths of corresponding sides are proportional.

$\dfrac{AB}{DE} = \dfrac{BC}{EF} \rightarrow \dfrac{6}{\boxed{}} \overset{?}{=} \dfrac{\boxed{}}{\boxed{}}$ *Substitute the lengths from the figure.*

    Simplify the ratios.

5. AC is congruent to BC and DF is congruent to EF, so you do not need to set up a second proportion.

Because the lengths of corresponding sides are _____, the triangles are _____.

© Houghton Mifflin Harcourt Publishing Company

Unit 12
Core Skills Math Review

Similar Triangles and Slope

For Exercises 1–9, use similar triangles to show that the slope of a line is constant. Use this space to make your drawing.

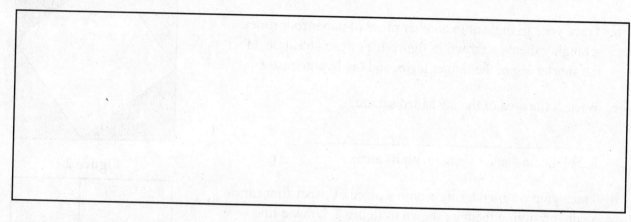

1. Draw line ℓ that is not a horizontal line. Label four points on the line as A, B, C, and D. You need to show that the slope between points A and B is the same as the slope between points C and D.

2. Draw the rise and run for the slope between points A and B. Label the intersection as point E. Draw the rise and run for the slope between points C and D. Label the intersection as point F.

3. Write expressions for the slope between A and B and between C and D.

   Slope between A and B: $\dfrac{BE}{\boxed{}}$. Slope between C and D: $\dfrac{\boxed{}}{CF}$

4. Extend $\overleftrightarrow{AE}$ and $\overleftrightarrow{CF}$. $\overleftrightarrow{AE}$ and $\overleftrightarrow{CF}$ are parallel. Line ℓ is a transversal that intersects parallel lines.

5. Complete the following statements:

   $\angle BAE$ and _____ are corresponding angles and are _____.

   $\angle BEA$ and _____ are right angles and are _____.

6. By Angle-Angle Similarity, $\triangle ABE$ and _____ are similar triangles.

7. Use the fact that the lengths of corresponding sides of similar triangles are proportional to complete the following ratios: $\dfrac{BE}{DF} = \dfrac{\boxed{}}{CF}$

8. Recall that you can also write the proportion so that the ratios compare parts of the same triangle: $\dfrac{\boxed{}}{AE} = \dfrac{DF}{\boxed{}}$.

9. The proportion you wrote in Exercise 8 shows that the ratios you wrote in step 3 are equal.

   So, the slope of the line is _____.

Proving the Pythagorean Theorem

Figure 1

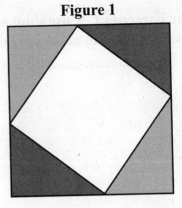

1. **a.** Draw a right triangle on a piece of paper and cut it out. Make one leg shorter than the other.

   b. Trace your triangle onto another piece of paper four times, arranging them as shown in figure 1. For each triangle, label the shorter leg *a*, the longer leg *b*, and the hypotenuse *c*.

   c. What is the area of the unshaded square?

   _____
   Label the unshaded square with its area.

Figure 2

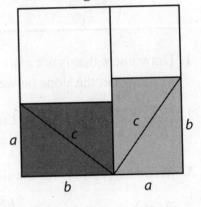

   d. Trace your original triangle onto a piece of paper four times again, arranging them as shown in figure 2. Draw a line outlining a larger square that is the same size as the figure you made in step b.

   e. What is the area of the unshaded square at the top right of the figure in step d? at the top left?

   _____
   Label the unshaded squares with their areas.

   f. What is the total area of the unshaded regions in figure 2?

   _____

2. Do the two large squares in figures 1 and 2 have the same area? Explain.

   _____

3. Do the unshaded regions of figures 1 and 2 have the same area? Explain.

   _____

   _____

4. Write an equation relating the area of the unshaded region in figure 1 to the unshaded region in figure 2.

   _____

   The Pythagorean Theorem says "If a triangle is a right triangle, then $a^2 + b^2 = c^2$."

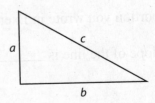

The Pythagorean Theorem

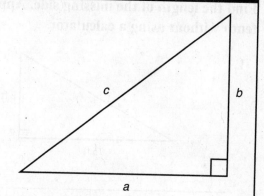

The side opposite the right angle in a right triangle is called the **hypotenuse.** Every right triangle has the property that the square of the hypotenuse is equal to the sum of the squares of the **legs.** This is called the **Pythagorean Theorem.**

The Pythagorean Theorem is written $a^2 + b^2 = c^2$. It can be used to find the length of one side of a right triangle if you know the lengths of the other two sides.

Solve for the hypotenuse.

$$a^2 + b^2 = c^2$$

$$c^2 = (8)^2 + (6)^2$$

$$c^2 = 64 + 36$$

$$c^2 = 100$$

$$c = \sqrt{100}$$

$$c = 10$$

The hypotenuse of the triangle is 10.

Solve for the missing leg.

$$a^2 + b^2 = c^2$$

$$(9)^2 + (b)^2 = (15)^2$$

$$81 + b^2 = 225$$

$$b^2 = 225 - 81$$

$$b^2 = 144$$

$$b = \sqrt{144}$$

$$b = 12$$

The missing leg of the triangle is 12.

Find the missing length in each right triangle, using $a^2 + b^2 = c^2$.

1. $a = 5, b = 12, c = ?$

2. $a = 7, c = 25, b = ?$

3. $a = 3, b = 4, c = ?$

4. $b = 40, c = 41, a = ?$

5. $a = 1.2, b = 1.6, c = ?$

6. $a = 15, c = 17, b = ?$

Using the Pythagorean Theorem

Find the length of the missing side. Approximate square roots of non-perfect squares to the nearest tenth without using a calculator.

1.

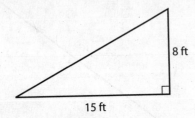

8 ft

15 ft

2.

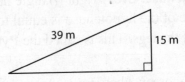

39 m

15 m

3.

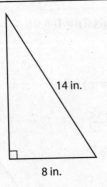

14 in.

8 in.

4.

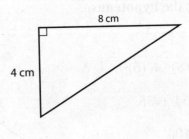

8 cm

4 cm

Approximate the length of the hypotenuse to the nearest tenth without using a calculator.

5.

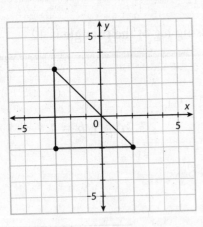

6.

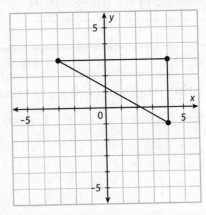

7. What is the longest flagpole (in whole feet) that could be shipped in a box that measures 1 ft by 2 ft by 12 ft?

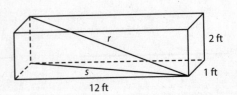

r

2 ft

s

1 ft

12 ft

Geometric Drawings

1. On a separate piece of paper, draw a triangle that has side lengths of 3 cm and 6 cm with an included angle of 120°. Determine whether the given information makes a unique triangle, more than one triangle, or no triangle.

_____

_____

2. Use geometry software to determine whether the given side lengths can be used to form *one unique triangle*, *more than one triangle*, or *no triangle*.

	Construction 1	Construction 2	Construction 3	Construction 4
Side 1 (units)	5	8	20	1
Side 2 (units)	5	9	20	1
Side 3 (units)	10	10	20	7
Triangle Formation?				

3. On a separate piece of paper, draw a triangle that has degrees of 30°, 60°, and 90°. Measure the side lengths.

4. Can you draw another triangle with the same angles but different side lengths?

_____

_____

5. If you are given 3 angles in one triangle, will the triangle be unique?

_____

_____

6. Draw a freehand sketch of a triangle with three angles that have the same measure. Explain how you made your drawing.

_____

_____

_____

_____

Name _____ Date _____

Unit 12 Review

Solve.

1. Angles *ABC* and *DBE* are vertical angles. If ∠*ABC* measures 80°, what is the measure of ∠*DBE*?

   _____

2. Angles *FGH* and *HGI* are supplementary angles. If ∠*FGH* measures 48°, what is the measure of ∠*HGI*?

   _____

3. Paul wants to draw a triangle that has side lengths of 4 cm, 8 cm, and 4 cm. Will this make one unique triangle, more than one triangle, or no triangle?

   _____

4. Meg wants to draw a triangle that has angle measures of 40°, 120°, and 20°. Will this make one unique triangle, more than one triangle, or no triangle?

   _____

Use the figures to answer the questions.

5. What is the measure of angle *x*?

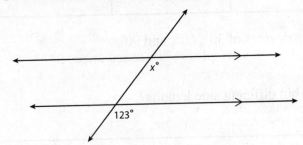

6. What is the value of *x*?

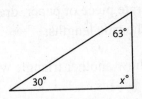

   _____   _____

Find the length of the missing side of each right triangle.

7.
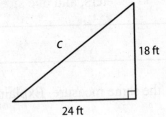

8.
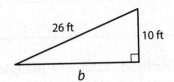

   _____   _____

Formula for Area of a Triangle

The **height** of a triangle is a perpendicular line segment from any vertex to the opposite side. The opposite side is called the **base**.

To find the **area** (number of square units) of a triangle, you can use a formula. The formula $A = \frac{1}{2}bh$ means the area of a triangle equals one half the base times the height. The answer will be in square units.

Find the area of this triangle.

Write the formula. $A = \frac{1}{2}bh$

Substitute the data. $A = \frac{1}{2} \times 12 \times 15$

Solve the problem. $A = \frac{12 \times 15}{2} = \frac{180}{2} = 90$

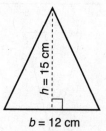

b = 12 cm

The area of the triangle is 90 square centimeters.

Use the formula for area of a triangle. Solve.

1. What is the area of a triangle that has a base of 16 meters and a height of 20 meters?

2. How much sod will be needed to cover a triangular-shaped park whose base measures 105 feet and height measures 87 feet?

3. A triangular-shaped park has one side, the base, measuring 120 meters, and one side, the height, measuring 80 meters. What is the area of the park?

4. A new highway cut off part of the town and formed a triangle. The base of the triangle measures 30 kilometers, and one side, the height, measures 25 kilometers. What is the area of this part of the town?

5. The top of the front wall of a barn forms a triangle. The triangle is 3.5 meters tall and 10 meters wide. What is the area of this part of the wall?

6. A group of students are making school banners shaped like triangles. The base of each triangle is 11 inches. The height of each triangle is 25 inches. How much fabric is needed to make each banner?

165

Area of Triangles

Find the area of each triangle.

1.

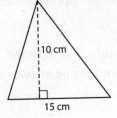

10 cm

15 cm

A = _____

2.

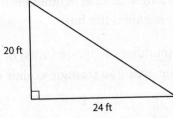

20 ft

24 ft

A = _____

3.

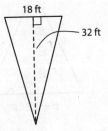

18 ft

32 ft

A = _____

4.

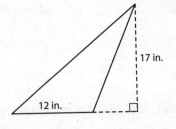

17 in.

12 in.

A = _____

5. $b = 8\frac{1}{2}$ inches; $h = 15$ inches

A = _____

6. $b = 15\frac{1}{4}$ inches; $h = 18$ inches

A = _____

7. $b = 132$ meters; $h = 72$ meters

A = _____

8. $b = 44$ feet; $h = 48$ feet

A = _____

9. What is the area of the triangular plot of land?

A = _____

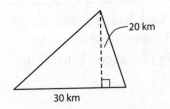

20 km

30 km

10. The sixth grade art students are making a mosaic using tiles in the shape of right triangles. Each tile has leg measures 3 centimeters and 5 centimeters. What is the area of one tile?

A = _____

11. A triangular piece of fabric has an area of 45 square inches. The height of the triangle is 15 inches. What is the length of the triangle's base?

b = _____

12. The front part of a tent is 8 feet wide and 5 feet tall. What is the area of this part of the tent?

A = _____

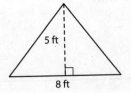

5 ft

8 ft

Formula for Area of a Rectangle

Area is the number of **square** units in a figure. A square unit measures 1 unit by 1 unit. The area of a rectangle is found by multiplying the length by the width. This verbal sentence can be written as the formula $A = lw$. To find A, substitute values for l and w into the formula and solve.

> The formula for area of a rectangle is
>
> $$A = lw,$$
>
> where A = area, l = length, and w = width.

Jaime's bedroom is 12 feet wide and 14 feet long. How many square feet of carpet will be needed to cover the bedroom floor?

Since both measurements are in feet, the area will be in square feet.

$A = lw$

$A = 12(14)$

$A = 168$

Jaime will need 168 square feet of carpet.

Solve. Use the formula for area of a rectangle.

1. How many square feet of tile are needed to cover a floor measuring 25 feet by 22 feet?

2. The school's playground measures 30 meters by 50 meters. How many square meters is the playground?

3. A den measures 20 feet by 12 feet. How many square feet is the den?

4. A kitchen measures 12 feet by 16 feet. How many square feet is the kitchen?

5. The dimensions of a professional football field are 120 yards by $53\frac{1}{3}$ yards. How many square yards is a professional football field?

6. A professional basketball court is 94 feet by 50 feet. How many square feet is a professional basketball court?

Area of Parallelograms and Trapezoids

A **parallelogram** is a quadrilateral with 2 sets of parallel sides.

The formula $A = b \times h$ means the area of a parallelogram is the product of the base and the height.

Find the area of the parallelogram.

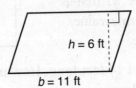

$A = bh = 11(6) = 66$

The area of the parallelogram is 66 square feet.

A **trapezoid** is a quadrilateral with exactly 1 pair of parallel sides.

The formula $A = \dfrac{(b_1 + b_2)h}{2}$ means the area of a trapezoid equals the sum of the bases times the height divided by 2.

Find the area of the trapezoid.

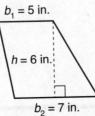

$A = \dfrac{(5 + 7)6}{2}$

$A = 36$

The area of the trapezoid is 36 square inches.

Find the area of each parallelogram or trapezoid.

1.

_____

2.

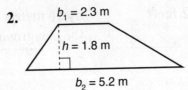

_____

3.

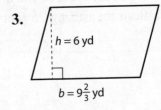

_____

4.

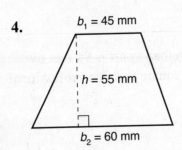

$b_1 = 45$ mm
$h = 55$ mm
$b_2 = 60$ mm

_____

5.

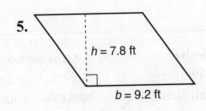

_____

6.

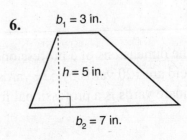

_____

© Houghton Mifflin Harcourt Publishing Company

Practice Area of Parallelograms and Trapezoids

Find the area of each parallelogram or trapezoid.

1.

$h = 10.5$ m
$b = 16$ m

_____

2.

$b_1 = 3.4$ yd
$h = 4.9$ yd
$b_2 = 5.6$ yd

_____

3.

$h = 17$ in.
$b = 27$ in.

_____

4.

$b_1 = 21$ cm
$h = 25$ cm
$b_2 = 29$ cm

_____

5.

$h = 30$ mm
$b = 65$ mm

_____

6.

$b_1 = 18$ ft
$h = 16$ ft
$b_2 = 20$ ft

_____

Solve.

7. What is the area of a trapezoid that is 8 inches high with bases that are 10 inches and 15 inches long?

_____

8. Dion drew a trapezoid with a height of 12 centimeters and bases of 25 centimeters and 17 centimeters. What is the area of Dion's trapezoid?

_____

9. What is the area of a parallelogram with a height of $3\frac{1}{4}$ feet and a base of $6\frac{1}{2}$ feet?

_____

10. What is the area of a parallelogram that is 16 yards long and 8 yards high?

_____

169

Area of Quadrilaterals

Find the area of each parallelogram.

1.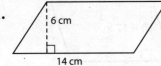
6 cm
14 cm

$A =$ _____ cm²

2.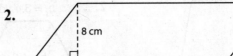
8 cm
21 cm

$A =$ _____ cm²

3. $b = 13$ meters; $h = 7$ meters

$A =$ _____ m²

4. $b = 12\frac{3}{4}$ inches; $h = 2\frac{1}{2}$ inches

$A =$ _____ in²

Find the area of each rhombus.

5.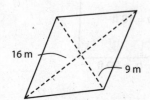
16 m
9 m

$A =$ _____ m²

6.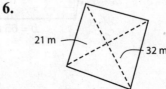
21 m
32 m

$A =$ _____ m²

7. $d_1 = 18$ feet; $d_2 = 7.25$ feet

$A =$ _____ ft²

8. $d_1 = 8$ inches; $d_2 = 2\frac{1}{2}$ inches

$A =$ _____ in²

Find the area of each trapezoid.

9.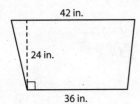
42 in.
24 in.
36 in.

$A =$ _____ in²

10.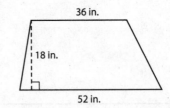
36 in.
18 in.
52 in.

$A =$ _____ in²

11. $b_1 = 9$ meters
$b_2 = 15$ meters
$h = 8$ meters

$A =$ _____ m²

12. $b_1 = 11$ meters
$b_2 = 14$ meters
$h = 10$ meters

$A =$ _____ m²

Solving Area Problems

Find the area of the figure.

1. Into what two figures can you divide this composite figure?

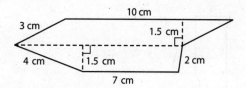

_____

2. Find the area of each shape.

Area of the Parallelogram

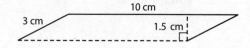

Area of the Trapezoid

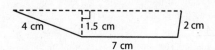

The base of the parallelogram is _____ cm.

The height of the parallelogram is _____ cm.

Use the formula.

$A = bh$

$A =$ _____ · _____

$A =$ _____

The area of the parallelogram is _____ cm².

The bottom base of the trapezoid is _____ cm.

The top base the trapezoid is _____ cm, since it is the same length as the base of the parallelogram.

The height of the trapezoid is _____ cm.

Use the formula.

$A = \frac{1}{2}h(b^1 + b^2)$

$A = \frac{1}{2}$ _____ (_____ + _____)

$A = \frac{1}{2}$ _____ (_____)

$A =$ _____

The area of the trapezoid is _____ cm².

Find the area of the composite figure.

3. _____ + _____ = _____

   Area of parallelogram   Area of trapezoid   Area of composite shape

4. Describe another way to divide the shape into simpler figures.

_____

_____

5. If you divide the composite figure into different shapes, what is the area? What does this tell you?

_____

_____

171

Area of Polygons

Find the area of each polygon.

1.
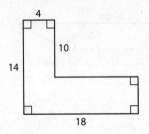

$A =$ _____ square units

2.
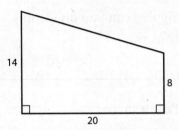

$A =$ _____ square units

3.
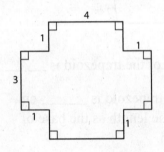

$A =$ _____ square units

4.
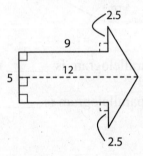

$A =$ _____ square units

5. In Hal's backyard, there is a patio, a walkway, and a garden.

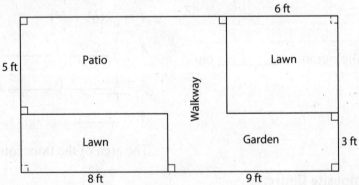

a. Show how to find the total area of the patio, walkway, and garden by adding areas of rectangles.

b. Show how to find the total area of the patio, walkway, and garden by subtracting areas of rectangles.

Unit 13
Core Skills Math Review

Name _____ Date _____

Polygons in the Coordinate Plane

Give the name of each polygon.

1.

_____

2.
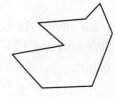

_____

3.
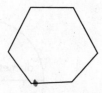

_____

4.

_____

5. A clothing designer makes letters for varsity jackets by graphing the letters as polygons on a coordinate plane. One of the letters is polygon *MNOPQRSTUV* with vertices *M*(2, 1), *N*(2, 9), *O*(7, 9), *P*(7, 7), *Q*(4, 7), *R*(4, 6), *S*(6, 6), *T*(6, 4), *U*(4, 4), and *V*(4, 1).

a. Graph the points on the coordinate plane and connect them in order.

b. What letter is formed? _____

c. Find the perimeter and area of the letter.

P = _____ units   A = _____ square units

Give the name of each polygon. Then find its perimeter and area. Some side lengths are given.

6.
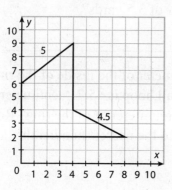

_____

P = _____ units

A = _____ square units

7.
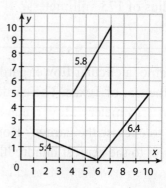

_____

P = _____ units

A = _____ square units

Name _____ Date _____

Formula for Circumference of a Circle

Circumference is the distance around a circle. To find the circumference, you can use a formula.

The formula $C = \pi d$ means the circumference equals **pi** times the **diameter.** This formula uses the symbol π for pi. We will use 3.14 for the value of π. The diameter is a straight line across the circle and through the center.

You can also use the formula $C = 2\pi r$, which means the circumference equals two times pi times the **radius.** The radius is a straight line from the center of the circle to the circumference. It is one half of the diameter, so $2r = d$.

Find the circumference of this circle.

Write the formula. $C = \pi d$

Substitute the data. $C = 3.14 \times 12$

Solve the problem. $C = 37.68$

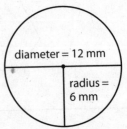

The circumference of the circle is 37.68 millimeters.

Use the formula for circumference of a circle. Solve.

1. What is the circumference of a circle that has a diameter of 7 inches?

2. The wheel of a bicycle has a radius of 35 centimeters. What is the circumference of the wheel?

3. What is the circumference of a circle with a radius of 175 millimeters?

4. What is the circumference of a circle with a diameter of 3.5 yards?

5. At the Alamo, a circular flower garden encloses the star of Texas. The garden has a radius of 3.15 meters. How much border is needed to enclose the garden? Round your answer to the nearest hundredth.

6. The diameter of the inside of the ring of a basketball hoop is 45.71 centimeters. What is the circumference of the ring? Round your answer to the nearest hundredth.

Name _____

Date _____

Formula for Area of a Circle

To find the area of a circle, you can use a formula.

The formula $A = \pi r^2$ means the area of a circle is equal to pi times the radius squared, or the radius times the radius.

Find the area of this circle.

Write the formula. $A = \pi r^2$

Substitute the data. $A = 3.14 (7 \times 7)$

Solve the problem. $A = 3.14 \times 49 = 153.86$

The area of the circle is 153.86 square centimeters.

Remember, write your answer in square units.

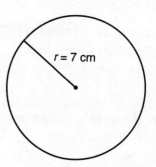

r = 7 cm

Use the formula for area of a circle. Solve.

1. Find the area of a circle that has a radius of 3.5 feet.

2. What is the area of a circle that has a diameter of 28 inches? (Hint: The radius is one half the diameter.)

3. A bandstand in the shape of a circle will be 7 meters across. How many square meters of flooring will be required? Round your answer to the nearest hundredth.

4. A circular canvas net used by firefighters has a radius of 2.1 meters. What is the area of the net?

5. A gallon of paint covers 56 square meters. How many gallons of paint will be needed to cover a circular ceiling that is 22 meters in diameter?

6. The circular top of an auto piston has a radius of 4.2 centimeters. What is the area of the top of the piston? Round your answer to the nearest hundredth.

Area of a Circle

Find the relationship between the circumference and area of a circle.

1. Start with a circle that has radius r.

    Solve the equation $C = 2\pi r$ for r.

    $r = \dfrac{\boxed{}}{\boxed{}}$

    Substitute your expression for r in the formula for area of a circle.

    $A = \pi \left(\dfrac{\boxed{}}{\boxed{}}\right)^2$

    Square the term in the parenthesis.

    $A = \pi \left(\dfrac{\boxed{}^2}{\boxed{}^2 \cdot \boxed{}^2}\right)$

    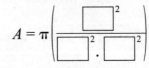

    Evaluate the power.

    $A = \dfrac{\boxed{} \cdot \boxed{}^2}{\boxed{} \cdot \boxed{}^2}$

    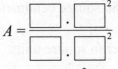

    Simplify.

    $A = \dfrac{\boxed{}^2}{\boxed{} \cdot \boxed{}}$

    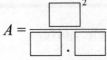

    Solve for C^2.

    $C^2 = 4\boxed{}\boxed{}$

2. The circumference of the circle squared is equal to _____

3. Does this formula work for a circle with a radius of 3 inches? Show your work below.

Find the area of the circles given the circumference. Give your answers in terms of π.

4. $C = 8\pi$; $A = $ _____

5. $C = \pi$; $A = $ _____

6. $C = 2\pi$; $A = $ _____

Name _____   Date _____

Unit 13 Review

Find the area of each polygon.

1.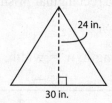
24 in.
30 in.

A = _____

2.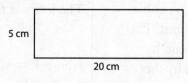
5 cm
20 cm

A = _____

3.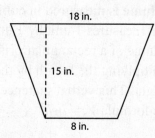
18 in.
15 in.
8 in.

A = _____

Find the circumference and area of each circle to the nearest hundredth. Use 3.14 for π. Remember that the diameter is 2 times the radius.

4.
12 mm

C = _____
A = _____

5.
14 m

C = _____
A = _____

6.
2 mm

C = _____
A = _____

Solve.

7. What is the area of a triangle that has a height of 16 centimeters and a base of 20 centimeters?

8. Find the area of a parallelogram with a base of 10 feet and a height of 7.5 feet.

9. How much sod is needed to cover a rectangular yard that measures 20 meters by 15 meters?

10. To the nearest hundredth inch, what is the area of a circle with a radius of 8 inches?

Unit 13
Core Skills Math Review

Formula for Volume of a Rectangular Prism

Volume is measured in **cubic** units. A cubic unit measures 1 unit by 1 unit by 1 unit. The volume of a rectangular prism is found by multiplying the length by the width by the height. This verbal sentence can be written as the formula $V = lwh$.

The formula for volume of a rectangular prism is

$$V = lwh,$$

where V = volume, l = length, w = width, and h = height.

What is the volume of a tank that measures 6 meters by 5 meters by 0.5 meter?

$V = lwh$

$V = (6)(5)(0.5)$

$V = 15$

The volume is 15 cubic meters.

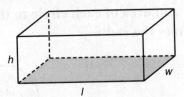

Solve. Use the formula for volume of a rectangular prism.

1. In building a new house, Al dug a basement measuring 30 feet by 32 feet by 9 feet. How many cubic feet of dirt had to be removed?

   _____

2. The floor of a railroad boxcar measures 6 feet by 36 feet. The car has been filled to a depth of 6 feet with grain. How many cubic feet of grain are in the boxcar?

   _____

3. A construction crew dug a ditch 2 meters wide, 3 meters deep, and 150 meters long. What was the volume of the ditch?

   _____

4. The trunk in Tina's car is shaped like a rectangular prism. It measures 4 feet by 2 feet by 3 feet. How many cubic feet is the trunk?

   _____

5. Cut wood is usually sold by the cord. A stack of wood 8 feet long, 4 feet wide, and 4 feet high is a cord. How many cubic feet are there in a cord?

   _____

6. What is the volume in cubic feet of a box whose inside dimensions are 48 inches by 3 feet by 4 feet? (Hint: Change the inches measurement to feet. There are 12 inches in 1 foot.)

   _____

Volume of Prisms

Find the volume of each rectangular prism.

1.
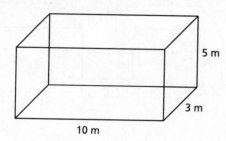

$V =$ _____ cubic meters

2.
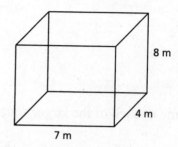

$V =$ _____ cubic meters

3.
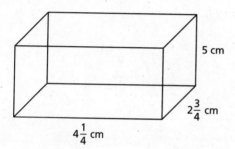

$V =$ _____ cubic centimeters

4.
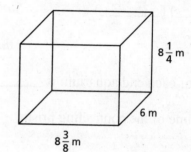

$V =$ _____ cubic meters

5.
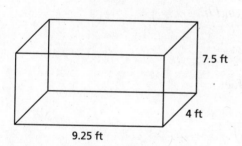

$V =$ _____ cubic feet

6.
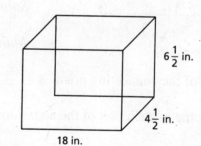

$V =$ _____ cubic inches

7. A block of wood measures 4.5 centimeters by 3.5 centimeters by 7 centimeters. What is the volume of the block of wood?

$V =$ _____ cubic centimeters

8. A restaurant buys a freezer in the shape of a rectangular prism. The dimensions of the freezer are shown. What is the volume of the freezer?

$V =$ _____ cubic inches

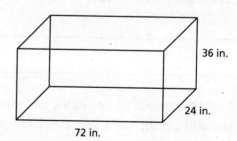

9. Conjecture The length, width, and height of a rectangular prism are doubled. How many times greater is the volume compared to the original prism?

Solving Volume Problems

Allie has two aquariums connected by a small square prism. Find the volume of the double aquarium.

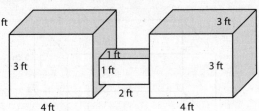

1. Find the volume of each of the larger aquariums.

   $V = Bh$ *Use the formula.*

   $V = ($_____$)($_____$)$ *Substitute for B and h.*

   $V = $ _____   *Multiply.*

   The volume of each end aquarium is _____ cubic feet.

2. Find the volume of the connecting prism.

   $V = Bh$ *Use the formula.*

   $V = ($_____$)($_____$)$ *Substitute for B and h.*

   $V = $ _____   *Multiply.*

   The volume of the connecting prism is _____ cubic feet.

3. Add the volume of each part of the aquarium.

   $V = $ _____ $+$ _____ $+$ _____ $=$ _____

   The volume of the aquarium is _____ cubic feet.

4. **What If?** Find the volume of the aquarium if all of the dimensions were doubled. What is the relationship between the original volume and the new volume?

   _____

   _____

5. Find the volume of one of the end aquariums using another pair of opposite sides as the base. Do you still get the same volume? Explain.

   _____

   _____

Name _____   Date _____

Formula for Volume of a Cylinder

To find the volume of a cylinder, you can use a formula.

The formula $V = \pi r^2 h$ means the volume of a cylinder equals pi times the radius squared times the height.

Remember, diameter = $2r$.

Find the volume of this cylinder.

Write the formula. $V = \pi r^2 h$

Substitute the data. $V = 3.14\,(1.4 \times 1.4) \times 20$

Solve the problem. $V = 123.088$

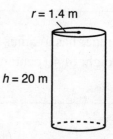

r = 1.4 m

h = 20 m

The volume of the cylinder is 123.088 cubic meters.

Remember, write your answer in cubic units.

Use the formula for volume of a cylinder. Solve.

1. A cylindrical water tank has a diameter of 2.8 yards and is 6.5 yards tall. What is the volume of the tank? Round your answer to the nearest hundredth.

   _____

2. The inside radius of a pipe is 0.35 meter. One section of the pipe is 6 meters long. How much water will this piece of pipe hold?

   _____

3. A small pipe has a radius of 1 inch and is 3.5 inches long. How much liquid can the pipe hold?

   _____

4. A storage tank has a radius of 5.25 meters and a height of 12 meters. How much liquid can the storage tank hold? Round your answer to the nearest hundredth.

   _____

5. The tank of a gasoline truck has a radius of 1.75 meters and is 7 meters long. What is the volume of the tank? Round your answer to the nearest hundredth.

   _____

6. A cylinder-shaped container is 9 centimeters in diameter and 15 centimeters in height. How much liquid will this container hold? Round your answer to the nearest hundredth.

   _____

Volume Formulas

Find the volume of each figure. Round your answers to the nearest tenth if necessary. Use 3.14 for π.

1.

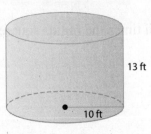

13 ft
10 ft

_____

2.

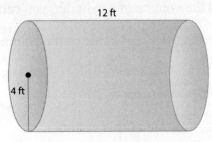

12 ft
4 ft

_____

3. A cylinder has a radius of 4 centimeters and height of 40 centimeters.

_____

4. A cylinder has a radius of 8 meters and height of 4 meters.

_____

5.

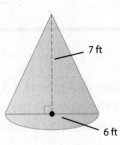

7 ft
6 ft

_____

6.

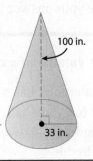

100 in.
33 in.

_____

7. A sphere has a radius of 3.1 meters.

_____

8. A sphere has a diameter of 18 inches.

_____

9. A farmer stores corn in a silo that is in the shape of a cylinder with a hemisphere on top. The diameter of the silo is 30 feet, and the total height of the silo is 60 feet.

   a. Find the radius of the hemisphere. _____

   b. Find the height of the cylinder. _____

   c. Find the volume of the cylinder. _____

   d. Find the volume of the hemisphere. _____

   e. Find the volume of the silo. _____

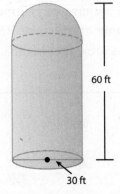

60 ft
30 ft

Surface Area of a Rectangular Prism

The **surface area** of a rectangular **prism** is the sum of the areas of each **face**. Because the surface area measures two **dimensions,** it is measured in square units.

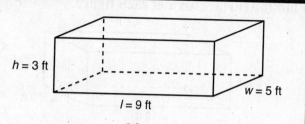

Find the surface area of this figure.

Find the sum of the areas of each face.

$A = 9 \times 3 = 27$ square ft

$B = 9 \times 5 = 45$ square ft

$C = 9 \times 3 = 27$ square ft

$D = 9 \times 5 = 45$ square ft

$E = 5 \times 3 = 15$ square ft

$F = 5 \times 3 = 15$ square ft

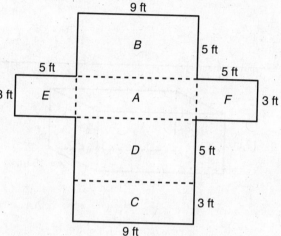

The sum of the areas of each face is:

$27 + 45 + 27 + 45 + 15 + 15 = 174$ square ft

The surface area of the rectangular prism is 174 square feet.

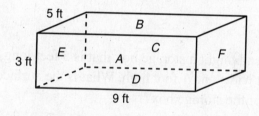

Find the surface area of each figure.

1.

2.

3.

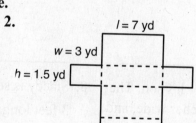

Practice Surface Area of a Rectangular Prism

Find the surface area of each figure.

1.
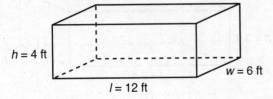
$h = 4$ ft
$l = 12$ ft
$w = 6$ ft

2.
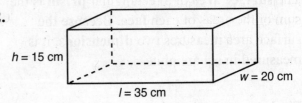
$h = 15$ cm
$l = 35$ cm
$w = 20$ cm

3.
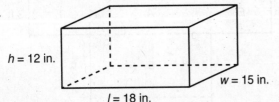
$h = 12$ in.
$l = 18$ in.
$w = 15$ in.

4.
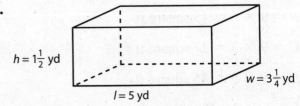
$h = 1\frac{1}{2}$ yd
$l = 5$ yd
$w = 3\frac{1}{4}$ yd

Solve.

5. Doreen bought a storage box that is 5 feet long, 3 feet wide, and 1 foot high. What is the surface area of the storage box?

6. A necklace came in a box that is 5 cm by 8 cm by 15 cm. What is the surface area of the box?

7. Antonio is building a toy chest for his son. The toy chest is 30 inches high, 40 inches wide, and 50 inches long. What is the surface area of the toy chest?

8. Stacey is sending her mother a package that is 3 feet long, 1 foot wide, and $1\frac{1}{2}$ feet tall. What is the surface area of the package?

Solving Surface Area Problems

Matthew builds a model of a simple flat-roofed house with a
chimney on top. He wants to paint both the house and chimney
with red paint. How many square inches will he paint?

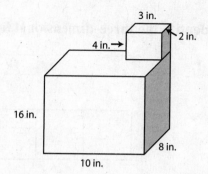

1. Find the surface area of the chimney.

$S = 2lw + 2lh + 2wh$

$S = 2 ($ _____ $\cdot$ _____ $) + 2($ _____ $\cdot$ _____ $) + 2($ _____ $\cdot$ _____ $)$

$S = $ _____ $+$ _____ $+$ _____

$S = $ _____

The surface area of the chimney is _____ square inches.

2. Find the surface area of the house. Do not include the bottom of the house.

$S = lw + 2lh + 2wh$

$S = ($ _____ $\cdot$ _____ $) + 2($ _____ $\cdot$ _____ $) + 2($ _____ $\cdot$ _____ $)$

$S = $ _____ $+$ _____ $+$ _____

$S = $ _____

The surface area of the house is _____ square inches.

3. Add the surface areas of the chimney and the house.

$S = $ _____ $+$ _____ $=$ _____ square inches

4. Part of the chimney and house overlap. The overlapping area has a length of 3 inches and a width of
2 inches, or an area of 6 square inches. Subtract two times that area.

$S = $ _____ $- 2$ _____ $=$ _____

Matthew will paint _____ square inches.

5. Explain why you subtract the overlap area two times.

_____

Nets and Surface Area

Identify the three-dimensional figure formed by each net.

1.

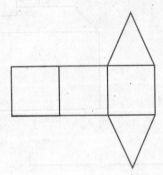

2.

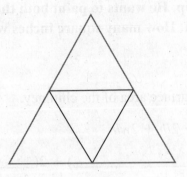

_____   _____

Draw a net for each three-dimensional figure.

3.

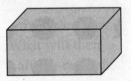

4.

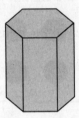

Find the surface area of each figure.

5.

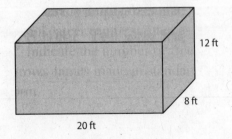

12 ft

8 ft

20 ft

_____ square feet

6.

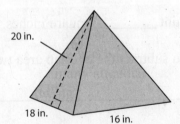

20 in.

18 in.   16 in.

_____ square inches

Cross Sections

Describe the shape of the cross section shown on each right rectangular prism.

1.

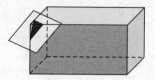

_____

2.

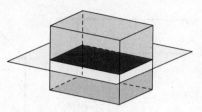

3.

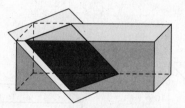

_____

4.

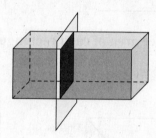

_____

Use the right rectangular pyramid that is shown below.

5. The shape of the base is a _____.

The shape of each side is a _____.

6. Circle the cross sections that are possible.

   square   rectangle   triangle   circle   trapezoid

7. Sketch the cross sections of the right rectangular pyramid below. Hint: Use the style shown in Exercises 1–4 as a guide.

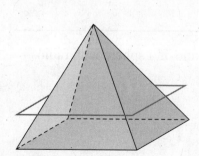
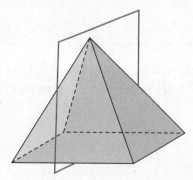
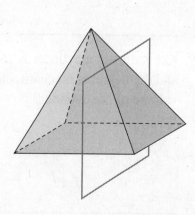

Name _____ Date _____

Unit 14 Review

Find the volume of each rectangular prism.

1.

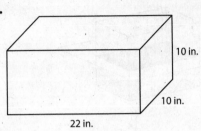

10 in.
10 in.
22 in.

$V =$ _____

2.

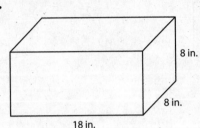

8 in.
8 in.
18 in.

$V =$ _____

3.

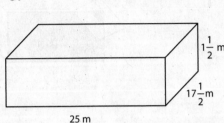

$1\frac{1}{2}$ m
$17\frac{1}{2}$ m
25 m

$V =$ _____

Find the surface area of each rectangular prism.

4.

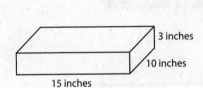

3 inches
10 inches
15 inches

$SA =$ _____

5.

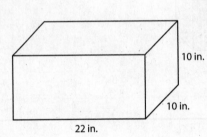

10 in.
10 in.
22 in.

$SA =$ _____

6.

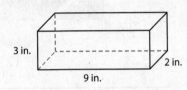

3 in.
2 in.
9 in.

$SA =$ _____

Solve.

7. What is the volume of a cone with radius 5 centimeters and height 3 centimeters?

8. How much dirt was removed to form a hole that measures 80 feet long, 54 feet wide, and 4 feet deep?

_____

9. The radius of a cylinder is 16 centimeters, and the height is 60 centimeters. What is the volume of the cylinder?

10. What is the volume of a sphere with radius 6 inches?

_____

Understanding Probability

1. In a hat, you have index cards with the numbers 1 through 10 written on them. You pick one card at random. Order the events from least likely to happen to most likely to happen.

You pick a number greater than 0.   You pick a number that is at least 2.

You pick an even number.   You pick a number that is at most 0.

_____

_____

Determine whether each event is impossible, unlikely, as likely as not, likely, or certain. Then, tell whether the probability is 0, close to 0, $\frac{1}{2}$, close to 1, or 1.

2. randomly picking a green card from a standard deck of playing cards

3. randomly picking a red card from a standard deck of playing cards

_____   _____

4. picking a number less than 15 from a jar with papers labeled from 1 to 12

5. picking a number that is divisible by 5 from a jar with papers labeled from 1 to 12

_____   _____

Find the probability.

6. The probability of rolling a 5 on a number cube is $\frac{1}{6}$. What is the probability of not rolling a 5?

7. The probability that a coin will land heads when flipping a coin is $\frac{1}{2}$. What is the probability of getting tails?

_____   _____

8. The probability of spinning a 4 on a spinner with 5 equal sections marked 1 through 5 is $\frac{1}{5}$. What is the probability of not landing on 4?

9. The probability of picking a queen from a standard deck of cards is $\frac{1}{13}$. What is the probability of not picking a queen?

_____   _____

10. Describe an event that has a probability of 0% and an event that has a probability of 100%.

_____

_____

Name _____ Date _____

Exploring Probability

Look at the spinner. Find the probability of landing on

1. green. _____

2. blue. _____

3. yellow. _____

4. red. _____

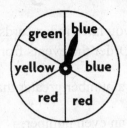

Look at the jar. Find the probability of picking a

5. black marble. _____

6. striped marble. _____

7. white marble. _____

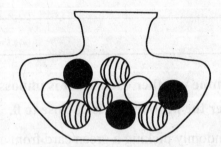

8. A bag contains 10 marbles. There are 5 red marbles, 2 green marbles, and 3 blue marbles. If you pick a marble without looking, would you be more likely to get a red or a blue marble?

_____

9. Ted has a nickel, 5 quarters, and 2 dimes in his pocket. Which type of coin is he most likely to pull out of his pocket? Which type of coin is he least likely to pull out of his pocket?

_____

10. A jar contains 3 red marbles, 2 blue marbles, and 1 black marble. What is the probability of picking a blue marble?

_____

11. A spinner has 5 equal sections marked with the numbers 1 through 5. What is the probability of landing on an odd number?

_____

12. The winner of the Crafts Fair Raffle will be the person whose name is drawn from among 100 name cards. The probability of a seventh grader winning is $\frac{1}{20}$. How many of the cards have the name of a seventh grader?

_____

190

Unit 15
Core Skills Math Review

Probability of Simple Events

You spin the spinner. Find each probability.

1. P(2) _____

2. P(not 4) _____

3. P(3 or 2) _____

4. P(1, 4, or 5) _____

5. P(5 and white) _____

6. P(5 or white) _____

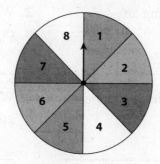

You roll a number cube numbered from 1 to 6. Find each probability.

7. P(5) _____   8. P(3 or 4) _____

9. P(not 5) _____   10. P(number > 3) _____

11. P(odd number) _____   12. P(number > 1) _____

13. What is the sample space when you flip three coins?

_____

14. What is the probability of getting exactly 2 heads if you flip 3 coins?

_____

15. What is the probability of getting exactly 2 tails if you flip 3 coins?

_____

16. If you throw a cube numbered 1–6, an even number gets you a prize. What is the probability that you will win a prize on a throw?

17. Free science catalogs are being distributed. They have even numbers of blue, green, red, and orange covers. What is the probability that the catalog you receive will have a green cover?

_____   _____

191

More Probability of Simple Events

For Exercises 1–4, think about rolling a number cube labeled 1, 3, 5, 7, 9, and 11.

1. What is the probability of rolling an odd number?

   _____

2. What is the probability of rolling an even number?

   _____

3. What is the probability of rolling a number less than 5?

   _____

4. What is the probability of rolling a number greater than 3?

   _____

Complete the table.

5.

Experiment	Possible Outcomes	Probability
Draw a card from 2 white, 4 red, and 3 blue cards without looking.	_____	P(white) = _____ P(blue) = _____ P(red or blue) = _____

6. In Exercise 5, which color has the least probability of being drawn?

   _____

7. In Exercise 5, which color has the greatest probability of being drawn?

   _____

8. A die rolls a 2. What is the probability of rolling a 2 on the next roll?

   _____

9. A coin shows tails seven times in a row. What is the probability of tails on the next toss?

   _____

10. Marty is given three answers to choose from on a multiple-choice test. He does not know the answer, so he guesses. What is the probability that he will guess the correct answer?

    _____

Random Numbers

The random numbers 0–9 in the table were generated by a computer. Use the table for Exercises 1–6.

50 random numbers

1	2	4	5	8	7	3	5	7	9
3	5	7	2	6	9	4	7	2	0
2	6	0	7	4	2	7	8	3	8
2	6	5	4	8	0	9	2	5	6
2	8	7	4	5	0	8	9	2	5

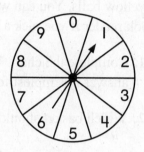

1. You are playing a game using the spinner shown. Use the table to simulate 50 spins. How many spins will it take before you get all the numbers from 0–9?

_____

2. Use the spinner again with the table. How many spins will it take to get number 7 twice?

_____

3. Using the mathematical probability, predict how many times the spinner will stop on 5 if you spin 40 times.

_____

4. What is the probability of getting number 3 in 10 spins? Use the data from the table.

_____

5. Jean put 10 cards numbered 0–9 in a bag. Amy takes a card out and puts it back. Predict the number of times Amy will pick the 2-card if she picks 50 times. How does your prediction compare with the results of the table?

_____

6. Using the table, what is the experimental probability of spinning a 0?

_____

7. Computer programmers often use random numbers in writing many different kinds of programs. Describe two kinds of programs in which random numbers might be useful.

_____

_____

_____

Theoretical Probability

At a school fair, you have a choice of randomly picking a ball from Basket A or Basket B. Basket A has 5 green balls, 3 red balls, and 8 yellow balls. Basket B has 7 green balls, 4 red balls, and 9 yellow balls. You can win a digital book reader if you pick a red ball.

	Basket A	Basket B
Total Number of Balls		
Number of Red Balls		
P(win) = Number of red balls Total number of balls		

1. Complete the chart. Write each answer in simplest form.

2. Which basket should you choose if you want the better chance of winning?

   _____

3. Jim has 4 nickels, 6 pennies, 4 dimes and 2 quarters in his pocket. He picks a coin at random. What is the probability that he will pick a nickel or a dime? Write your answer as a fraction, as a decimal, and as a percent.

   _____

4. A class has 12 boys and 15 girls. The teacher randomly picks one child to lead the class in singing.

   a. What is the probability that the teacher picks a boy? _____

   b. What is the probability that the teacher picks a girl? _____

   c. Describe two different ways you could find the answer to part b.

   _____

Use the spinner for Exercises 5–8.

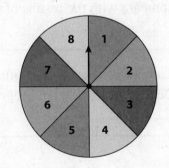

5. In 20 spins, about how often can you expect to land on a number evenly divisible by 2? _____

6. In 150 spins, about how often can you expect to land on a number less than 6? _____

7. In 200 spins, about how often can you expect to land on a 1? _____

8. Rudolfo says there is a greater chance of landing on an even number than on an odd number. What is his error?

   _____

Experimental Probability

1. You roll a number cube once. Complete the table of theoretical probabilities for the different outcomes. Remember that theoretical probability is the ratio of the number of ways an event can occur to the total number of equally likely outcomes.

Number	1	2	3	4	5	6
Theoretical Probability						

2. Using your knowledge of theoretical probability, predict the number of times each number will be rolled out of 30 total rolls.

   1: _____ times   3: _____ times   5: _____ times

   2: _____ times   4: _____ times   6: _____ times

3. Roll a number cube 30 times. Complete the table for the frequency of each number and then find its experimental probability.

Number	1	2	3	4	5	6
Frequency						
Experimental Probability						

4. Look at the tables you completed. How do the experimental probabilities compare with the theoretical probabilities?

   _____

5. By performing more trials, you tend to get experimental results that are closer to the theoretical probabilities. Combine your table from 3 with those of your classmates to make one table for the class. How do the class experimental probabilities compare with the theoretical probabilities?

   _____

6. Could the experimental probabilities ever be exactly equal to the theoretical probability? Why or why not?

   _____

   _____

195

Predictions

Frank tosses a baseball card into the air. The card lands faceup 30 out of 50 times. Use this information for Exercises 1–4.

1. What is the experimental probability that the card will land faceup on the next toss?

   _____

2. What is the experimental probability that the card will land facedown on the next toss?

   _____

3. How many times can you expect the card to land faceup in the next 75 tosses?

   _____

4. How many times can you expect the card to land facedown in the next 25 tosses?

   _____

Alison is on the basketball team. She has made 7 out of 10 free throws. Use this information for Exercises 5 and 6.

5. What is the experimental probability that she will make her next free throw?

   _____

6. How many of the next 20 free throws can she expect to miss?

   _____

The table shows the TV show preferences of 500 students. Use the table for Exercises 7–10.

7. What is the experimental probability that a seventh grader will prefer comedy?

   _____

TV Show Preferences			
	Comedy	News	Cartoons
Sixth Graders	20	26	34
Seventh Graders	30	46	44
Eighth Graders	44	46	30

8. What is the experimental probability that a sixth grader will prefer news?

   _____

9. Of 280 eighth graders, how many could be expected to prefer comedy?

   _____

10. What percent of seventh graders prefer news?

   _____

Using a Table with Compound Events

A **compound event** consists of two or more single events. To find the probability of a compound event, write a ratio of the number of ways the compound event can happen to the total number of possible outcomes. The sample space of an experiment is the set of all possible outcomes. To find the sample space for an experiment, you can use tables, lists, and tree diagrams.

Jacob rolls two fair number cubes. Find the probability that the sum of the numbers he rolls is 8.

1. Use the table to find the sample space for rolling a particular sum on two number cubes. Each cell is the sum of the first number in that row and column.

2. How many possible outcomes are in the sample space?

    _____

3. Circle the outcomes that give the sum of 8.

4. How many ways are there to roll a sum of 8?

    _____

	1	2	3	4	5	6
1						
2						
3						
4						
5						
6						

5. What is the probability of rolling a sum of 8? _____

Find the probability of each event.

6. Rolling a sum less than 5 _____

7. Rolling a sum of 7 or a sum of 9 _____

8. Give an example of an event that is more likely than rolling a sum of 8.

    _____

9. Give an example of an event that is less likely than rolling a sum of 8.

    _____

Using a Tree Diagram with Compound Events

A deli prepares a selection of grab-and-go sandwiches with one type of bread (white or wheat), one type of meat (ham, turkey, or chicken), and one type of cheese (cheddar or Swiss). Each combination is equally likely. Find the probability of choosing a sandwich at random and getting turkey and Swiss on wheat bread.

1. Complete the tree diagram to find the sample space for the compound event.

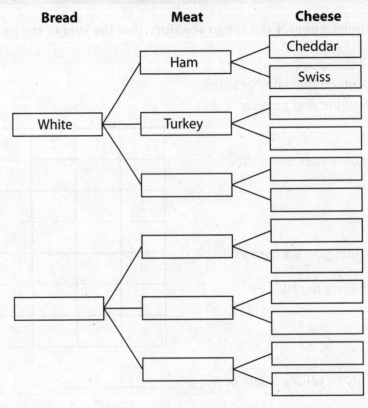

Bread   **Meat**   **Cheese**

2. How many possible outcomes are in the sample space? _____

3. What is the probability of choosing turkey and Swiss on wheat bread at random? _____

4. How can you find the probability of choosing a sandwich at random that is on wheat bread?

_____

_____

_____

5. How can you find the probability of choosing a sandwich at random that does not have ham?

_____

_____

Conducting a Simulation

There are winning prize codes in 30% of a cereal company's cereal boxes. What is the probability that you have to buy at least 3 boxes of cereal to find a winning prize code?

1. Design a simulation to model the situation.

   Represent each box by a random number from 1 to 10. Since 30% of the boxes have a winning prize code, the numbers 1 to 3 will represent the boxes containing a winning code. The numbers 4 to 10 represent the boxes not containing a winning code.

   Conduct trials and record the results in the second column of the table.

   For each trial, use a random number generator on a graphing calculator to generate a random integer from 1 to 10. Continue generating random numbers until you get a number from 1 to 3 (representing a winning code). Conduct 10 trials.

2. In the third column of the table, record how many boxes were needed to find a winning code. Circle the trials that required 3 or more boxes.

3. Calculate the experimental probability of needing to buy at least 3 boxes of cereal in order to find a winning code.

   _____

Trial	Random Numbers	Boxes Bought
1		
2		
3		
4		
5		
6		
7		
8		
9		
10		

4. Combine your results with your classmates and calculate the experimental probability. Do you think this value is a better approximation of the theoretical probability than your result from only 10 trials?

   _____

   _____

5. At a local restaurant, about 50% of the customers order an appetizer. Design a simulation to estimate the probability that 4 of the next 10 customers order an appetizer. Explain your methods.

   _____

   _____

199

Name _____   Date _____

Unit 15 Review

Determine whether each event is impossible, unlikely, as likely as not, likely, or certain. Then tell whether the probability is 0, close to 0, $\frac{1}{2}$, close to 1, or 1.

1. randomly picking a pair of white socks from a drawer of a dozen white pairs and a dozen black pairs

_____

2. randomly picking a quarter from a pocket full of dimes and nickels

_____

3. rolling a total of 2 from a pair of number cubes that are each marked 1 to 6

_____

4. picking a number greater than 10 from a jar with papers that are marked 11 to 29

_____

Find each probability of where the spinner may land.

5. P(Juan) _____

6. P(Jim) _____

7. P(John) _____

8. P(Joel) _____

9. P(Jack or Joe) _____

10. P(name starting with J) _____

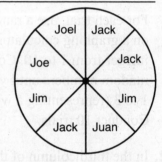

Solve.

11. Yvonne draws a marble from a basket. She records the color and puts the marble back into the basket. She does this several times. She records the frequency of each color in the table.

Color	Frequency
Red	7
Yellow	9
Green	14
Purple	10

What is the experimental probability of choosing a green marble?

_____

12. Ian packs for a trip. He has 4 shirts that are each a solid color. They are white, blue, red, and gray. He packs a tan pair of shorts and a blue pair of shorts. Use a tree diagram to solve. How many possible outcomes are there for wearing 1 shirt and 1 pair of shorts?

_____

13. Cameron's basket contains 5 red, 5 yellow, 10 green, and 15 purple marbles. What is the theoretical probability of randomly choosing a red marble?

_____

14. Malia tosses a coin. It lands on heads 52 out of 80 times. What is the experimental probability that the coin will land on heads on the next toss?

_____

200

Name _____   Date _____

Displaying Numerical Data

Tell whether each question is *statistical* or *non-statistical*.

1. What are the incomes of your neighbors? _____

2. How old are the homes on your street? _____

3. What is your favorite movie? _____

The dot plot shows the number of runs scored by a baseball team in games played during the month of April. Use the dot plot for Exercises 4–9.

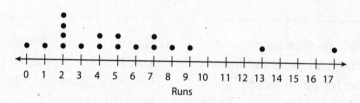

Runs Scored

4. What does each dot represent? _____

5. How many games did the team play in April? _____

6. Make a frequency table and histogram for the data.

Interval	Frequency
0–4	

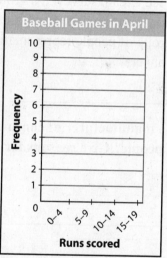

7. Give an example of information provided by the dot plot that is not provided by the histogram.

_____

_____

8. The numbers of runs scored by the same team in games played during May are: 3, 5, 2, 5, 4, 7, 1, 0, 6, 4, 8, 5, 3, 2, 4, 5, 9. Add these data to the dot plot. Describe the shape of the data. Are there any data values that do not fit the overall shape? If so, which ones?

_____

_____

201

Choosing Samples

Use geometric shapes, draw a number line, or list multiples to solve.

1. Surveyors called 200 parents (every 20th parent on the list) in the Tulane School District to collect data about their support of the school board. Is this a random sample? Is the sample large enough to claim that 15 out of 17 parents support the school board?

_____

_____

2. A commercial claims that 7 out of 8 teenagers prefer white bread. This claim is based on a random sample of 16 teenagers from the same school in Chicago. Is the sample large enough to represent all teenagers?

_____

_____

3. A local TV station polls its viewers on issues in the upcoming election. Viewers call in to vote *yes* or *no*. Are the results of these polls representative of all of the TV station's viewers?

_____

_____

4. Ray surveys 100 people in a room of 200 people and determines that 0.9 of them like to read. Can Ray claim that 90 out of 100 people in the room like to read?

_____

_____

5. Northpole Ice Cream surveyed a group of senior citizens about their favorite flavors of ice cream. Was this group of people representative of all ice cream buyers?

_____

_____

6. Globe Magazine surveyed 0.15 of its 940 subscribers at random. How many Globe subscribers were questioned?

_____

_____

If you were the manufacturer of consumer products, about what type of products would you survey each group of people? Give reasons for your answers.

7. children

_____

_____

8. athletes

_____

_____

9. business people

_____

_____

Populations and Samples

Determine whether each sample is a random sample or a biased sample. Explain your reasoning.

1. Roberto wants to know the favorite sport of adults in his hometown. He surveys 50 adults at a baseball game.

   _____

   _____

2. Paula wants to know the favorite type of music for students at her school. She surveys the first 60 people who enter the school doors in the morning.

   _____

   _____

A shipment to a warehouse consists of 3,500 MP3 players. The manager chooses a random sample of 50 MP3 players and finds that 3 are defective. How many MP3 players in the shipment are likely to be defective?

3. It is reasonable to make a prediction about the population because

   this sample is _____.

4. Determine what percentage of the sample is damaged.

   $\frac{3}{50} = \frac{\boxed{}}{100}$, so _____ % of the MP3s are damaged.

5. Find 6% of the population, which is 6% of _____.

   _____ × _____ = _____

6. You could also set up a proportion to make a prediction.

   $$\frac{\text{defective MP3s in sample}}{\text{size of sample}} = \frac{\text{defective MP3s in population}}{\text{size of population}}$$

   $\frac{3}{50} = \frac{\boxed{}}{3,500}$

   Based on the sample, you can predict that _____ MP3s in the shipment would be defective.

Generating Multiple Samples

A store gets a shipment of 1,000 light bulbs, 200 of which are defective upon arrival. The store's manager does not know this. She wants to predict the number of defective light bulbs by testing a sample of the shipment. The manager will want to use a random sample to represent the entire shipment. One way to simulate a random sample is to use a graphing calculator to generate random integers.

1. To simulate picking out random light bulbs between 1 and 1,000:
   • Press MATH, scroll right and select PRB. Then select 5: randInt(.
   • Enter the smallest value, comma, largest possible value.
   • Hit ENTER to generate random numbers.

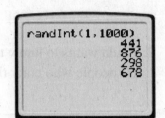

   In this specific case, you will enter **randInt** (_____ , _____)

   because there are _____ light bulbs in the shipment.

2. The numbers that are generated will each represent bulbs in the shipment.

   Let numbers 1 to 200 represent bulbs that are _____.

   Numbers 201 to 1,000 will represent bulbs that are _____.

3. Generate four numbers and record your results in the table below.

Random Sample of Light Bulbs		
Bulb	**Random Number Generated**	**Defective or Working?**
1		
2		
3		
4		

4. Based on this sample, how many defective light bulbs should the manager expect to find in the shipment?

   _____

5. You and your classmates have generated multiple samples. Compare your results to those of your classmates. How do your predictions compare?

   _____

   _____

Finding the Average

Find the average

1. 44; 49; 54

_____

2. 42; 90; 87

_____

3. 34; 440; 42; 44

_____

4. 100; 130; 133

_____

5. 310; 421; 424

_____

6. 345; 676; 432; 651

_____

7. 493; 383; 273; 163

_____

8. 848; 327; 838

_____

9. 1,240; 3,218; 390

_____

For the month of March, Mary kept a record of four types of books taken out of the library. Use the table for Exercises 10–13.

Week	Adventure	Travel	Biography	Children's Books
1	30	30	19	25
2	24	18	23	32
3	20	21	33	22
4	22	23	17	25

10. What was the average number of travel books taken out in these 4 weeks?

_____

11. Which type of book averaged more take-outs in the 4 weeks, adventure books or children's books?

_____

12. Which type of book averaged the most take-outs for this 4-week period?

_____

13. Which week averaged the most take-outs?

_____

Here is a way to estimate the average of four numbers mentally. Apply this method to Exercises 14–16.

Step 1 ⟶
Divide each number by 4.

Step 2 ⟶
Leave off the remainder.

Step 3
Add the quotients.

14. 31, 43, 23, 42

_____

15. 46, 57, 68, 79

_____

16. 50, 24, 100, 65

_____

205

Range, Mode, Median, and Mean

Find the range, mode, median, and mean.

1. 32, 37, 32, 32, 32

_____

2. $75, $38, $65, $38, $84

_____

3. 19, 22, 23, 24, 22

_____

4. 55, 59, 59, 60, 57

_____

5. 150, 150, 162

_____

6. $200, $300, $255, $255, $240

_____

7. Team A scored 16 points, 12 points, and 17 points in three games. Find the mean score.

_____

8. Sheila scored 90%, 92%, 85%, and 93% on four tests. After the fifth test, the mode of her scores was 92%. What was her score on the fifth test?

_____

9. Will a set of data always have a mode? Explain.

_____

_____

10. Can a set of data have more than one mode? Explain.

_____

_____

11. In 1810, the population of the United States was about 7 million people. In 1830, the population was about 13 million people. How can you use an average to predict the population in 1820? What is your prediction?

_____

_____

_____

Measures of Center

The **mode** of a data set is the data value that occurs most often. If all data values occur the same number of times, the data set is said to have no mode. Otherwise, a data set may have one or more modes.

Find the mode(s) of each data set.

1. 5, 3, 7, 3, 9, 1, 7, 11

2. 34, 66, 22, 55, 23, 77

3. 400, 340, 870, 400

_____   _____   _____

Several students' scores on a history test are shown. Use these data for Exercises 4 and 5.

4. Mean ≈ _____   Median = _____

History Test Scores
73 45 88 90 90 81 83

5. Which measure better describes the typical score for these students? Explain.

_____

The points scored by a basketball team in its last 6 games are shown. Use these data for Exercises 6 and 7.

6. Mean ≈ _____   Median = _____

Points Scored
73 77 85 84 35 115

7. Which measure better describes the typical number of points scored? Explain.

_____

For two weeks, the school librarian recorded the number of library books returned each morning. The data are shown in the dot plot. The librarian found the mean number of books returned each morning.

Books Returned

$$\frac{8 + 6 + 10 + 5 + 9 + 8 + 3 + 6}{8} = \frac{55}{8} = 6.9$$

8. Is this the correct mean of this data set? If not, explain and correct the error.

_____

_____

_____

Name _____ Date _____

Measures of Variability

The RBIs (Runs Batted In) for 15 players from the 2010 Seattle
Mariners are shown. Use this data set for Exercises 1–6.

Mariners' RBIs
15 51 35 25 58 33 64
43 33 29 14 13 11 4 10

1. Find the median. _____

2. Find the lower quartile. _____

3. Find the upper quartile. _____

4. Make a box plot for the data.

Mariners' RBIs

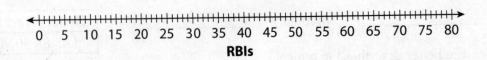

RBIs

5. Find the interquartile range (IQR). _____

6. Find the mean average deviation (MAD). Round to the nearest whole number.

_____

The RBIs for 15 players from the 2010 Baltimore Orioles
are shown. Use this data set for Exercises 7–12.

Orioles' RBIs
55 76 15 28 39 31 69
60 72 32 20 12 9 14 9

7. Find the median. _____

8. Find the lower quartile. _____

9. Find the upper quartile. _____

10. Make a box plot for the data.

Orioles' RBIs

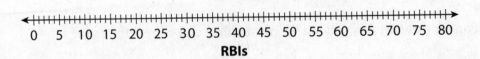

RBIs

11. Find the IQR. Round to the nearest whole number. _____

12. Find the MAD. Round to the nearest whole number. _____

Comparing Populations

Paula and Dean wanted to determine the average word length in two books. They took a random sample of 12 words each and counted the length of each word from each book.

Book 1 Word Length Count
3, 7, 5, 2, 4, 3, 1, 6, 4, 8, 2, 3

Book 2 Word Length Count
5, 4, 3, 6, 4, 5, 5, 2, 3, 4, 2, 5

1. Calculate the mean for Book 1. Show your work below.

2. Calculate the MAD for Book 1. _____

3. Calculate the mean for Book 2. Show your work below.

4. Calculate the MAD for Book 2. _____

5. What can you infer about each population?

_____

_____

Carol wants to know how many people live in each household in her town. She conducts two random surveys of 10 people each and asks how many people live in their home. Her results are listed below. Use the data for Exercises 6 and 7.

Sample A: 1, 6, 2, 4, 4, 3, 5, 5, 2, 8   Sample B: 3, 4, 5, 4, 3, 2, 4, 5, 4, 4

6. Find the mean and MAD for Sample A.   7. Find the mean and MAD for Sample B.

Mean: _____   Mean: _____

MAD: _____   MAD: _____

Scatter Plots and Association

A set of **bivariate data** involves two variables. Bivariate data are used to explore the relationship between two variables. You can graph bivariate data on a scatter plot. A **scatter plot** is a graph with points plotted to show the relationship between two sets of data.

The final question on a math test reads, "How many hours did you spend studying for this test?" The teacher records the number of hours each student studied and the grade the student received on the test.

Hours Spent Studying	Test Grade
0	75
0.5	80
1	80
1	85
1.5	85
1.5	95
2	90
3	100
4	90

1. Make a prediction about the relationship between the number of hours spent studying and test grades.

    _____

    _____

2. Make a scatter plot. Graph hours spent studying as the independent variable and test grade as the dependent variable.

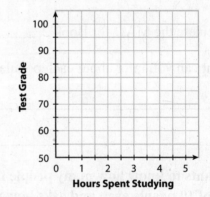

3. What trend do you see in the data?

    _____

    _____

4. Do you think that studying for 10 hours would greatly increase a student's grade?

    _____

    _____

5. Why might a student who studied fewer hours make a higher score?

    _____

    _____

Finding the Equation of a Trend Line

The scatter plot shows the relationship between the number
of chapters and the total number of pages for several books.
Draw a trend line, write an equation for the trend line, and
describe the meanings of the slope and *y*-intercept.

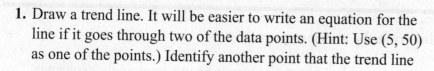

1. Draw a trend line. It will be easier to write an equation for the
   line if it goes through two of the data points. (Hint: Use (5, 50)
   as one of the points.) Identify another point that the trend line

   goes through: (_____, _____).

2. What type(s) of association does the
   scatter plot show?

   _____

3. Do you expect the slope of the line to be
   positive or negative?

   _____

4. Find the slope of the trend line.

   $$m = \dfrac{\boxed{} - 50}{\boxed{} - 5} = \dfrac{\boxed{}}{\boxed{}} = \boxed{}$$

5. Use the equation $y = mx + b$, the slope, and the point (5, 50). Substitute values
   for *y*, *m*, and *x* into the equation and solve for *b*.

   $y = mx + b$

   $\boxed{} = \boxed{} \cdot \boxed{} + b$ *Substitute for y, m, and b.*

   $\boxed{} = \boxed{} + b$ *Simplify on the right side.*

   $\dfrac{-\boxed{} \quad -\boxed{}}{\boxed{} =\qquad b}$ *Subtract the number that is added to b from both sides.*

   Use your slope and *y*-intercept values to write an equation in slope-intercept form.

   $y = \boxed{}x + \boxed{}$

6. What is the meaning of the slope in this situation?

   _____

7. What is the meaning of the *y*-intercept in this situation?

   _____

Making Predictions

When you use a trend line or its equation to predict a value between data points that you already know, you **interpolate** the predicted value. When you make a prediction that is outside the data that you know, you **extrapolate** the predicted value.

Refer to the scatter plot and trend line from the previous page.

1. Use the equation of the trend line to predict how many pages would be in a book with 26 chapters. Is this prediction an example of interpolation or extrapolation?

_____

$y =$ _____   *Write the equation for your trend line.*

$y =$ _____   *Substitute the number of chapters for x.*

$y =$ _____   *Simplify.*

I predict that a book with 26 chapters would have _____ pages.

2. Use the equation of the trend line to predict how many pages would be in a book with 14 chapters. Is this prediction an example of interpolation or extrapolation?

_____

$y =$ _____   *Write the equation for your trend line.*

$y =$ _____   *Substitute the number of chapters for x.*

$y =$ _____   *Simplify.*

I predict that a book with 14 chapters would have _____ pages.

3. How well do your new points fit the original data?

_____

_____

4. Do you think that extrapolation or interpolation is more accurate? Explain.

_____

_____

_____

_____

Two-Way Tables

One hundred teens were polled about whether they are required to do chores and whether they have a curfew. Is there an association between having a curfew and having to do chores?

	Curfew	No Curfew	TOTAL
Chores	16	4	20
No Chores	16	64	80
TOTAL	32	68	100

1. Find the relative frequency of having to do chores.

   Total who have to do chores →
   Total number of teens polled → $\dfrac{\boxed{}}{100} = \boxed{} = \boxed{}$ %

2. Find the relative frequency of having to do chores among those who have a curfew.

   Number with a curfew who have to do chores →
   Total number with a curfew → $\dfrac{\boxed{}}{32} = \boxed{} = \boxed{}$ %

3. Compare the relative frequencies. Students who have a curfew are less likely/more likely to have to do chores than the general population.

   Is there an association between having a curfew and having to do chores? Explain.

   _____

   _____

   _____

4. Compare the relative frequency of having a curfew and having chores to the relative frequency of not having a curfew and having chores. Does this comparison help you draw a conclusion about whether there is an association between having a curfew and having chores? Explain.

   _____

   _____

   _____

   _____

Name _____   Date _____

Unit 16 Review

The weights of Ann's chickens are shown.
Use the data in the table to answer Exercises 1–6.

Chickens' Weights (lb)											
14	6	5	7	7	5	6	7	6	6	4	5

1. How many chickens does Ann have?

   _____

2. What unit of measurement is used?

   _____

3. What is the mean weight of the chickens?

   _____

4. What is the median weight of the chickens?

   _____

5. Make a dot plot for the weights.

   Ann's Chickens

   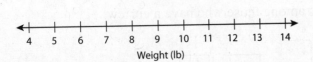

6. Make a histogram for the weights.

   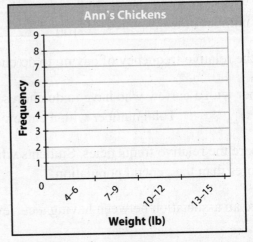

Solve.

7. Marty surveys 20 grocery store customers to find out what type of bread they usually buy. How can she make her random sample more accurately reflect the population it represents?

   _____

8. A department store receives a shipment of 1,000 glasses. Out of a random sample of 10 glasses, 2 are broken. How many glasses would you expect to be broken in the entire shipment?

   _____

Interpret the data in the scatter plots.

9. Does the scatter plot show a positive association, negative association, or no association?

   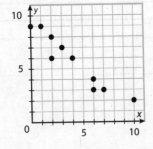

10. The scatter plot shows the price of different numbers of ounces of bulk grains. Is the trend line a good fit for the data? Why?

    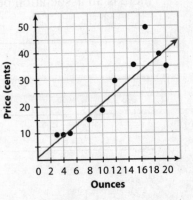

    _____

_____

Converting Measurements

Convert each measurement. Round to the nearest hundredth.

1. A ruler is 12 inches long. What is the length of this ruler in centimeters?

   _____ centimeters

2. A bottle contains 4 fluid ounces of medicine. About how many milliliters of medicine are in the bottle?

   _____ milliliters

3. Miguel rode 19 miles on his bicycle. About how many kilometers did he ride?

   _____ kilometers

4. A gas can contains 2.5 gallons of gas. About how many liters of gas are in the gas can?

   _____ liters

5. A kitten weighs 4 pounds. About how many kilograms does the kitten weigh?

   _____ kilograms

Convert each measurement. Round to the nearest hundredth.

6. 20 yards ≈ _____ meters

7. 12 ounces ≈ _____ grams

8. 5 quarts ≈ _____ liters

9. 30 inches ≈ _____ centimeters

10. 42 feet ≈ _____ meters

11. 7 gallons ≈ _____ liters

12. 5 miles ≈ _____ kilometers

13. 400 meters ≈ _____ yards

14. 165 centimeters ≈ _____ inches

15. 137.25 meters ≈ _____ feet

16. 10 liters ≈ _____ gallons

17. 10,000 kilometers ≈ _____ miles

18. A countertop is 16 feet long and 3 feet wide.

   a. What is the area of the countertop in square meters? _____ square meters

   b. Tile costs $28 per square meter. How much will it cost to cover the countertop with new tile?

   $ _____

Name _____   Date _____

Problem-Solving Strategy: Work Backwards

Work backwards to solve each problem.

1. Rita had $14.25 left after a day at the county fair. She had spent $12.75 for her ticket. Then she had bought lunch for $6.50 and souvenirs for $15.99. How much money had Rita brought to the fair?

2. Deanne is writing invitations for her party. She will have 70 guests. When she writes twice as many as she has already written, she'll have only 10 more invitations to write. How many has she written so far?

3. This week, Gretchen earned $20.50 mowing lawns and she spent $4.00 on lunch. She has $28.59 left. How much did Gretchen have at the beginning of the week?

4. Mario is driving in the Indianapolis 500-mile race. When he has driven twice as far as he's gone already, he'll be 50 miles from the finish line. How far has he driven?

5. Mei spends 50 minutes getting ready for work each day. After leaving the house, she walks 10 minutes to a diner, where she eats breakfast for 25 minutes. Then she walks 5 minutes to the bus stop for the 15-minute ride to work. What time must Mei wake up to reach her office by 9 A.M.?

6. From 1990 to 1997, the price of a monthly commuter train ticket doubled. In 1998 the price dropped $4.00, and in 1999 it dropped $6.00 more. Then in 2000 it doubled again to $32.00. How much did a monthly train ticket cost in 1990?

Name _____ Date _____

Problem-Solving Applications: Decimals

Solve.

1. Paulo is paid $14.10 per hour and 1.5 times that rate for every hour worked more than 40 hours in a week. How much will he earn for working 42 hours in a week?

   _____

2. Mary wanted to find the length of her average stride. She walked 100 strides and found that the distance she covered was 92 meters. What was the length of her average stride?

   _____

3. Dan bought three books for $29.85. Each book was the same price. About how much did each book cost?

   _____

4. Sam paid $41.97 for 3 CDs. Latoya paid $51.00 for 4 CDs. Who paid more per CD? How much more?

   _____

5. Kim's family drove to Montréal yesterday. The trip took 8.5 hours, and their car averaged 75.4 kilometers per hour. How far did Kim's family drive to get to Montréal?

   _____

6. Ms. Soto planted a tree that was 1.2 meters tall. She was told that it would grow at the rate of 0.15 meter per year. At that rate, what will be the tree's height after 12 years?

   _____

7. Tavon bought 500 bricks for a patio project. If each brick weighs 2.2 pounds, what is the total weight of all the bricks?

   _____

8. Tavon paid $85.00 for the 500 bricks. What was the cost per brick?

   _____

Problem-Solving Applications: Expressions and Equations

Fill in the numbered circles to show the answers.

1. Evaluate the following expression when $x = 5$ and $y = 10$.

$$\frac{2(x + 4y)}{5}$$

2. The distance from Theron's house to the beach can be written as 8^3 miles. Indicate the distance from Theron's house to the beach in standard form.

3. The mountain-hiking team plans to descend 1,200 feet per day from their current elevation of 7,500 feet. What will their elevation be after 6 days of descent?

4. What is the value of the following expression: $(2^6)^2 \div 2^5$?

5. Juan has a balance of $285 in his checking account. What will his new balance be after he withdraws $40 and pays a utility bill of $72 from his checking account?

6. Evaluate the following expression when $s = 230$.

$$\frac{1}{2}s + 20$$

7. The number of free throws James made during his high school career can be written as 3^5. Indicate the number of free throws James made in standard form.

8. Attendance at the first showing of a movie was 644 people. Attendance at the second showing was 87 fewer people. How many attended the second showing?

Problem-Solving Applications: Functions, Graphs, and Inequalities

Solve.

1. The temperature on the first day of winter was 12 °C. Wanda represented this fact on a coordinate plane with the ordered pair (1, 12). On the ninth day of winter, the temperature was 8 °C, which Wanda represented with (9, 8). What is the slope of the line through these two points?

2. There are fewer than 30 seats on Jill's bus. Shanell's bus has 5 more seats than Jill's bus has. Write an inequality that shows the possible number of seats on Shanell's bus.

3. Tonya's age plus two times Stephen's age is equal to 24. Let Tonya's age be x and let Stephen's age be y. Find Tonya's age if Stephen is 10 years old.

4. The least number of points the Hawks scored during the first football game of the season was 7. The Tigers scored twice as many points as the Hawks did. Write an inequality to show the possible points scored by the Tigers.

5. Leslie has a dozen eggs for baking. If she uses 3 eggs per day, what is the maximum number of days she can bake before buying more eggs?

6. Jacob planted a tree and kept track of its growth on a coordinate plane. The growth rate during April was given by the slope of the line from (2, 6) to (3, 10). The rate for May was given by the slope from (3, 10) to (4, 13). Which month had the higher rate of growth?

7. The bonuses for employees of the Fresh-Baked Pie Company are given by the equation $-x + 4y = 8$. Which of the following points would not lie on the graph of this equation? (4, 3), (8, 4), (10, 5)

8. The Jackson family income is $800 per week. If their regular expenses are $510 per week, what is the maximum amount they can save each week?

Problem-Solving Strategy: Use a Formula

Solve using a formula.

1. The area of a trapezoid is 45 square centimeters. The bases of the trapezoid are 10 centimeters and 8 centimeters. What is the height of the trapezoid?

2. The height of a cylinder is 3 feet. The volume of the cylinder is 2.355 cubic feet. What is the diameter of the cylinder?

3. The volume of a rectangular prism is 84 cubic inches. The height of the prism is 3 inches. The length is 7 inches. What is the width of the prism?

4. The area of a triangle is 12 square inches. The height of the triangle is 4 inches. What is the base of the triangle?

5. One triangular face of a pyramid has a base of 20 meters and a height of 30 meters. What is the area of the triangular face?

6. A triangular stained-glass window has a base of 36 inches and a height of 48 inches. What is the area of the window?

7. A rectangular wastebasket has a length of 20 inches, a width of 10 inches, and a height of 24 inches. What is the volume of the wastebasket?

8. A rectangular mailbox has a length of 18 inches, a width of 20 inches, and a height of 5 inches. What is the volume of the box?

Name _____ Date _____

Problem-Solving Applications: Geometry

Solve.

1. What is the length of a side of an equilateral triangle whose perimeter is 375 feet?

   _____

2. What is the radius of a circle whose area is 113.04 meters? (Hint: Use 3.14 for π.)

   _____

3. The volume of a rectangular shed is 700 cubic yards. If the shed's length is 7 yards and the width is 10 yards, what is the height?

   _____

4. The area of a triangle is 88 square feet. The height is 8 feet. What is the base of the triangle?

   _____

5. The volume of a cylinder that is 25 inches high is 2,826 cubic inches. What is the diameter of the cylinder?

   _____

6. What is the radius of a circle with a circumference of 78.5 centimeters?

   _____

7. A professional football field measures $53\frac{1}{3}$ yards wide. Its area is 6,400 square yards. What is the length of a professional football field?

   _____

8. The volume of a rectangular prism is 160 cubic inches. The length and width of the rectangular prism are 5 inches and 2 inches. What is the height of this rectangular prism?

   _____

Problem-Solving Strategy: Write an Equation

Write an equation for the problem. Then solve.

1. Eric has saved $8,587.46 to buy a used car. The car he wants costs $8,675. How much more money does he need?

   _____

2. A custom-made pair of shoes costs $225. This is 3 times the cost of a regular pair of shoes. What is the cost of a regular pair of shoes?

3. A truck can carry 7 tons of logs. Suppose that a truck is carrying a load of 4.7 tons. How much more could it haul?

   _____

4. A newspaper began publication in 1897 and was printed daily for 76 years. In what year did the newspaper stop publication?

5. Vera used 2.4 gallons of paint to paint her living room. This is 4 times the amount she used for her kitchen. How much paint was used for the kitchen?

   _____

6. The cost of a dinner is divided equally among 12 diners. Each diner pays $12.50 for his or her portion. What was the cost of the dinner?

Choose a strategy and solve.

┌─────────────────────────────────────┐
│ • Write an Equation • Guess and Check │
│   • Find a Pattern • Use Estimation   │
└─────────────────────────────────────┘

7. Roy has a total of 10 quarters and dimes. The value of the coins is $2.05. He has more quarters than dimes. How many of each coin does he have?

8. Dot wants to buy meat for $7.57, milk for $2.69, cereal for $4.08, and juice for $2.99. She has $16.00. Does she have enough money for all the items?

   _____

9. Harvey bought a used car. He installed a $212 stereo system and 4 new tires valued at $285. His car is now worth $10,742. How much did he pay for the car?

   _____

10. Marsha sold 2 cameras in January, 4 in February, 7 in March, and 11 in April. If the number sold increases at the same rate, how many cameras will she sell in December?

   _____

Problem-Solving Applications:
Expressions, Equations, and Inequalities

1. Mary got 8 out of 10 questions right on her test. With what percentage increase of correct answers could her test score have been at least a 90?

_____

2. Joe's balance in his checking account is $132. At the end of the month, it is 15.3% higher. What is his balance at the end of the month?

_____

3. Diane is centering a $3\frac{1}{2}$-inch-wide picture on a 12-inch-wide scrapbook page. How far from the side edges should she put the picture?

_____

4. The quarterback was sacked x yards from his own goal as the first quarter ended. He walked to the other end of the field and lined up on the other x yard line. He walked $41\frac{3}{4}$ yards between the two yard lines. How far from his end zone was he sacked? Hint: A football field is 100 yards long.

_____

5. Last year, Mr. Jones made $30,000. His boss just informed him that he will be receiving an 11.2% raise for this year. How much will he make this year?

_____

6. In March, a share of stock was worth $55. Six months later the value of the stock decreased by 7.2%. Find the final value of the stock.

_____

7. There were 348 students in the school last year. The school expects a 7.25% increase in enrollment this year. How many students do they expect to be in the school this year?

_____

8. A company has 350 workers. The president of the company wants to know what percent increase in employment would be necessary for the number of workers to be greater than 375.

_____

9. A town has a population of 53,000. The mayor wants to know what percent increase would be necessary for the town's population to be greater than 55,000. Write and solve an inequality that represents the situation. Round your answer to the nearest thousandth.

_____

10. Suppose the population of the town in Exercise 9 increases to more than 60,000. This would reflect a percent increase greater than what percent? Round your answer to the nearest thousandth.

_____

Name _____ Date _____

Unit 17 Review

Use the following units of conversion to solve.

> 1 inch = 2.54 centimeters
> 1 pound ≈ 0.454 kilogram

1. The length of a poster is 16 inches. What is the length of this poster in centimeters?

2. Paula's dog, Toby, weighs 95 pounds. What is the dog's weight in kilograms?

Use problem-solving strategies to solve.

> **STRATEGIES**
> • Use a Formula • Guess and Check • Write an Equation
> • Choose an Operation • Use Estimation • Work Backwards

3. Hannah bought 4 books for $38.89. Each book was the same price. About how much did each book cost?

4. David is taking a road trip that is 400 miles total. When he has driven twice as far as he's gone already, he'll be 80 miles from the end. How far has he driven?

5. The distance from Karla's house to her state capitol building can be written as $142 + 8$ miles. What is the distance?

6. There are fewer than 40 seats on one carnival ride. Another carnival ride has 12 more seats. Write an inequality that shows the possible number of seats on the second ride.

7. Niko's age plus 3 times Adam's age is equal to 54. Find Niko's age if Adam is 13 years old.

8. The area of a triangle is 93 square feet. The height is 6 feet. How long is the base of the triangle?

224

© Houghton Mifflin Harcourt Publishing Company

Unit 17
Core Skills Math Review

Final Review

Solve.

1. $\frac{5}{6} \times 12 =$ _____

2. $1\frac{3}{5} \times 10 =$ _____

3. $1\frac{2}{3} \times 2\frac{1}{4} =$ _____

4. $\frac{3}{5} \div \frac{2}{5} =$ _____

5. $3\frac{3}{10} \div \frac{2}{5} =$ _____

6. $2\frac{1}{4} \div 1\frac{1}{2} =$ _____

Write each decimal as a fraction or mixed number.

7. $0.3 =$ _____

8. $1.17 =$ _____

9. $0.009 =$ _____

10. $0.01 =$ _____

Write each fraction as a decimal.

11. $\frac{8}{10} =$ _____

12. $\frac{23}{100} =$ _____

13. $\frac{5}{100} =$ _____

14. $\frac{8}{1000} =$ _____

Find each answer. Write zeros as needed.

15.
$$\begin{array}{r} 7.38 \\ + 0.19 \\ \hline \end{array}$$

16.
$$\begin{array}{r} 48.02 \\ + 21.086 \\ \hline \end{array}$$

17.
$$\begin{array}{r} 8.95 \\ - 1.68 \\ \hline \end{array}$$

18.
$$\begin{array}{r} 15.3 \\ - 7.29 \\ \hline \end{array}$$

19.
$$\begin{array}{r} 9.06 \\ \times 13 \\ \hline \end{array}$$

20.
$$\begin{array}{r} 7.69 \\ \times 0.13 \\ \hline \end{array}$$

21. $92\overline{)22.77}$

22. $1.5\overline{)10.05}$

Write each percent as a decimal and as a fraction. Simplify.

23. $35\% =$ _____ $=$ _____

24. $8\% =$ _____ $=$ _____

Find each number.

25. 25% of 80 _____

26. What percent of 40 is 8? _____

27. 10% of what number is 9? _____

28. 72% of 50 _____

Find the simple interest.

29. \$350 at $4\frac{1}{2}\%$ for 1 year

30. \$600 at 7.1% for 2 years

_____

_____

Final Review

Evaluate each expression if $x = 2$, $y = -3$, and $z = 5$.

31. $12 \div 2y =$ _____   **32.** $4x - y =$ _____   **33.** $-3z^2 =$ _____   **34.** $\dfrac{x^2 + 16}{z} =$ _____

Find the slope of each line that passes through the given points.

35. (2,3), (4,5) _____   **36.** (-9,1), (2,-8) _____   **37.** (6,0), (7,-6) _____

Solve each equation using the given value of x or y. Write the ordered pair that makes the equation true.

38. $3x + 2y = 9$ when $x = -3$ **39.** $4x - y = 3$ when $y = 1$ **40.** $-2x + 3y = 7$ when $x = 4$

_____   _____   _____

Solve.

41. $x - 15 = 7$ **42.** $6x + 9 = 29 + 2x$ **43.** $7x = -42$ **44.** $6x + 1 = 61$

_____   _____   _____   _____

45. $3x + 5x = 72$ **46.** $10x - 4x = 36$ **47.** $x + 5 = 19$ **48.** $\dfrac{12}{5} = \dfrac{x}{15}$

_____   _____   _____   _____

49. $\dfrac{5}{x} = \dfrac{40}{64}$ **50.** $\dfrac{x}{8} = \dfrac{12}{16}$ **51.** $5x - 1 = 24$ **52.** $6 = 2x - 20$

_____   _____   _____   _____

Write a fraction for each ratio. Simplify.

53. the ratio of days in a week to months in a year

54. the ratio of 3 teachers to 24 students

Ratio: _____   Ratio: _____

Solve.

55. $3 + 10x \geq 33$ **56.** $17 < 2 + x$ **57.** $10x > 5x + 15$ **58.** $-2x - 50 \leq 30$

_____   _____

59. A right triangle with a hypotenuse 17 centimeters long has a side 15 centimeters long. What is the length of the third side?

60. A triangle has a base of 9 meters and a height of 12 meters. What is the area?

_____   _____

Final Review

Find the LCM of each pair of numbers.

61. 7, 10

62. 4, 12

63. 6, 9

64. 9, 15

_____   _____   _____   _____

Evaluate each expression.

65. $10^3 \times 10^2 =$

66. $(52)^2 + (23)^2 =$

67. $7^2 - 2^4 =$

68. $6^2 \times 4^0 =$

_____   _____   _____   _____

Change each number to scientific notation or standard form.

69. $350,000,000 =$

70. $128,400 =$

71. $7.5 \times 10^3 =$

72. $0.12 \times 10^6 =$

_____   _____   _____   _____

Simplify each expression.

73. $\sqrt{100} - \sqrt{25} =$

74. $\sqrt{121} + \sqrt{16} =$

75. $\sqrt{144} \div 2 =$

76. $\sqrt{81} \times 5 =$

_____   _____   _____   _____

77. Write an equation for the line with the given slope and y-intercept.

slope 6; y-intercept 2

78. Graph the equation in Exercise 77.

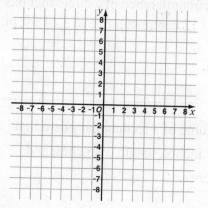

_____

Solve.

79. A tree cast a 20-foot shadow at the same time a fence post 6 feet high cast a 4-foot shadow. How tall is the tree?

_____

80. Jocelyn is thinking of a number. Three times that number equals 5 more than 22. What is the number?

_____

Final Review

Add or subtract each expression.

81. $(2x + 3) + (5x - 3)$

82. $(x + 8) - (3x + 1)$

83. $(9x - 1) - (4x - 2)$

_____   _____   _____

Solve each system algebraically.

84. $5x + 4y = 12$
$x + 2y = -2$

85. $x - 5y = 10$
$-3x + 3y = 6$

86. $4x + y = 16$
$2x - 4y = 8$

_____   _____   _____

Solve.

87. Angles *ABC* and *DBE* are vertical angles. If $\angle ABC$ measures 60°, what is the measure of $\angle DBE$?

88. Angles *FGH* and *HGI* are complementary angles. If $\angle FGH$ measures 35°, what is the measure of $\angle HGI$?

_____   _____

89. What is the circumference of a circle that has a diameter of 12 centimeters? Use 3.14 for pi.

90. What is the area of a circle that has a radius of 11 feet? Use 3.14 for pi.

_____   _____

91. Find the volume of a rectangular prism that has height 2 inches, length $3\frac{1}{4}$ inches, and width $4\frac{1}{2}$ inches.

92. The radius of a cylinder is 1.4 meters, and the height is 16 meters. What is the volume of the cylinder? Use 3.14 for pi. Round to the nearest tenth.

_____   _____

93. A box contains 5 purple shirts, 14 white shirts, 15 blue shirts, and 6 gray shirts. What is the theoretical probability of randomly choosing a purple shirt?

94. Sanjaya tosses a coin. It lands on heads 54 out of 90 times. What is the experimental probability that the coin will land on heads on the next toss?

_____   _____

Answer Key

Page 1

1. 79 R5
2. 62
3. 137 R7
4. 45 R14
5. 15
6. 12
7. 2
8. 32
9. -2
10. -11
11. 19
12. -78
13. 4
14. 18
15. 100
16. 19
17. $\frac{3}{10}$
18. $4\frac{13}{20}$
19. $3\frac{3}{50}$
20. $\frac{1}{8}$
21. 6.7
22. 2.55
23. 0.16
24. 0.005
25. 4.54
26. 76.67
27. 0.06006
28. 40.1
29. $4\frac{4}{7}$
30. $1\frac{2}{3}$
31. $\frac{7}{10}$
32. $28\frac{4}{5}$
33. 40
34. 85

Page 2

35. $13.13
36. $36.80
37. 3
38. 2
39. 4
40. 601
41. $50x$
42. $z - 17$
43. -11
44. 32
45. -24
46. 7
47. $x = 29$
48. $x = 24$
49. $x = 5$
50. $x = 9$
51. $x = 12$
52. $x = 6$
53. $x = 13$
54. $x = 5$
55. 36
56. -8
57. 7
58. 81
59. 3,000
60. 12,000
61. 607,000
62. 890
63. (2, 3) and (-4, -3)
64. $301.50
65. $8.75

Page 3

66. (2, -4)
67. $(-1, -3\frac{1}{3})$
68. (3, 4)
69.–70.

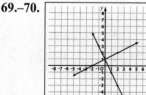

71. -1
72. $\frac{7}{2}$
73. $\frac{9}{7}$
74. $x > -17$
75. $x \le 32$
76. $x \ge -15$
77. $x < -8$
78. 3
79. 11
80. $3.45

Page 4

81. 3 gal 3 qt
82. 0.04 km
83. 2 lb
84. 3 ft 4 in.
85. 56,000 g
86. 0.334 L
87. $\frac{1}{4}$
88. $\frac{7}{12}$
89. $x = 35$
90. $x = 30$
91. $x = 2$
92. 12 feet
93. 30 feet
94. $b = 4$
95. $c = 10$
96. $a = 5$
97. 168 square inches
98. 108 square inches

Page 5

99. $10x + 2$
100. $4x + 9$
101. $5x - 3$
102. $(-3, \frac{1}{4})$
103. (-8, -5)
104. (7, 4)
105.

106.

107. 43.96 cm
108. 254.34 ft²
109. $52\frac{1}{2}$ in³
110. 79.6 cubic cm
111. $\frac{6}{28}$ or $\frac{3}{14}$
112. $\frac{33}{60}$ or $\frac{11}{20}$

Page 6

1. 314
2. 1,294 R16
3. 971
4. 1,075 R45
5. 845 R37
6. 504 R6
7. 1,733 R25
8. 183 R33

Page 7

1. 233 R107
2. 40 R207
3. 14 R13
4. 9 R132
5. 73 R44
6. 82 R872
7. 860
8. 501 R210
9. 97 R12

Page 8

1. 288
2. 957
3. 15,552
4. 203,200
5. 888
6. 4,368
7. 44,620
8. 618,372
9. 358,812
10. 2,980,055
11. 136,752
12. 2,270,436
13. 13 R15
14. 939 R1
15. 640 R3
16. 5,219
17. 4
18. 213 R25
19. 73 R10
20. 30 R134
21. 847
22. 483 R8
23. 608 R20
24. 126

Page 9

1. 1, 2, 4, 8, 16
2. 1, 3, 13, 39
3. 1, 2, 5, 10, 25, 50
4. 8
5. 5
6. 3
7. 12
8. 1
9. 4
10. 14
11. 9
12. 15
13. 11
14. 8
15. 9
16. 21
17. 18
18. $15 \times (5 + 6)$
19. $9 \times (4 + 5)$
20. $8 \times (7 + 8)$
21. $2 \times (24 + 7)$

Page 10

1. 18: 1, 2, 3, 6, 9, 18; 27: 1, 3, 9, 27; GCF: 9
2. 28: 1, 2, 4, 7, 14, 28; 35: 1, 5, 7, 35; GCF: 7
3. 12: 1, 2, 3, 4, 6, 12; 15: 1, 3, 5, 15; GCF: 3
4. 3×5; 5×7; 5
5. $2 \times 2 \times 2 \times 3$; $2 \times 2 \times 3 \times 3$; 12
6. 3×7; $3 \times 3 \times 5$; 3
7. yes, no, yes
8. 18 groups; 2 maple trees and 3 dogwood trees
9. 5
10. 14
11. 50
12. 16
9–12. Pattern: The numbers are factors of the last number in the set.

Page 11

1–4. Answers will vary. Possible answers are given.

229

1. 4, 8, 12
2. 5, 10, 15
3. 12, 24
4. 18, 36
5. 12
6. 40
7. 108 beads
8. 72 beads
9. 24 beads
10. 12

Page 12

1. 36
2. 72
3. The LCM is the greater of the two numbers. Possible example: The LCM of 4 and 8 is 8.
4. The LCM is the product of the two numbers. Possible example: The LCM of 4 and 9 is 36.
5. 18
6. 63
7. 56
8. 48
9. 60
10. 30
11. 60
12. 15
13. 40
14. 120

Page 13

1. 42 days
2. 3 inches
3. 12 vases
4. 40 minutes
5. 36 Venus' flytraps
6. 42 inches
7. $2^3 \times 3$
8. 2^5
9. 2×29

Page 14

1. 6
2. 9
3. 8
4. 13
5. 18
6. 3
7. 10
8. 15
9. 7
10. 0
11. 17
12. 22
13. 12
14. 19
15. 11
16. 26
17. 30, -30
18. 14, -14
19. 32, -32
20. 29, -29
21. 21, -21
22. 23, -23
23. 42, -42
24. 99, -99

Page 15

1. The number line will show points marked at -7, -4, -2, 4, 5, and 7.
2. 7
3. 5
4. 7
5. 2
6. 4
7. 4
8. -7 and 7; 4 and -4; They are opposites.
9. yes; |0| = 0 because the distance between 0 and 0 is 0.
10. positive; negative
11. no; Explanations will vary.

Page 16

1. The number line will show points C, B, E, A, and D marked at -8.5, -5, -3, 5, and 8.
2. 0
3. Juniper Trail; Its elevation is closest to 0 on the number line.
4. below
5. Little Butte (above) and Cradle Creek (below)
6. The number line will show points I, H, F, K, J, and G marked at -10, -6, -4, 6, 7, and 9.

Page 17

1. -4
2. 7
3. 21
4. -45
5. 19
6. -33
7. 66
8. 0
9. +33
10. -8
11. +150
12. -10
13. +6
14. +88
15. +3,500
16. -50
17. +7
18. -4
19. -30
20. -9

Page 18

1. <
2. <
3. >
4. >
5. =
6. <
7. >
8. <
9. >
10. <
11. <
12. >
13. =
14. >
15. =
16. >
17. >
18. <
19. >
20. =
21. >
22. <
23. <
24. >
25. -6, 0, 7
26. -9, -5, 7
27. -1, 1, 11
28. -21, 12, 27
29. -2, 3, 8
30. -13, -3, 0
31. -11, 4, 5
32. -20, -16, 19

Page 19

1. 2
2. -10
3. 2
4. -4
5. -12
6. 7
7. -7
8. -18
9. -3
10. -8
11. 9
12. 13
13. 5 + 3 = 8
14. -7 + -1 = -8
15. -9 + 9 = 0
16. 4 + -8 = -4
17. -8 + 1 = -7
18. -6 + 2 = -4
19. -12 + 7 = -5
20. -9 + -10 = -19

Page 20

1. -9
2. 4
3. 12
4. -42
5. 27
6. -12
7. -20
8. 18
9. 24
10. -24
11. 30
12. -10
13. 0
14. 20
15. 21
16. 32
17. -6
18. -4
19. 3
20. -6
21. 4
22. -2
23. 8
24. -9
25. 6
26. -7
27. 0
28. -1
29. 7
30. 4
31. 9
32. -4

Page 21

1. 30
2. 7
3. -20
4. 8
5. 18
6. 2
7. 21
8. -20
9. 35
10. -12
11. 30
12. 4
13. 8
14. 20
15. 28
16. 30
17. 10
18. 2
19. -50
20. 11
21. 3
22. 2
23. -8
24. -13

Page 22

1. 232 R31
2. 117 R8
3. 230 R3
4. 389
5. 14
6. 4
7. 6
8. 27
9. 40
10. 30
11. 52
12. 9
13. 51
14. 0
15. 16
16. 43
17. -5
18. 10
19. 3
20. 8
21. 15
22. 28
23. 33
24. 14
25. -8, -4, 4
26. -9, 6, 7

Page 23

1. $\frac{2}{5}$
2. $\frac{3}{5}$
3. $\frac{2}{25}$
4. $\frac{1}{500}$
5. $\frac{21}{100}$
6. $\frac{83}{1000}$
7. $\frac{901}{1000}$
8. $\frac{9}{500}$
9. $4\frac{1}{2}$

Answer Key
Core Skills Math Review

10. $1\frac{31}{50}$

11. $10\frac{1}{10}$

12. $1\frac{11}{40}$

13. $9\frac{7}{100}$

14. $38\frac{6}{25}$

15. $5\frac{23}{50}$

16. $13\frac{4}{5}$

17. 0.1

18. 0.2

19. 0.5

20. 0.7

21. 0.06

22. 0.8

23. 0.052

24. 0.416

25. 5.6

26. 3.1

27. 7.6

28. 0.65

29. 1.03

30. 5.09

31. 1.643

32. 2.051

Page 24

1. 0.125

2. 0.4

3. 0.15

4. 0.8

5. 0.34

6. 0.44

7. 0.035

8. 0.32

9. 0.375

10. 6.5

11. 2.15

12. 7.4

13. 6.25

14. 1.38

15. 1.56

16. 1.45

17. 2.84

18. 6.12

19. 13.02

20. 19.5

21. 4.875

Page 25

1. $5.41

2. $0.59

3. $16.86

4. $42.24

5. 0.306

6. 29.228

7. 315.3

8. 54.25

9. $11.43

10. 37.525

11. 1.603

12. 16.737

13. 72.204

14. 23.294

15. $535.00

16. 99.068

Page 26

1. 9.52

2. 10.345

3. 22.536

4. 20.401

5. 38.662

6. 82.233

7. 88.183

8. 44.739

9. $23.63

10. 45.475

11. 1.815

12. 22.771

13. 5.755

14. 2.849

15. 8.87

16. 7.901

17. 13.1

18. $24.89

19. 58.2

20. 54.073

Page 27

1. 3.136

2. 1.16

3. 5.599

4. $23.77

5. 3.915

6. 4.75

7. 2.04

8. 1.897

9. 4.242

10. 17.20

11. 0.808

12. $4.14

13. 3.834

14. 1.112

15. 22.36

16. 10.63

Page 28

1. 5.122

2. 2.158

3. 2.014

4. 0.16

5. $6.96

6. $24.50

7. $79.78

8. $9,032.30

9. 1.625

10. 1.226

11. 1.089

12. 7.45

13. 3.834

14. 79.78

15. 4.505

16. 1.112

17. 4.015

18. 2.04

19. 22.26

20. 7.45

21. 4.75

22. 1.089

23. 0.006

24. 0.12

25. 0.020

26. 0.04

27. 0.9

28. 0.040

29. 3.3

30. 6.008

Page 29

1. 0.9

2. 0.08

3. 3.55

4. 12.37

5. 10.24

6. 0.19

7. 0.83

8. 1

9. 3.761

10. 5.653

11. 10.31

12. 442.96

13. 0.6

14. 9.2

15. 0.19

16. 0.07

17. 0.281

18. 11.9

19. 3.704

20. 6.54

21. 0.2322

22. 0.9283

23. 47.4

24. 6.258

25. 4.218

26. 16.1357

27. 248.692

28. 159.59

Page 30

1. 4.846

2. 21.31

3. 18.337

4. 27.97

5. 16.9594

6. 16.57

7. 45.92

8. 390.44

9. 12.174

10. 39.254

11. 8.25

12. 56.85

13. 0.234

14. 21.77

15. 3.828

16. 2.76

17. 11.257

18. 5.7645

19. 4.5008

20. 53.997

21. 11.486

22. 3.125

23. 6.42

24. 26.9933

25. 0.0266

26. 15.47

Page 31

1. 5.1

2. 2.16

3. 1.414

4. 0.4

5. 0.84

6. 0.95

7. 0.012

8. 0.06

9. 0.054

10. 134.4

11. 5.94

12. 2,134.4

13. 468.66

14. 2,622.87

15. 116.256

Page 32

1. 1.724

2. 0.252

3. 9.78

4. 11.7

5. 40.8

6. 114.08

7. 16.9

8. 33.8

9. 98.4

10. 21.7

11. 350

12. 49.5

13. 76.75

14. 3.936

15. 13.806

16. 487.83

17. 91.2

18. 28.148

19. 855.65

20. 19.432

21. 155.61

22. 3.5812

Page 33

1. 0.64

2. 0.477

3. 0.38

4. 0.072

5. 0.027

6. 0.0008

7. 0.01288

8. 0.408

9. 0.1557

10. 1.425

11. 4.858

12. 46.2

13. 182.508

14. 16.324

15. 14.6016

Page 34

1. 0.18

2. 0.018

3. 4.9

4. 0.252

5. 0.0032

6. 0.0024

7. 1.096

8. 0.01096

9. 0.0021

10. 0.0165

11. 32.86

12. 14.382

13. 0.0086

14. 0.07622

15. 53.4432

16. 0.01701

17. 0.0016

18. 7.3476

19. 1.0404

20. 3.672

21. 0.408

Page 35

1. 8.2

2. $0.69

3. 2.76

4. 0.112

5. 0.04

6. $1.50

7. 0.203

8. $3.14

9. 4.16

10. $4.12

11. 0.018

12. 0.007

13. 1.5

14. $0.67

15. 1.4

Page 36

1. 4.8

2. 5.29

3. 0.003

4. $13.70

5. 29.9

6. 6.2

7. $81.00

8. 4.5

9. 2.06

10. 0.7

11. $46.00

Page 37

1. 160

2. 30

3. 5

4. $340

5. 150

6. 500

7. $650

8. 400

9. $35

10. 26

11. 600

12. $140

231

13. $15
14. 108
15. 820

Page 38
1. 0.5
2. $0.30
3. 0.4
4. $0.75
5. 0.02
6. 0.05
7. $0.80
8. 0.95
9. 0.25
10. 0.125
11. 0.025
12. 0.6
13. 0.5
14. 0.75
15. 0.004
16. 0.25

Page 39
1. 2.4
2. 1.032
3. 30.186
4. 4.7173
5. 36
6. 0.06
7. 0.098
8. 0.008
9. 56.52
10. 0.18
11. 0.06
12. 0.348
13. 2.3
14. 826
15. 26,078
16. 12,483
17. 1.28
18. 18.5
19. 5.9
20. 25.3
21. 2.664
22. 1.12
23. 8.96
24. 934.16

Page 40
1. 123.93
2. 6.888
3. 315.375
4. 4.176
5. 0.084

6. 0.2072
7. 0.0005
8. 0.729
9. 30.52875
10. 0.00441
11. 2.3562
12. 0.003776
13. 0.092
14. 0.017
15. 0.03
16. 0.04
17. 2.54
18. 90.6
19. 93.8
20. 1,250
21. 0.625
22. 20
23. 200
24. 430

Page 41
1. 0.1
2. 0.03
3. 0.2
4. 0.75
5. 0.125
6. 0.625
7. 1.25
8. 2.6
9. $1\frac{1}{10}$
10. $1\frac{1}{2}$
11. $\frac{3}{4}$
12. $5\frac{1}{2}$
13. 18.82
14. 6.309
15. 1.608
16. 40.317
17. 3.38
18. 0.3168
19. 259.64
20. 0.9996
21. 0.05
22. 36.96
23. 8.4
24. 0.166
25. 0.06
26. 0.12
27. 1,200
28. 6

Page 42
1. $\frac{9}{2}$
2. $\frac{4}{3}$
3. $\frac{6}{5}$
4. $\frac{10}{7}$
5. $\frac{8}{1}$
6. $\frac{9}{8}$
7. $\frac{7}{1}$
8. $\frac{2}{1}$
9. $\frac{5}{2}$
10. $\frac{11}{5}$
11. $\frac{1}{2}$
12. $1\frac{1}{9}$
13. $1\frac{1}{4}$
14. $\frac{2}{3}$
15. $\frac{2}{3}$
16. $1\frac{13}{32}$
17. $5\frac{1}{3}$
18. $1\frac{1}{2}$
19. $1\frac{7}{9}$
20. $1\frac{5}{11}$
21. $1\frac{1}{5}$
22. $1\frac{1}{2}$

Page 43
1. $\frac{3}{8}$
2. $\frac{5}{9}$
3. $1\frac{1}{2}$
4. $2\frac{1}{3}$
5. $2\frac{1}{10}$
6. $6\frac{2}{3}$
7. 1
8. $\frac{5}{8}$
9. $\frac{8}{27}$
10. 2
11. $\frac{24}{35}$
12. $\frac{2}{3}$
13. $1\frac{1}{3}$
14. $\frac{2}{3}$
15. 2
16. $1\frac{2}{3}$
17. $\frac{10}{21}$
18. $\frac{9}{16}$
19. $\frac{3}{20}$
20. 1
21. $1\frac{1}{2}$
22. 3

Page 44
1. 14
2. 2
3. $2\frac{1}{9}$
4. $7\frac{1}{2}$
5. 11
6. $7\frac{3}{4}$
7. 2
8. $1\frac{1}{2}$
9. $2\frac{3}{4}$
10. $2\frac{7}{9}$
11. $2\frac{7}{10}$
12. 11
13. $15\frac{3}{4}$
14. 4
15. 6
16. 9

Page 45
1. $\frac{1}{2}$
2. $1\frac{29}{46}$
3. $3\frac{2}{3}$
4. $1\frac{29}{41}$
5. $3\frac{3}{10}$
6. $\frac{2}{3}$
7. $3\frac{1}{33}$
8. $6\frac{1}{2}$
9. 2
10. $5\frac{2}{3}$
11. $3\frac{3}{5}$
12. $5\frac{1}{3}$
13. $1\frac{7}{8}$
14. $\frac{3}{8}$
15. $2\frac{26}{27}$
16. $2\frac{2}{3}$

Page 46
1. −2
2. −5
3. 5
4. −1
5. $1 + (-4) = -3$
6. $-2 + 6 = 4$
7. $-\frac{1}{4} + 1 = \frac{3}{4}$
8. $\frac{1}{4} + \left(-\frac{3}{4}\right) = -\frac{1}{2}$
9. −4
10. −28.8
11. −15
12. −48
13. 1
14. −36
15. Sample answer: A person owed her friend $13. Then she earned $20 and used it to pay her friend. She has $7 to keep.
16. 46 points
17. Sample answer: He added 3 instead of −3.

Page 47
1. 12
2. −7
3. −13
4. $-3\frac{1}{2}$
5. −46
6. −1.4
7. $3\frac{2}{3}$
8. −32
9. $2\frac{2}{7}$
10. −10
11. 3 meters

12. 59 points below zero
13. 622 feet
14. −18 °C
15. 9 °C
16. $58.46

Page 48
1. −8
2. $\frac{10}{27}$
3. 21
4. −150
5. −84
6. −87.6
7. $-1\frac{5}{13}$
8. 0
9. −133
10. $850
11. 45 yards
12. $2\frac{1}{3}$ miles
13. $220
14. 21 °F
15. $14.25
16. Sample answer: A stock dropped 12 points each day for 2 days. The result was $(-12)(2) = -24$; the stock dropped 24 points.

Page 49
1. −0.8
2. $-\frac{1}{8}$
3. −7
4. $-\frac{928}{3}$ or $-309\frac{1}{3}$
5. −540
6. 5
7. $-\frac{12}{49}$
8. −500
9. −1.3
10. −24
11. $-2\frac{2}{9}$
12. 30
13. 35 meters
14. $7
15. Sample answer: The temperature dropped 55° over 13 days. This can

232

be shown by -55 ÷ 13 = -4.23.
The average change in temperature
was -4.23 per day.

16. Yes, it is a rational number because the unsimplified quotient is a ratio of two integers and the denominator is not zero.

17. No, since an integer that has zero in the denominator is not rational by definition.

Page 50

1. rational
2. irrational
3. irrational
4. rational
5. rational
6. irrational
7. rational
8. rational
9. real, rational, integer
10. real, rational
11. real, irrational
12. real, rational
13. real, irrational
14. No; She bought only $16\frac{1}{12}$ yd; she is short by $\frac{7}{12}$ yd.
15. Yes; The square will be 14 ft × 14 ft.
16. 2.45 seconds

Page 51

1.

2. A
3. B
4. -9, -6, -3, 0, 1, 4, 8
5. -9, -0.1, 1, 1.5, 5, 7, 31
6. -80, -32, -14, 59, 75, 88, 96
7. -65, -13, -7.6, 7.6, 34, 55, 62.5
8. -17 > -22; -22 < -17
9. 16 > -2; -2 < 16
10. > 12. > 14. > 16. <
11. < 13. > 15. < 17. >
16. veggies and dip; 2.86 > 2.49
17. pretzels; 1.71 < 1.97
18. -12 < -3, so it will be colder.

Page 52

1. 0.875
2. $0.\overline{6}$
3. 2.8
4. $0.958\overline{3}$
5. 0.85
6. 0.72
7. $7\frac{4}{9}$
8. $\frac{14}{25}$
9. $\frac{9}{20}$
10. $\frac{31}{33}$
11. $\frac{6}{11}$
12. $6\frac{1}{50}$
13. >
14. =
15. >
16. =
17. <
18. <
19. $\frac{3}{200}$ m
20. $0.1\overline{6}$
21. 0.6
22. 0.24; Sample answer: $\frac{6}{25}$ is 6 times $\frac{1}{25}$, so I multiplied 6 times 0.04.

Page 53

1. 1, 2; 1.5
2. 1.7, 1.8; 1.75
3.
4. 1.5, $\sqrt{3}$, π
5. $\sqrt{3}$, $\sqrt{5}$, 2.5
6. $\sqrt{75}$, π^2, 10
7. >
8. <

Page 54

1. $\frac{1}{8}$
2. 2
3. $\frac{40}{43}$
4. 2
5. $6\frac{2}{3}$
6. $3\frac{7}{9}$
7. $21\frac{3}{7}$
8. $\frac{4}{5}$
9. -5
10. 3
11. 15
12. -3.6
13. 63
14. -126.9
15. -0.8
16. 20
17. >
18. <
19. <
20. >
21. 0.3125 inch
22. $-\sqrt{121}$

Page 55

1. 45
2. 180
3. 96
4. 60
5. 30
6. 180
7. 250
8. 54.45
9. $237.60
10. $65.70

Page 56

1. 4
2. $\frac{2}{3}$
3. 34
4. $1\frac{1}{3}$
5. 33
6. 3
7. $1\frac{1}{5}$
8. $4\frac{2}{3}$
9. $22.00
10. 400 students

Page 57

1. 68
2. 125
3. 80
4. 200
5. 55
6. 200
7. 730
8. 160
9. $40.00
10. $3,000.00
11. 13,000 miles
12. 40 questions

Page 58

1. $13.75
2. $14.63
3. $144.00
4. $100.00
5. $8.25
6. $36.00
7. $700.00
8. $17.00

Page 59

1. $112.45
2. $3.94
3. $13.36
4. $577.80
5. $79.95
6. $1,072.00
7. $58.59
8. $32.81
9. $317.52
10. $33.13
11. $1,207.50
12. $2,846.25

Page 60

1. 63.6 pounds
2. $7.80
3. $108,972
4. 19,812 students
5. $23,540
6. $24.75

Page 61

1. 475 students
2. $24.00
3. $12,800
4. 69 points
5. 548,800 people
6. $119.38

Page 62

1. 99
2. 450
3. 75
4. 860
5. 25% increase
6. $320
7. 20%
8. $320

Page 63

1. $52.50
2. $36.80

233

3. $165
4. $18; $19.53
5. $700
6. $715
7. Sample answer: February sales are up 25% of $1,000, or $1,250. Sales for March are down 25% of $1,250, or $937.50.
8. 2%
9. 24% Increase; 13% Decrease

Page 64
1. 40.5
2. 18
3. 35
4. $1\frac{1}{8}$
5. 15%
6. 200%
7. 30
8. 50
9. $445.20
10. $18.80
11. $24.75
12. $24.00
13. $75.60
14. $31.50
15. $23.10
16. $1,020.00
17. 50% increase
18. 20% decrease

Page 65
1. 8^{10}
2. 10^8
3. $\left(\frac{1}{2}\right)^{11}$
4. $\left(\frac{2}{3}\right)^6$
5. 6^3
6. 10^7
7. $\left(\frac{3}{4}\right)^5$
8. $\left(\frac{7}{9}\right)^8$
9. 512
10. 2,401
11. 125
12. 16
13. $\frac{1}{16}$
14. $\frac{1}{27}$
15. $\frac{36}{49}$
16. $\frac{9}{10}$
17. 2
18. 3
19. 2
20. 3
21. 2
22. 1
23. 5
24. 2
25. 10
26. 4
27. 2
28. 3
29. $\frac{1}{3}$
30. $\frac{8}{3}$
31. $\frac{3}{4}$
32. 9
33. 27 players

34. 1; No matter how many 1s are multiplied, the product is always 1.

Page 66
1. 2,352
2. 6,561
3. 32,768
4. 1,280
5. 2,187
6. 240
7. 117,649
8. 65,536
9. 262,144
10. 4,096
11. 16
12. 600
13. 8
14. 1,024
15. 720
16. 8
17. 6,588
18. 32,256
19. 9,765,625
20. 729

Page 67
1. 7,812
2. 100
3. 4,096
4. -531,360
5. 7
6. 625
7. 4,160
8. 6,561
9. 4
10. 392
11. 7,776
12. 279,936
13. 1,000,000
14. 4,096
15. 3,250
16. 49,152
17. 343
18. 387,420,489
19. 1,000,000,000
20. 320
21. 7,560
22. 10
23. 512
24. 48

Page 68
1. $\frac{1}{49}$
2. 1
3. $\frac{1}{1000}$
4. $\frac{1}{32}$
5. $\frac{1}{125}$
6. 343
7. 15^{-3}
8. 20^3
9. 14^{-5}
10. 8^{48}
11. 12^{-15}
12. 4^{-24}
13. m^5
14. r^3
15. a^{-9}
16. 6
17. 7
18. 0
19. 4,132
20. 2,176,782,579
21. No; $\frac{4^3}{16^3} =$
$$\frac{4 \times 4 \times 4}{(4 \times 4) \times (4 \times 4) \times (4 \times 4)}$$
$$= \frac{1}{4 \times 4 \times 4} = \frac{1}{64}$$
22. x^2; x^2; You can write $\frac{x^5}{x^3}$ as $x^5 \cdot \frac{1}{x^3}$ which is equal to $x^5 \cdot x^{-3}$.

Page 69
1. 5.6×10^6
2. 6.04×10^6
3. 6.7×10^3
4. 1.013×10^6
5. 3.3×10^5
6. 7.16×10^8
7. 2.021×10^9
8. 2.07×10^6
9. 410,000
10. 599
11. 110,000
12. 22,300
13. 8,900
14. 50,300,000
15. 3,120,000,000
16. 75,000
17. 101,100
18. 600,000,000
19. 31,400
20. 10

Page 70
1. 5.8927×10^4
2. 1.304×10^9
3. 4.87×10^{-4}
4. 2.8×10^{-5}
5. 5.9×10^{-5}
6. 6.73×10^6
7. 1.33×10^4
8. 4.17×10^{-2}
9. 400,000

10. 1,849,900,000
11. 0.00083
12. 0.000003582
13. 0.0297
14. 6,410
15. 84,560,000
16. 0.0000906
17. 2,000
18. 3,000
19. 0.2
20. 0.0001
21. km

Page 71
1. 3.1×10^8; 0.338×10^8; 1.1×10^8
2. 0.338; 4.538
3. 4.538×10^8
4. 310,000,000; 33,800,000; 110,000,000
5. 33,800,000; 110,000,000; 453,800,000
6. 4.538×10^8
7. 7.62×10^7 or 76,200,000

Page 72
1. 2.025×10^{14}; 225,000,000
2. 2.25×10^8
3. 2.025×10^{14}; 2.25×10^8
4. 2.25; 0.9
5. $14 - 8$; 6
6. 9.0×10^5 km per year
7. 1.86, 4.8; 1.86, 10^5; 8.928, $5 + 3$; 8.928, 8

Page 73
1. 64; 8
2. 225; 15
3. 1; 1
4. 36; 6
5. 5
6. 3
7. 10
8. 2
9. 12
10. 4

Page 74
1. 12
2. 16
3. $\frac{1}{9}$
4. $\frac{7}{30}$
5. 20

234

6. $\frac{1}{10}$
7. 6
8. 20
9. $\frac{3}{5}$
10. $\frac{1}{3}$
11. $\frac{3}{4}$
12. 8
13. 9
14. 15
15. 15
16. 0
17. 3
18. 4
19. 6 feet
20. 8 squares
21. 3 feet
22. Multiply the square root by itself. The product should be the number you started with.
23. No; 12 is not a perfect square. No; 20 is not a perfect cube.

Page 75
1. 343
2. 81
3. $\frac{1}{125}$
4. $\frac{5}{7}$
5. $\frac{1}{16}$
6. $\frac{1}{15}$
7. $\frac{1}{289}$
8. $\frac{1}{16}$
9. 1,332
10. 593
11. 33
12. 100
13. 3
14. 216
15. 100,000
16. 512
17. 2.15×10^8
18. 5.62×10^4
19. 89,000
20. 9,400,000
21. 1
22. 8
23. 1
24. 24
25. 2.43×10^4 or 24,300 people

26. store A; 7.418×10^7 dollars or $74,180,000

Page 76
1. $\frac{1}{3}$
2. $\frac{1}{7}$
3. $\frac{1}{2}$
4. $\frac{1}{2}$
5. $\frac{1}{4}$
6. $\frac{4}{5}$
7. 5
8. $\frac{5}{4}$
9. $\frac{17}{20}$
10. $\frac{5}{3}$
11. 1
12. $\frac{1}{2}$
13. 2
14. 1

Page 77
1. 5:3, 5 to 3; $\frac{5}{3}$
2. 46:24, 46 to 24, $\frac{46}{24}$ or 23:12, 23 to 12, $\frac{23}{12}$
3. 2:5, 2 to 5, $\frac{2}{5}$
4. 12:46, 12 to 46, $\frac{12}{46}$ or 6:23, 6 to 23, $\frac{6}{23}$
5. Sample answers: $\frac{3}{7}, \frac{6}{14}, \frac{24}{56}$
6. Sample answers: $\frac{10}{4}, \frac{15}{6}, \frac{20}{8}$
7. Sample answers: $\frac{20}{6}, \frac{30}{9}, \frac{40}{12}$
8. 15; There is no whole number that 15 can be multiplied/divided by to get 9.
9. 3, 3, 5, 15, 3
10. Multiplying/dividing both terms by the same number is equivalent to multiplying/dividing by 1.

Page 78
1. 0.15; 0.12; 0.14
2. B
3. 0.21; 0.19
4. family size
5. 16
6. 72
7. 300
8. 6.00
9. Yes; Sample answer: Each has a unit rate of 2.5 windows per hour.

Page 79
1. 17, $25\frac{1}{2}$, 34, $42\frac{1}{2}$
2. $1\frac{1}{8}$
3. $\frac{4}{5}$
4. $1\frac{1}{5}$
5. 6
6. $2\frac{4}{5}$ miles per hour
7. $\frac{15}{16}$ page per minute
8. $1\frac{1}{2}$ cups per recipe
9. $3\frac{3}{4}$ square yards per hour
10. about $2.86 per hour
11. $2.50 per hour
12. Talk Time; Their rate per hour is lower.
13. Multiply 0.05 times 60 because there are 60 minutes in 1 hour.

Page 80
1. $\frac{1}{9}$
2. $\frac{1}{16}$
3. $\frac{1}{125}$
4. $\frac{27}{64}$
5. $\frac{8}{27}$
6. $\frac{100}{1}$

Page 81
1. true
2. false
3. true
4. false
5. true
6. true
7. true
8. true
9. false

Page 82
1. $36.10
2. $1.30
3. $4.00
4. $290.40
5. 50 miles
6. $26.25

Page 83
1. 100; 150; 200; 250
2. 40; 60; 80; 100; 120; 140
3. 12; 18; 24; 30; 36; 42

Page 84
1. $\frac{120}{2}$
2. 60 miles
3. $\frac{60}{1}$
4. equivalent
5. Sample answer:

Multiply the number of hours by $\frac{60}{1}$, or 60.
6. 180; 240, 300; 2.5, 3; 4, 5
7. 2.5, 180, 4, 300; straight line through the origin

Page 85
1. yes; 60
2. no
3. yes; 3
4. yes; 8
5. x is number of hours; y is miles driven; $y = 65x$
6. x is cups of batter; y is number of muffins; $y = 2.5x$
7. $y = 18.5x$
8. $22.50
9. Rent-All has the best deal because it has the lowest rate per day, $18.50.

Page 86
1. proportional; The number of pages is always 65 times the number of hours.
2. proportional; Earnings are always 7.5 times the number of hours.
3. not proportional; The line will not pass through the origin.
4. proportional; The line will pass through the origin.
5. A: 8 minutes; B: 5 minutes
6. At 0 minutes, the start of the race, each horse has run 0 miles.
7. A: $y = \frac{1}{8}x$; B: $y = \frac{1}{5}x$

Page 87
1. 5, 10, 15, 20, 25, 30
2. The wall is 30 feet long.
3. 1.5 inches
4. The length is 28 feet and the width is 14 feet. The area is 392 square feet.

235

5. The length is 25 meters and the width is 15 meters. The area is 375 square meters.

6. Drawing should be a 4 by 6 rectangle.

Page 88

1. YZ; 3
2. XZ; 4
3. YZ; 3
4. XZ; 4
5. $\frac{AC}{XZ} = \frac{AB}{XY}, \frac{2}{4} = \frac{1}{2}$
6. $\frac{BC}{AB} = \frac{YZ}{XY}, \frac{1.5}{1} = \frac{3}{2}$
7. $\frac{YZ}{BC} = \frac{XZ}{AC}, \frac{3}{1.5} = \frac{4}{2}$
8. $\frac{XY}{AB} = \frac{XZ}{AC}, \frac{2}{1} = \frac{4}{2}$
9. $\frac{XY}{XZ} = \frac{AB}{AC}, \frac{2}{4} = \frac{1}{2}$
10. $\frac{YZ}{XZ} = \frac{BC}{AC}, \frac{3}{4} = \frac{1.5}{2}$
11. $\frac{AC}{BC} = \frac{XZ}{YZ}, \frac{2}{1.5} = \frac{4}{3}$
12. $\frac{AC}{AB} = \frac{XZ}{XY}, \frac{2}{1} = \frac{4}{2}$

Page 89

1. 21 in.
2. $3\frac{2}{3}$ ft
3. 8 m
4. 8 cm
5. $\frac{1}{2}$ yd
6. 2 ft

Page 90

1. 50 feet
2. 555 feet
3. 40 feet
4. 100 feet

Page 91

1. $\frac{1}{2}$
2. $\frac{7}{13}$
3. 4
4. 140
5. true
6. false
7. true
8. 30 feet
9. 37.4
10. 4
11. 24 meters

Page 92

1. $a \times b = b \times a$
2. $x - x = 0$
3. $n + n = 2n$
4. $0 \times m = 0$
5. Answers may vary.
   $0 + 3 = 3$
   $0 + 5 = 5$
   $0 + 8 = 8$
6. Answers may vary.
   $8 \div 2 = 4$
   $10 \div 2 = 5$
   $12 \div 2 = 6$

Page 93

1. 9
2. 30
3. 13
4. 16
5. 16
6. 26
7. 16
8. 24
9. 14
10. 5
11. 56
12. 10
13. 3
14. 8
15. 5
16. $\frac{5}{2}$ or $2\frac{1}{2}$
17. 1
18. 1
19. $\frac{1}{2}$
20. 7
21. 1
22. $\frac{5}{3}$
23. 3
24. 4

Page 94

1. $10 + r$ or $r + 10$
2. $t - 9$
3. $7s$
4. $w \div 3$ or $\frac{w}{3}$
5. $m + 12$ or $12 + m$
6. $2hx$ or $2xh$
7. $25 - n$
8. $p - g$
9. $24 \div k$ or $\frac{24}{k}$
10. $13 + b$ or $b + 13$
11. $c - 7$
12. $y \div 5$ or $\frac{y}{5}$

Page 95

1. 4, 2; t, n
2. $x - 79$; $a + b$; $13t$; $\frac{n}{16}$; $24 - 3h$; r
3. $\frac{n}{8}$ or $n \div 8$
4. $4p$
5. $b + 14$ or $14 + b$
6. $90x$
7. $a - 16$
8. $24 - k$
9. $3w$
10. $1 + q$ or $q + 1$
11. $\frac{13}{z}$ or $13 \div z$
12. $45 + c$ or $c + 45$
13–20. Sample answers given.
13. 83 added to m
14. 42 times s
15. 9 divided by d
16. t minus 29
17. g more than 2
18. the product of 11 and x
19. the quotient of h and 12
20. k less than 5
21. $k - 12$
22. $g + 6$ or $6 + g$
23. $\frac{48}{b}$ or $48 \div b$

Page 96

1. sum
2. product
3. quotient
4. difference
5. algebraic expression; sum of two terms; sum of a quotient and a constant
6. algebraic expression; product of two factors
7. algebraic expression; product of two factors; product of a coefficient and a variable
8. sum of two terms
9–12. Sample answers given.
9. xy
10. $3x + 2$
11. $7a + b - 9$

Page 97

1. 5 is a coefficient, 9 is a constant
2. 3 is a coefficient, -1 is a coefficient
3. 6 is a coefficient, -2 is a coefficient
4. 10 is a coefficient, -7 is a constant
5. 20
6. 8
7. 36
8. 30
9. $\frac{1}{4}$
10. 10
11. 3
12. 5
13. 85
14. 25
15. 600
16. 300
17. 7
18. 8
19. 1
20. 40

Page 98

1. 16
2. 18
3. 2
4. 10.5
5. 17
6. $\frac{1}{2}$
7. 0.7
8. 16
9. 4
10. 32
11. 3
12. 66
13. $2\frac{1}{18}$
14. 50
15. 136
16. 95
17. 48
18. 15
19. 32
20. 49
21. 160
22. 86

23. $3x$ means that 3 should be multiplied by the value of x; 17

Page 99

1. $4 + 4b = 4(b + 1)$; $4(b - 1) = 4b - 4$; $4b + 1 = 1 + 4b$
2. ba; Commutative Property of Multiplication
3. $13 + x$; Commutative Property of Addition
4. $15x - 10$; Distributive Property
5. $(2 + a) + b$; Associative Property of Addition
6. $3a$, $16a$
7. $5x^3$, $7x^3$
8. $6b^2$, b^2
9. $12t^2$, $4t^2$, $2t^2$
10. 5, 17, 6
11. m, $2m$
12. $2x^4$
13. $5x + 4$
14. $13b - 10$
15. $37y$
16. $4y + 10$
17. $6a^2 + 16$
18. $5y$
19. $10x^2 - 4$
20. $2a^5 + 5b$
21. $8m + 2 + 4n$
22. 10, Commutative, 13; $13a + 2b$

Page 100

1. $6.9x + 3.3$
2. $4x - 4$
3. $x + \frac{1}{2}$
4. $5x + 15$
5. Joey: $20; Julie: $20; total; $40
6. $210
7. $\frac{1}{4}(6a + 9m)$
8. $12(2 + 3x)$
9. $5(x - 5)$
10. $2(6x + 5)$
11. $10(x - 6)$
12. Multiply the factors. The result should match the original expression.

Answer Key
Core Skills Math Review

Page 101

1. 42
2. s, 42, s, 0.42s
3. 0.42s, 1s, 0.42s
4. 1.42s
5. 24
6. b; 24, b; 0.24b
7. 0.24b, 1b, 0.24b
8. 0.76b

Page 102

1. Distributive Property
2. Multiplicative Property of Zero
3. Additive Identity Property
4. Commutative Property of Multiplication
5. 15
6. 28
7. 4
8. 2
9. $\frac{n}{4m}$ or $n \div 4m$
10. Sample: $8n + 2$
11. 30
12. –3
13. $-1\frac{4}{5}$
14. $32 + 4d$
15. $5(3s + 2t)$
16. $3g$
17. $24x + 1$
18. $x + 10$
19. $8x - 11$
20. Sample answers: $1c + 0.1c$; $1.1c$
21. $1p - 0.05p$; $0.95p$

Page 103

1. no
2. yes
3. yes
4. yes
5. no
6. yes
7. no
8. yes
9. no
10. no
11. yes
12. no
13. yes
14. yes
15. no
16. no

17–22. Sample answers given.

17. $8r = 256$
18. $b + 5 = 18$
19. $\frac{f}{2} = 5$
20. 71 students
21. 68°F

Page 104

1. $x = 3$
2. $x = 4$
3. $y = 10$
4. $m = 8$
5. $n = 17$
6. $x = 12$
7. $x = 21\frac{1}{3}$
8. $k = 13$
9. $x = 53$

Page 105

1. $x = \frac{1}{2}$
2. $n = 35$
3. $x = 2\frac{1}{3}$
4. $x = 3\frac{1}{3}$
5. $k = 25$
6. $x = 5\frac{5}{8}$
7. $m = 1\frac{3}{8}$
8. $k = 13$
9. $x = 7\frac{2}{5}$
10. $k = 11$
11. $x = \frac{3}{4}$
12. $x = 52$
13. $k = 11\frac{2}{3}$
14. $x = 29$
15. $x = 87$
16. $x = 5\frac{1}{8}$
17. $n = 5$
18. $n = 2\frac{1}{7}$
19. $x = 16$
20. $n = 7\frac{1}{2}$
21. $x = 68$
22. $x = 8\frac{3}{5}$
23. $x = 12$
24. $x = 98$

Page 106

1. 4
2. 8
3. 88
4. 180
5. 15
6. 48
7. 4.5
8. 8.2
9. 40
10. $\frac{5}{4}$ or $1\frac{1}{4}$

Page 107

1. 3
2. 7
3. 5
4. 14
5. 8
6. 7
7. 115
8. 9
9. 272
10. 108
11. 36
12. 512
13. 108
14. 96
15. 81
16. 11 books
17. 28 mi/gal
18. 7.6 hours
19. 4 days
20. $\frac{1}{4}$

Page 108

1. $x = 6$
2. $x = 12$
3. $x = 10\frac{4}{5}$
4. $x = 5$
5. $x = 67\frac{5}{8}$
6. $x = 14$
7. $x = 21$
8. $x = 7$
9. $x = 10$

Page 109

1. $x = 5$
2. $x = \frac{1}{2}$
3. $x = 8$
4. $x = 2\frac{1}{2}$
5. $x = 5$

11. $\frac{19}{15}$ or $1\frac{4}{15}$
12. 10
13. 141
14. 4
15. 64

16–18. Sample equations given.

16. $x + 8.95 = 21.35$; $12.40
17. $x + 8 = 37$; 29 compact cars
18. $x - 2.6 = 58.4$; 61 seconds
19. If the equation contains addition, subtract on both sides. If the equation contains subtraction, add on both sides.

Page 110

1. $x = 10$
2. $x = 5$
3. $x = 2$
4. $x = 7$
5. $x = 3$
6. $x = 2$
7. $x = 15$
8. $x = 3$
9. $x = 3$

Page 111

1. $x = 1$
2. $x = 5$
3. $x = 4$
4. $x = 12$
5. $x = 7$
6. $x = \frac{3}{4}$
7. $x = \frac{1}{2}$
8. $x = 6$
9. $x = 5$
10. $x = \frac{3}{14}$
11. $x = 1$
12. $x = \frac{1}{15}$
13. $x = 13$
14. $x = 9$
15. $x = 10$
16. $x = 9$
17. $x = 2$
18. $x = 2\frac{1}{3}$

Page 112

1. $x = 5$
2. $x = 3$
3. $x = 2$
4. $x = -4$
5. $x = 3$
6. $x = 5$

6. $x = \frac{3}{4}$
7. $x = 4$
8. $x = 9$
9. $x = \frac{1}{5}$
10. $x = \frac{1}{24}$
11. $x = \frac{3}{10}$
12. $x = 4$
13. $x = 4$
14. $x = 2\frac{13}{17}$
15. $x = \frac{1}{7}$
16. $x = \frac{1}{12}$
17. $x = 7$
18. $x = 6$

7. $x = 2$
8. $x = -2$
9. $x = 16$
10. $x = 2.5$
11. 3 lessons
12. 1 lesson
13. 2 lessons

Page 113

1. $x = 6$
2. $x = 5$
3. $x = 1$
4. $x = 2$
5. $x = 8$
6. $x = 10$
7. $x = 2$
8. $x = 7$
9. $x = 15$

Page 114

1. $x = 10$
2. $x = 3$
3. $x = 6$
4. $x = 17$
5. $x = 1$
6. $x = 25$
7. $x = 5$
8. $x = 30$
9. $x = 8$
10. $x = 10$
11. $x = 24$
12. $x = 9$
13. $x = \frac{2}{7}$
14. $x = 11$
15. $x = -2$
16. $x = \frac{1}{2}$
17. $x = 1\frac{2}{3}$
18. $x = 25$

Page 115

1. $n = 28$
2. Malik has $40, and Arsenio has $105.
3. Jerry has $3.20, and Pat has $9.60.
4. $n = 48$

Page 116

1. Elena has $35, and Tori has $7.
2. DeWayne has $35, and Hakeem

237

has $20.

3. 1st package has 50. 2nd package has 30.
4. 1st lot has 75 cars. 2nd lot has 125 cars.
5. Mother is 54, and Ricardo is 18.
6. Father is 58, and Natasha is 20.
7. The three numbers are 30, 60, and 90.
8. The three numbers are 20, 40, and 80.

Page 117
1. (-1, 4)
2. (-3, 5)
3. (5, 1)
4. (3, 5)
5. (0, 11)
6. (-1, 13)
7. (-4, -2)
8. (-5, -1)
9. (-9, 3)

Page 118
1. 4, 2; 5; -4x, -4x; -5; true
2. -2, -2; -4x, -4x; 0, -7; false
3. In problem 1, any value of x will result in a true statement. In problem 2, any value of x will result in a false statement.
4. one solution
5. infinitely many solutions
6. any value other than 1
7. 4

Page 119
1. $x = -14$; $y = -88$
   Solution: (-14, -88)
2. 6, 2x, y, 2x,
   -6 + 2x, 8x, 5, 4;
   Solution: (5, 4)

Page 120
1. no
2. yes
3. $n = 10\frac{1}{2}$
4. $a = 13$
5. $p = 2.5$
6. $x = 10$

7. $x = 10.58$
8. $x = 15$
9. $x = 24$
10. $x = \frac{3}{4}$
11. $x = 2$
12. (-2, 18)
13. (-2, 1)
14. (-2, -2)
15. zero
16. one
17. infinitely many
18. (-1, 2)
19. (2, 7)
20. (1, 9)
21. 14
22. 159 and 199 passengers

Page 121
1. (6, 3)
2. (3, -2)
3. (-2, 3)
4. (2, 4)
5. (-4, -4)
6. (-6, 2)
7. (5, -7)
8. (-2, -6)
9. (-2, 1)
10. (4, 6)
11. (1, -3)
12. (-3, -2)
13. P
14. N
15. K
16. M
17. Q
18. R

19–27.

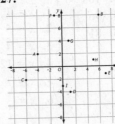

28. 4 blocks
29. 5 blocks
30. Base I (3, 7); Base II (5, -5); Base III (-3, 0)

Page 122
1. (3, 3); I
2. (2, 5); I
3. (2, -2); IV
4. (-4, -2); III
5. (0, 1); none or y-axis
6. (-3, 0); none or x-axis

7–10.

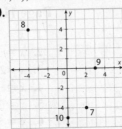

11. (-5, -1); (-2, -4)
12. a. Sample answer: (6, -5)
    b. Sample answer: (2, 0)
13. a. Jefferson Field (-1, 2); Madison Field (-2, -2); Hamilton Field (4, -3); Adams Field (-2, 2)
    b. I

Page 123
1. (2, 7)
2. (2, -7)
3. 14
4. 11
5. 12 miles
6. 6 miles
7. (-4, 1); 3 miles
8. (2, 1); 3 miles

Page 124
1. yes
2. no
3. yes
4. yes
5. domain: {-10, -2, 1, 9}
   range: {-1, 3, 4, 5}
6. domain: {-2, 1, 7}
   range: {-3, 6, 8}
7. domain: {-1, -0, 4}
   range: {-6, -5, 0, 9}
8. domain: {1, 2, 5}
   range: {-2, 1, 9}

Page 125
1. 5, 10
2. time, x
3. cost, y
4. time and cost
5. Cost depends on time.
6. time, x
7. cost, y
8. 15, 20, 25, 30, 35, 40
9. (1, 15), (2, 20), (3, 25), (4, 30), (5, 35), (6, 40)
10.

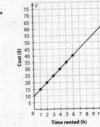

11. $50
12. (8, 50)
13. 10; (10, 60)

Page 126
1.

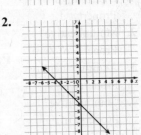

2.

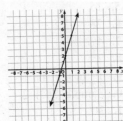

3.

Page 127
1.

2.

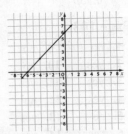

3.

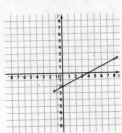

Page 128

1. $20x$, 200
2. $\frac{x}{2}$ or $x \div 2$, 30
3. $2.25x$, 40.50
4. no
5. yes
6. yes
7. no

8–9.

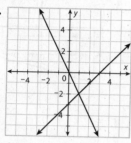

Page 129

1. 4, 5, 6
2. y is 3 more than x
3. Add 3 to the value of x to find y.
4. $y = x + 3$

5–6.

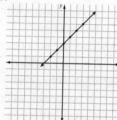

7. The value of y is three times the value of x.
8. $y = 3x$

9–10.

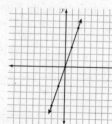

11. $y = 1$
12. $x = 2$

Page 130

1. no, no, no
2. no, yes, yes
3. yes, no, yes
4. no, no, no

Page 131

1. 7, 3, -1, -5; linear

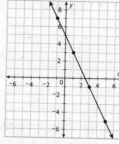

2. -2, 1, 2, 1, -2; non-linear

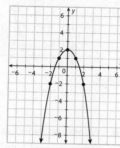

3. $y = 12x$; linear
4. $y = 20x + 100$; linear
5. No; the equation cannot be written in the form $y = mx + b$, and the graph of the solutions is not a straight line.
6. Yes, the equation can be written in the form $y = mx + b$, and the graph of the solutions is a straight line.
7. Disagree; the equation can be written in the form $y = mx + b$ where m is 0, and the graph of the solutions is a horizontal line.

Page 132

1. 15, 15, 15
2. $\frac{15}{1}$, $\frac{45}{3}$; 15
3. The graph appears to be a straight line through the origin.
4. 15 miles per hour.
5. They are the same.
6. No; in a proportional relationship, the rate of change is constant.
7. No; a situation may have variable rates of change or in a non-proportional relationship, the point $(1, r)$ will not include r as the unit rate.

Page 133

1. $\frac{1}{3}$, positive
2. $\frac{7}{-2}$, negative
3. $\frac{1}{-3}$, negative

Page 134

1. $-\frac{1}{3}$
2. 2
3. -1
4. 2
5. $-\frac{3}{4}$
6. $\frac{1}{2}$
7. $-\frac{6}{5}$
8. $\frac{5}{9}$
9. 3

Page 135

1. $(0, b)$; The value of x is 0 at the point that includes the y-intercept.
2. $y - b$
3. $x - 0$
4. b, x
5. $y = mx + b$
6. $y = -4x + 6$
7. $y = \frac{5}{2}x - 3$

Page 136

1. $m = \frac{51 - 59}{2000 - 0} = \frac{-8}{2000} = -0.004$
2. $b = 59$
3. $y = -0.004x + 59$
4. 39°F
5. 0.0625; the diver ascends at a rate of 0.0625 meter per second.
6. -5; the diver starts 5 meters below the water's surface.
7. $y = 0.0625x - 5$
8. $\frac{9}{5}$, 32, $y = \frac{9}{5}x + 32$
9. 98.6°F

Page 137

1. 15 words per minute
2. 20 words per minute
3. Brian
4. Both graphs go through the origin. Brian's graph is steeper than Morgan's because Brian's rate (slope) is greater.
5. Katie's graph would go through the origin. It would be less steep than Brian's, but steeper than Morgan's.
6. Jen's graph would go through the origin. It would be steeper than Brian's and Morgan's.

Page 138

1. Slowest growth: Phase 1; the curve is increasing, but not very steep. Fastest growth: Phase 2: the curve is increasing and much steeper than Phase 1.
2. The graph is almost horizontal. The population is stable (not increasing or decreasing).
3. The graph is decreasing, so the number of microbes is decreasing.
4.

5. The graph would show a steep decline at the point that represents the fire. Then as the forest regrows, the gradual increasing and decreasing pattern would resume.

Page 139

1. $(1, 3)$
2. parallel; no solution
3. infinitely many solutions

Page 140

1. yes
2. no
3. $-\frac{5}{9}$
4. $\frac{1}{3}$
5. $y = 5x + 2$

6. $y = -7x + 8$

7–8.

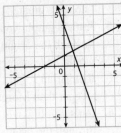

9. (1, 4)

Page 141

1. rectangle
2. trapezoid
3. triangle
4. parallelogram
5. isosceles right triangle
6. scalene right triangle
7. scalene right triangle
8. scalene triangle
9. scalene triangle
10. isosceles triangle
11. scalene triangle
12. scalene triangle
13. Answers will vary.

Page 142

1. translation
2. reflection
3. reflection
4. translation

5.

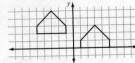

6.

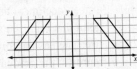

7.

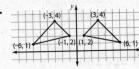

8.

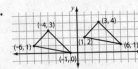

9.

Page 143

1. 90°
2. 180°
3. 270°
4. 180°

5. (0, -3), (2, -1), (4, -1), (6, -3)

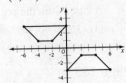

6–7.

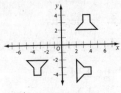

8. 60°

Page 144

1.

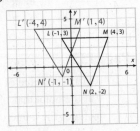

2.

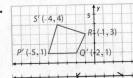

3.

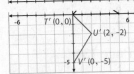

4.

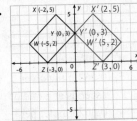

5. (2, -2), (2, -4), (-3, -4), (-3, -2)
6. (4, -3), (4, -1), (-1, -1), (-1, -3)
7. (-2, 2), (-2, 4), (3, 4), (3, 2)
8. (-2, -2), (-2, -4), (3, -4), (3, -2)
9. (-1, 3), (-1, 5), (-6, 5), (-6, 3)

Page 145

1–2.

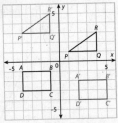

3. No; I can measure the line segments or the angles to see that they do not change.

4–5.

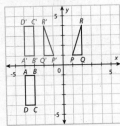

6. A rotation moves a figure around a point, but it does not change the size or shape of the figure.

Page 146

1.

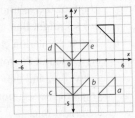

2. a. Possible answer:
$(x, y) \rightarrow (-x, y)$ and
$(x, y) \rightarrow (x - 1, y)$
b. Possible answer:
$(x, y) \rightarrow (x + 1, y)$ and
$(x, y) \rightarrow (-x, y)$

3. Yes; they have the same size and shape.

4. No; they do not have the same size and shape.

Page 147

1. Preimage: (0, 2), (-2, 0), (0, -2); Image: (0, 3), (-3, 0), (0, -3)

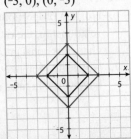

Page 145

2.

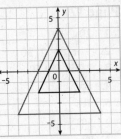

3.

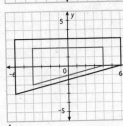

4. $\frac{1}{4}$

5. $\frac{1}{2}$

Page 148

1. dilation by scale factor 2 with center at origin and $(x, y) \rightarrow (x + 4, y + 6)$

2. If you translate the figure first, the center of the dilation will not be the origin.

3. They are not congruent. They are similar.

4. dilation by scale factor $\frac{1}{2}$, translation up 5 units, reflection across y-axis

5. rotation of 180° about the origin, dilation by scale factor $\frac{1}{2}$, translation up 5 units

6.

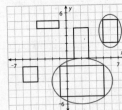

Page 149

1–5.

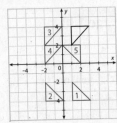

240

6.

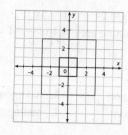

7. No; Explanations will vary.
8. The lengths of segments are changed, but the angle measures stay the same.
9. Possible answer: reflection across the x-axis; translation 2 units right
10. Possible answer: reflection across the x-axis; translation 4 units right and 1 unit down

Page 150

1. $x > 16$	10. $x > 24$
2. $x \le 15$	11. $x \ge 25$
3. $x < 25$	12. $x \ge 35$
4. $x \le 7$	13. $x < -2$
5. $x > 3$	14. $x \ge -4$
6. $x \ge 6$	15. $x < 9$
7. $x > 15$	16. $x \le -2$
8. $x \le 24$	17. $x < 8$
9. $x > 23$	18. $x \le -5$

Page 151

1. $x < 20$	9. $x \le -4$
2. $x \ge -16$	10. $x < 6$
3. $x \le -18$	11. $x \ge 7$
4. $x > 5$	12. $x > 5$
5. $x \ge -5$	13. $x \le -5$
6. $x < 4$	14. $x > -9$
7. $x < 3$	15. $x > 9$
8. $x < 7$	

Page 152

1. 8.5 feet	3. $2,300
2. 6 days	4. $240

Page 153

1. $0.03, 0, 1.5, \frac{1}{2}$
2.
3.
4.
5. a. $c \ge 48$

   b. No; 46 is not greater than or equal to 48.

6. $0 \le s < 15$
7. $p \le 150$
8. $s \ge 20$
9. $r \le 50$
10. $g > 250$
11. $m \le 6$
12. $t > 2$

Page 154

1. $x > 32$	6. $x \ge 2$
2. $x \le 66$	7. $x \le 10$
3. $x \ge -5$	8. $x > 36$
4. $x < 2$	9. $x \le -2$
5. $x > 4$	

10.
11.
12.
13. $t < 2$
14. $t > -4$

Page 155

1. Sample answer: $\angle AFB$ and $\angle CFB$
2. Sample answer: $\angle AFB$ and $\angle DFE$
3. Sample answer: $\angle AFB$ and $\angle CFB$
4. $\angle CFB$
5. Sample answer: $\angle BFA$
6. $\angle AFC$
7. $\angle DFE$ and $\angle CFB$
8. The measure of $\angle DFE$ is 40°. Angles DFE and BFA are vertical angles; therefore, $\angle DFE$ also has a measure of 40°.
9. No, they are not vertical angles because they are not opposite angles formed by intersecting lines.
10. Yes, they are vertical angles because they are opposite angles formed by intersecting lines.

Page 156

1. $\angle 5$
2. $\angle 5, \angle 5$

3. Sample answer: $\angle 3$ and $\angle 6$; rotate $\angle 3$ about the intersection point of line a and line t; then translate along line t to align with $\angle 6$.
4. 55; alternate interior angles
5. supplementary; 4x, 12, 12, 12; 120°

Page 157

1. 71°
2. 30°
3. 88°, 29°, 63°
4. 90°, 45°, 45°
5. 40°, 76°, 64°
6. 129°, 19°, 161°

Page 158

1. Missing angle measures: 109°, 41°; Missing values in first solution: 71°, 71°, 109°; Missing values in second solution: 109°, 30°; 139°; 139°, 139°, 139°; 41°
2. the angles, the angles, similar
3. $\overline{EF}, \overline{DF}$
4. $2, \frac{9}{3}; 1, \frac{3}{1}$
5. proportional, similar

Page 159

1-4.

3. AE, DF
5. $\angle DCF$; congruent; $\angle DFC$, congruent
6. $\triangle CDF$
7. AE
8. BE, CF
9. constant

Page 160

1. a–b. Check students' drawing.

   c. c^2 square units

   d. Check students' drawing.

   e. a^2 square units, b^2 square units

   f. $a^2 + b^2$ square units
2. Yes, the outlines of the figures are the same size.
3. Yes; they are made of congruent triangles. Subtracting the shaded region from the total area gives the same area for the unshaded regions.
4. $a^2 + b^2 = c^2$

Page 161

1. $c = 13$
2. $b = 24$
3. $c = 5$
4. $a = 9$
5. $c = 2$
6. $b = 8$

Page 162

1. 17 ft
2. 36 m
3. 11.5 in.
4. 8.9 cm
5. 7.1 units
6. 8.1 units
7. 12 feet

Page 163

1. The given conditions will make a unique triangle; check students' work.
2. no triangle; one; one; no triangle
3. Check students' drawings.
4. Sample answer: Yes, I can draw several triangles of different sizes that have 30°, 60°, and 90° angles.
5. No, several differently sized triangles can be drawn with the same angles.
6. Students should draw a triangle that is reasonably close to an equilateral triangle. Sample answer: Since a triangle has 180°, I drew angles that were about 60° and then connected them with lines that were about the same length.

Page 164

1. 80°
2. 132°
3. no triangle
4. more than one triangle
5. 123°
6. 87°
7. 30 ft
8. 24 ft

Page 165

1. 160 square meters
2. 4,567.5 square feet
3. 4,800 square meters
4. 375 square kilometers
5. 17.5 square meters
6. 137.5 square inches

Page 166

1. 75 cm²
2. 240 ft²
3. 288 ft²
4. 102 in²
5. $63\frac{3}{4}$ in²
6. $137\frac{1}{4}$ in²
7. 4,752 m²
8. 1,056 ft²
9. 300 km²
10. 7.5 cm²
11. 6 in.
12. 20 ft²

Page 167

1. 550 square feet
2. 1,500 square meters
3. 240 square feet
4. 192 square feet
5. 6,400 square yards
6. 4,700 square feet

Page 168

1. 70 cm²
2. 6.75 m²
3. 58 yd²
4. 2,887.5 mm²
5. 71.76 ft²
6. 25 in²

Page 169

1. 168 m²
2. 22.05 yd²
3. 459 in²
4. 625 cm²
5. 1,950 mm²
6. 304 ft²
7. 100 square inches
8. 252 square centimeters
9. $21\frac{1}{8}$ square feet
10. 128 square yards

Page 170

1. 84
2. 168
3. 91
4. $31\frac{7}{8}$
5. 72
6. 336
7. 65.25
8. 10
9. 936
10. 792
11. 96
12. 125

Page 171

1. parallelogram and trapezoid
2. parallelogram: 10; 1.5; 10 • 1.5; 15; 15 trapezoid: 7; 10; 1.5; $\frac{1}{2}$ • 1.5(7 + 10); $\frac{1}{2}$ • 1.5(17); 12.75; 12.75
3. 15, 12.75, 27.75 cm²
4. Sample answer: two triangles, and two trapezoids
5. 27.75 cm²; it does not matter how you divide the figure; the area is still the same.

Page 172

1. 112
2. 220
3. 26
4. 60
5. a. Area of patio = 5 • 8 = 40 ft²; Area of walkway = 8 • 3 = 24 ft²; Area of garden = 6 • 3 = 18 ft²; Total area = 40 + 24 + 18 = 82 ft²
   b. Area of backyard = 17 • 8 = 136 ft²; Area of lawns = (8 • 3) + (6 • 5) = 24 + 30 = 54 ft²; Remaining area = 136 − 54 = 82 ft²

Page 173

1. pentagon
2. octagon
3. hexagon
4. heptagon
5. a.

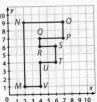

   b. F
   c. 30; 26
6. pentagon; 26.5; 26
7. heptagon; 31.6; 37.5

Page 174

1. 21.98 inches
2. 219.8 centimeters
3. 1,099 millimeters
4. 10.99 yards
5. 19.78 meters
6. 143.53 centimeters

Page 175

1. 38.465 square feet
2. 615.44 square inches
3. 38.47 square meters
4. 13.8474 square meters
5. 7 gallons
6. 55.39 square centimeters

Page 176

1. $\frac{C}{2\pi}$; $\frac{C}{2\pi}$; C, 2, π; π, C, 4, π; C, 4, π; π, A
2. four times pi times the area
3. Yes; $A = \pi r^2 \approx 28.26$, $C = 2\pi r \approx 18.84$, $C^2 \stackrel{?}{=} 4\pi A$, $18.84^2 \stackrel{?}{=} 4 \times 3.14 \times 28.26$ 354.9456 = 354.9456
4. 16π square units
5. $\frac{\pi}{4}$ square units
6. π square units

Page 177

1. 360 in²
2. 100 cm²
3. 195 in²
4. $C = 75.36$ mm; $A = 452.16$ mm²
5. $C = 43.96$ m; $A = 153.86$ m²
6. $C = 12.56$ mm; $A = 12.56$ mm²

7. 160 square centimeters
8. 75 square feet
9. 300 square meters
10. 200.96 square inches

Page 178

1. 8,640 cubic feet
2. 1,296 cubic feet
3. 900 cubic meters
4. 24 cubic feet
5. 128 cubic feet
6. 48 cubic feet

Page 179

1. 150
2. 224
3. $58\frac{7}{16}$
4. $414\frac{9}{16}$
5. 277.5
6. $526\frac{1}{2}$
7. 110.25
8. 62,208
9. The volume is 8 times as great as the original volume.

Page 180

1. 12, 3; 36; 36
2. 1, 2; 2; 2
3. 36, 36, 2, 74; 74
4. 592 ft²; the new volume is eight times the original volume.
5. 36 ft³; yes, if you use a base that is 3 ft by 3 ft, the height of the prism is 4 ft. $V = (3 \times 3)(4) = 9 \times 4 = 36$

Page 181

1. 40 cubic yards
2. 2.3079 cubic meters
3. 10.99 cubic inches
4. 1,038.56 cubic meters
5. 67.31 cubic meters
6. 953.78 cubic centimeters

Page 182

1. 4,082 ft³
2. 602.9 ft³
3. 2,009.6 cm³
4. 803.8 m³
5. 65.9 ft³
6. 113,982 in³
7. 124.72 m³
8. 3,052.08 in³
9. a. 15 ft
   b. 45 ft
   c. 31,792.5 ft³
   d. 7,065 ft³
   e. 38,857.5 ft³

Page 183

1. 550 in²
2. 72 yd²
3. 85.5 m²

Page 184

1. 288 ft²
2. 3,050 cm²
3. 1,332 in²
4. $57\frac{1}{4}$ yd²
5. 46 ft²
6. 470 cm²
7. 9,400 in²
8. 18 ft²

Page 185

1. 3, 2, 3, 4, 2, 4; 12, 24, 16; 52; 52
2. 10, 8, 10, 16, 8, 16; 80, 320, 256; 656; 656
3. 52, 656; 708
4. 708, 6; 696; 696
5. Sample answer: You have to subtract it from the surface area of both the chimney and the house, or two times.

Page 186

1. triangular prism
2. triangular pyramid
3. Check students' drawing.
4. Check students' drawing.
5. 992
6. 1,008

Page 187

1. triangle
2. rectangle
3. parallelogram
4. square
5. rectangle, triangle
6. rectangle, triangle, trapezoid
7. Check students' drawing.

Page 188

1. 2,200 in³
2. 1,152 in³
3. $656\frac{1}{4}$ m³
4. 450 in²
5. 1,080 in²
6. 102 in²
7. 25 cm³
8. 17,280 ft³
9. 48,230.4 cm³
10. 904.32 in³

Page 189

1. You pick a number that is at most 0. You pick an even number. You pick a number that is at least 2. You pick a number that is greater than 0.
2. impossible; 0
3. as likely as not; $\frac{1}{2}$
4. certain; 1
5. unlikely; close to 0
6. $\frac{5}{6}$
7. $\frac{1}{2}$
8. $\frac{4}{5}$
9. $\frac{12}{13}$
10. Sample answers: pulling a red marble out of a bag that contains blue marbles; pulling a white marble out of a bag that contains only white marbles.

Page 190

1. $\frac{1}{6}$
2. $\frac{1}{3}$
3. $\frac{1}{6}$
4. $\frac{1}{3}$
5. $\frac{1}{3}$
6. $\frac{4}{9}$
7. $\frac{2}{9}$
8. a red marble
9. a quarter; a nickel
10. $\frac{2}{6}$ or $\frac{1}{3}$
11. $\frac{3}{5}$
12. 5 cards

Page 191

1. $\frac{1}{8}$
2. $\frac{7}{8}$
3. $\frac{1}{4}$
4. $\frac{3}{8}$
5. 0
6. $\frac{3}{8}$
7. $\frac{1}{6}$
8. $\frac{1}{3}$
9. $\frac{5}{6}$
10. $\frac{1}{2}$
11. $\frac{1}{2}$
12. $\frac{5}{6}$
13. hhh, hht, hth, thh, tth, htt, tht, ttt
14. $\frac{3}{8}$
15. $\frac{3}{8}$
16. $\frac{1}{2}$
17. $\frac{1}{4}$

Page 192

1. 1
2. 0
3. $\frac{1}{3}$
4. $\frac{2}{3}$
5. white, red, or blue; $\frac{2}{9}, \frac{1}{3}, \frac{7}{9}$
6. white
7. red
8. $\frac{1}{6}$

9. $\frac{1}{2}$

10. $\frac{1}{3}$

Page 193
1. 20 spins
2. 9 spins
3. 4 times
4. $\frac{1}{10}$
5. 5 times; 4 times fewer
6. $\frac{2}{5}$
7. Answers will vary.

Page 194
1. Basket A: 16, 3, $\frac{3}{16}$; Basket B: 20, 4, $\frac{1}{5}$
2. Basket B
3. $\frac{1}{2}$; 0.50; 50%
4. a. $\frac{4}{9}$

   b. $\frac{5}{9}$

   c. You could find the complement of part a or you could find the theoretical probability.
5. 10 times
6. 94 times
7. 25 times
8. The chances of landing on an even number are $\frac{1}{2}$, which is the same probability as landing on an odd number.

Page 195
1. $\frac{1}{6}; \frac{1}{6}; \frac{1}{6}; \frac{1}{6}; \frac{1}{6}; \frac{1}{6}$
2. 5, 5, 5, 5, 5, 5
3–5. Answers will vary.
6. Sample answer: Yes, the experimental probabilities could eventually come out to be equal to the theoretical probabilities, but it is unlikely.

Page 196
1. $\frac{3}{5}$ or 0.6
2. $\frac{2}{5}$ or 0.4
3. 45 times
4. 10 times
5. $\frac{7}{10}$ or 0.7
6. 6 free throws
7. $\frac{1}{4}$ or 0.25
8. $\frac{13}{40}$ or 0.325

9. 103
10. $38.\overline{3}\%$

Page 197
1.

	1	2	3	4	5	6
1	2	3	4	5	6	7
2	3	4	5	6	7	8
3	4	5	6	7	8	9
4	5	6	7	8	9	10
5	6	7	8	9	10	11
6	7	8	9	10	11	12

2. 36
3. The 8s in the table should be circled.
4. 5
5. $\frac{5}{36}$
6. $\frac{6}{36} = \frac{1}{6}$
7. $\frac{10}{36} = \frac{5}{18}$
8. Sample answer: rolling a sum of 7
9. Sample answer: rolling a sum of 1

Page 198
1.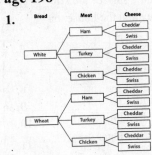
2. 12
3. $\frac{1}{12}$
4. Count the number of total number of sandwiches available (12). Then count the branches on the tree diagram that lead back to wheat bread (6). The probability is $\frac{6}{12}$ or $\frac{1}{2}$.
5. Sample answer: Count the outcomes that do not include ham. The probability is $\frac{8}{12}$ or $\frac{2}{3}$.

Page 199
1–4. Answers will vary.
5. Sample answer: I think the experimental probability from the combined trials is closer to the theoretical probability.
6. Answers will vary.

Page 200
1. as likely as not; $\frac{1}{2}$
2. impossible; 0
3. unlikely; close to 0
4. certain; 1
5. $\frac{1}{8}$
6. $\frac{2}{8}$ or $\frac{1}{4}$
7. 0
8. $\frac{1}{8}$
9. $\frac{4}{8}$ or $\frac{1}{2}$
10. 1
11. $\frac{14}{40}$ or $\frac{7}{20}$
12. 8 possible outcomes
13. $\frac{5}{35}$ or $\frac{1}{7}$
14. $\frac{52}{80}$ or $\frac{13}{20}$

Page 201
1. statistical
2. statistical
3. non-statistical
4. the number of runs scored by the team in one game
5. 18
6.

Interval	Frequency
0–4	9
5–9	7
10–14	1
15–19	1

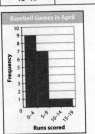

7. Answers will vary.
8. Almost all of the data are between 0 and 9, with peaks at 2, 4, and 5; 13 and 17 do not fit.

Page 202
1. Yes; answers will vary. Many will think the 10% sample is large enough.
2. no
3. no

4. yes
5. no
6. 141 subscribers
7–9. Answers will vary. Possible answers are given.
7. toys
8. sport shoes
9. computers

Page 203
1. The sample is biased because people at a baseball game are more likely to say baseball is their favorite sport.
2. The sample is random because arriving early to school has nothing to do with a person's musical preference.
3. random
4. 6, 6
5. 3,500; 0.06 × 3,500 = 210
6. 210, 210

Page 204
1. 1; 1,000; 1,000
2. defective, working
3–5. Answers will vary.

Page 205
1. 49
2. 73
3. 140
4. 121
5. 385
6. 526
7. 328
8. 671
9. 1,616
10. 23 travel books
11. children books
12. children books
13. week 1
14. 32
15. 61
16. 59

Page 206
1. 5; 32; 32; 33
2. $46; $38; $65; $60
3. 5; 22; 22; 22
4. 5; 59; 59; 58
5. 12; 150; 150; 154
6. $100; $255; $255; $250
7. 15 points
8. 92%
9. No; a set of data might not have any numbers

Answer Key
Core Skills Math Review

that repeat.

10. Yes; a set of data can have several numbers repeated.

11. Answers will vary. Possible answer: Find the average of 7 million and 13 million. The prediction would be 10 million.

Page 207

1. 3 and 7
2. no mode
3. 400
4. Mean 78.6; Median 83
5. Median; the mean is affected by the low score of 45.
6. Mean 78; Median 80.5
7. Both describe the number of points equally well.
8. No; although it is not strictly necessary to include the two data values of 0 in the sum, they must be included in the number of data values. The sum should be divided by 10, not by 8. The correct mean is 5.5.

Page 208

1. 29
2. 13
3. 43
4.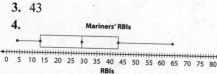
Mariners' RBIs
5. 30
6. 15
7. 31
8. 14
9. 60
10. Orioles' RBIs
11. 46
12. 36

Page 209

1. 4 letters
2. 1.$\overline{6}$ letters
3. 4 letters
4. 1 letter
5. The length of the words in the first population varies more than the second, but overall the average length is the same.
6. 4, 1.6
7. 3.8, 0.68

Page 210

1. Sample answer: A greater number of study hours should correlate to higher test grades.

2.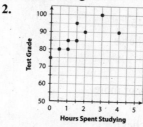

3. In general, test scores increase as the number of study hours increase.

4. No; the graph shows a general upward trend, but the grade cannot exceed 100.

5. The subject matter might be easy for a student to understand, so that student may not need to spend much time studying for the test.

Page 211

1. Possible answer: 17, 70
2. positive, linear
3. positive
4–7. Answers will vary based on the point selected.
4. 170, 17; $\frac{120}{12}$; 10
5. 50, 10, 5; 50, 50; 50, 50; 0; 10, 0
6. There is an average of 10 pages per chapter; an additional chapter is associated with 10 additional pages.
7. The number of pages in a book with 0 chapters is 0.

Page 212

1. extrapolation; 10x; 10(26); 260; 260
2. interpolation; 10x; 10(14); 140; 140
3. They fall close to the original data, so they fit well.
4. Possible answer: Interpolation is more accurate because the predicted value fits between known points where the trend is known. There is no guarantee that a trend will continue beyond the known data points.

Page 213

1. 20; 0.20; 20
2. 16; 0.50; 50

3. more likely; Yes; the relative frequencies show that having a curfew makes it more likely that a student will have to do chores.

4. The relative frequency of having a curfew and having chores ($\frac{16}{32} = 50\%$) is greater than the relative frequency of not having a curfew and having chores ($\frac{4}{68} \approx 6\%$), so there seems to be an association between the two events.

Page 214

1. 12 chickens
2. pounds
3. 6.58 pounds
4. 6 pounds
5.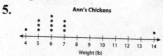
Ann's Chickens
Weight (lb)

6.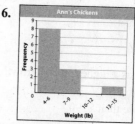
Ann's Chickens
Weight (lb)

7. increase the number of people surveyed
8. 200 glasses
9. negative association
10. yes; Possible answer: Most of the data points are close to the trend line. There are about the same number of points above and below the line.

Page 215

1. 30.48
2. 118.4
3. 30.60
4. 9.48
5. 1.82
6. 18.28
7. 340.8
8. 4.73
9. 76.2
10. 12.81
11. 26.53
12. 8.05
13. 437.64
14. 64.96
15. 450
16. 2.64
17. 6,211
18. a. 4.47
    b. 125.16

Page 216

1. $49.49
2. 30 invitations
3. $12.09
4. 225 miles
5. 7:15 A.M.

6. $13.00

Page 217
1. $606.30
2. 0.92 meter
3. about $10.00
4. Sam paid $1.24 more per CD.
5. 640.9 kilometers
6. 3 meters tall
7. 1,100 pounds
8. $0.17 per brick

Page 218
1. 18
2. 512
3. 300
4. 128
5. $173
6. 135
7. 243
8. 557

Page 219
1. $-\frac{1}{2}$
2. $x < 35$
3. Tonya is 4.
4. $t \geq 14$
5. 4 days
6. April has a higher rate of growth.
7. (10, 5)
8. No more than $290

Page 220
1. 5 centimeters
2. 1 foot
3. 4 inches
4. 6 inches
5. 300 square meters
6. 864 square inches
7. 4,800 cubic inches
8. 1,800 cubic inches

Page 221
1. 125 feet
2. 6 meters
3. 10 yards
4. 22 feet
5. 12 inches
6. 12.5 centimeters
7. 120 yards
8. 16 inches

Page 222
1. $x + 587.46 = 675$;
   $x = 87.54$; $87.54
2. $3s = 225$; $s = 75$; $75
3. $l + 4.7 = 7$; $l = 2.3$; 2.3 T more
4. $p - 76 = 1897$;
   $p = 1973$; 1973

---

5. $4k = 2.4$; $k = 0.6$;
   0.6 gal
6. $\frac{d}{12} = 12.50$; $d = 150$; $150
7. 7 quarters and 3 dimes
8. no
9. $10,245
10. 79 cameras

Page 223
1. 12.5% or more
2. $152.20
3. $4\frac{1}{4}$ inches
4. $29\frac{1}{8}$ yards
5. $33,360 or more
6. $51.04
7. 373 students
8. 7.1%
9. $53,000 + 53,000x > 55,000$; $x > 3.8\%$
10. 13.2

Page 224
1. 40.64 cm
2. 43.13 kg
3. about $10.00
4. 160 miles
5. 150 miles
6. $r < 40 + 12$; $r < 52$
7. 15 years old
8. 31 feet

Page 225
1. 10
2. 16
3. $3\frac{3}{4}$
4. $1\frac{1}{2}$
5. $8\frac{1}{4}$
6. $1\frac{1}{2}$
7. $\frac{3}{10}$
8. $1\frac{17}{100}$
9. $\frac{9}{1000}$
10. $\frac{1}{100}$
11. 0.8
12. 0.23
13. 0.05
14. 0.008
15. 7.57
16. 69.106
17. 7.27
18. 8.01
19. 117.78
20. 0.9997
21. 0.2475
22. 6.7
23. $0.35 = \frac{7}{20}$
24. $0.08 = \frac{2}{25}$
25. 20
26. 20%
27. 90
28. 36
29. $15.75
30. $85.20

Page 226
31. -2
32. 11
33. -75
34. 4
35. 1
36. $-\frac{9}{11}$
37. -6
38. (-3, 9)
39. (1, 1)
40. (4, 5)
41. $x = 22$
42. $x = 5$
43. $x = -6$
44. $x = 10$
45. $x = 9$
46. $x = 6$
47. $x = 14$
48. $x = 36$
49. $x = 8$
50. $x = 6$
51. $x = 5$
52. $x = 13$
53. $\frac{7}{12}$
54. $\frac{1}{8}$
55. $x \geq 3$
56. $x > 15$
57. $x > 3$
58. $x \geq -40$
59. 8 centimeters
60. 54 square meters

Page 227
61. 70
62. 12
63. 18
64. 45
65. 100,000
66. 3,233
67. 33
68. 36
69. 3.5×10^8
70. 1.284×10^5
71. 7,500
72. 120,000
73. 5
74. 15
75. 6
76. 45
77. $y = 6x + 2$
78.

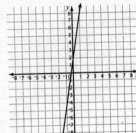

79. 30 feet
80. 9

Page 228
81. $7x$
82. $-2x + 7$
83. $5x + 1$
84. $(5\frac{1}{3}, -3\frac{2}{3})$
85. (-5, -3)
86. (4, 0)
87. 60°
88. 55°
89. 37.68 cm
90. 379.94 square feet
91. $29\frac{1}{4}$ cubic inches
92. 98.5 cubic meters
93. $\frac{1}{8}$
94. $\frac{3}{5}$

246

Answer Key
Core Skills Math Review